A Disability of the Soul

A Disability of the Soul

An Ethnography of Schizophrenia and Mental Illness in Contemporary Japan

KAREN NAKAMURA

CORNELL UNIVERSITY PRESS

ITHACA AND LONDON

Reprinted without accompanying DVD in 2017 with ISBN 978-1-5017-1704-8. Materials formerly available on DVD may now be found at www.disability.jp/soul/films.

Cornell University Press gratefully acknowledges receipt of a grant from the Council on East Asian Studies of Yale University, which assisted in the publication of this book. The book was also published with the assistance of the Frederick W. Hilles Publication Fund of Yale University.

First published 2013 by Cornell University Press
First printing, Cornell Paperbacks, 2013

Printed in the United States of America

Library of Congress Cataloging-in-Publication Data

Nakamura, Karen, 1970– author.
A disability of the soul : an ethnography of schizophrenia and mental illness in contemporary Japan / Karen Nakamura.
pages cm
Includes bibliographical references and index.
ISBN 978-0-8014-5192-8 (cloth : alk. paper)
ISBN 978-0-8014-7861-1 (pbk. : alk. paper)
1. Mentally ill—Rehabilitation—Japan—Urakawa-cho. 2. Schizophrenics—Rehabilitation—Japan—Urakawa-cho. 3. Community mental health services—Japan—Urakawa-cho. 4. Mental illness—Social aspects—Japan. 5. Schizophrenia—Social aspects—Japan. 6. Beteru no Ie (Urakawa-cho, Japan) I. Title.
RC439.5.N35 2013
362.2'6—dc23 2012050910

Cornell University Press strives to use environmentally responsible suppliers and materials to the fullest extent possible in the publishing of its books. Such materials include vegetable-based, low-VOC inks and acid-free papers that are recycled, totally chlorine-free, or partly composed of nonwood fibers. For further information, visit our website at www.cornellpress.cornell.edu.

This book is dedicated to the memory of
Gen'ichi Nakayama (1969–2006) and
Tsutomu Shimono (1969–2010),
two young Bethel members whose paths and
lives overlapped with mine. Their absence is
deeply felt in all of our hearts.

Contents

Acknowledgments

This was a difficult book to research and to write. I have seen and experienced many things at Bethel over the past seven years that have deeply affected me. There is much pain and suffering in the worlds of people with severe mental illnesses, and these are only partly compensated by the strong personal bonds, mutual support, laughter, and warmth that can also be found there.

I wrote this book so that people who might have never thought seriously about mental illness, let alone what it would be like to live with mental illness in another country, might learn not to be afraid when a child, coworker, or spouse tells them of his or her condition. I hope that after reading this book, you, the reader, can understand that another world is possible, but only if all of us—those with mental illnesses as well as those without—are totally committed to building it.

I wrote this book for the many students who have lived or are living with a mental illness. In my ten years of teaching, many students have come out of the closet, so to speak, to me privately, but not to their friends and classmates. In an era where being gay or lesbian or trans has become almost passé, there is still a profound stigma attached to mental illness. For a college student, being diagnosed with a mental illness can be devastating. Schizophrenia often appears in one's late teens or early twenties, and becoming ill can mean a forced medical leave and many years of struggling without a job or education.

I wrote this book for all my friends at Bethel who trusted me with their life stories. One of their great fears is that their lives will have meant nothing; that they will live and die without contributing to society. They talked to me as part of achieving the eighth and final step of the Urakawa Schizophrenics Anonymous program. By listening and engaging with them, I took on the burden of responsibility to make sure that their stories would be told and their lives remembered.

Finally, I must admit that I wrote this book for myself, as living in Bethel and then collecting my thoughts as I wrote this book has involved a long and painful—but also illuminating—discovery of my self.

THIS book would not have been possible without the full cooperation of Bethel House and the Urakawa Red Cross Hospital. I am particularly indebted to Dr. Kawamura, who not only allowed me access to the hospital but also arranged for me to stay in staff housing on the hospital grounds and lent me his beloved "Porsche"—a tiny white pickup truck, so named because it was a two-seater with rear-wheel drive and a tiny 600cc engine—to buzz around town. I also profusely thank Mr. and Mrs. Mukaiyachi of Bethel House for their support for this project from the very start.

I acknowledge various Bethel members and staff, including Rika Shimizu, Kiyoshi Hayasaka, Tsutomu Shimono, Kohei Yamane, Shio Hayasaka, Mai Suzuki, Katsuko Miyanishi, Masako Yoshino, Yanagi-kun, Akao-san, IwaMeg, YoshiMeg, KashiMeg, Nakahara-san, Ogawa-san, Ohinata-san, and countless others that I cannot name. Thank you for allowing me to serve as a witness to your lives. I could not include in this book all of the stories that you told me, but they are sealed in my heart. I am deeply appreciative of Dr. Muneharu and Mrs. Chika Nakayama for their permission to write about their family, including their late son Gen'ichi Nakayama.

THE research for this book was made possible by an Abe Fellowship from the Social Science Research Council and the Japan Foundation Center for Global Partnership as well as a Yale University Junior Faculty Fellowship. I thank Sophia University in Tokyo and Doshisha University in Kyoto for hosting me during the Abe Fellowship period. I also thank Professor Glenda Roberts of Waseda University and Yale University's Waseda Asakawa Kan'ichi Fellowship for providing a particularly conducive environment in which to finish the final manuscript.

Among my professional colleagues, I am particularly indebted to Junko Kitanaka for her critical evaluation of an early version of this manuscript. William Kelly has been my intellectual mentor for the past decade and a half. I can never repay the debt that I owe him, so I only hope that I will be able to pay it forward to my own students. I thank the doctoral students in the Kelly-Nakamura seminar, especially Ellen Rubinstein, who was a fellow traveler in the world of the mentally ill during her studies at Yale.

I recognize the help of numerous librarians, in particular Haruko Nakamura at the Yale University East Asia library, who, in my insatiable quest for materials, has been my tireless, indispensable ally. My editor at Cornell University Press, Roger Haydon, provided the right balance of gentle suasion, good humor, and achievable deadlines. The two anonymous readers of the manuscript also provided essential feedback in shaping this book's final form.

Finally, this book would never have been finished without the constant love and support of my partner, Hisako Matsuo, and the forbearance of our beagle, Momosuke. We will go for a walk now.

A Note on Language

When referencing historical documents that use archaic and discriminatory phrases such as *tenkyō* and *chiokure,* I use the analogous English translations *lunacy* and *mental retardation.* I mean no offense to readers who may dislike these terms—I dislike them too—but I think that pretending that people were not using hostile and discriminatory language in the past whitewashes history unnecessarily.[1]

When translating the word *byōki* (illness or disease) in the context of mental illness, I have used the English word *illness* in situations when it is clear that the speaker is not referring to a *disease.* Here I am differentiating between *illness* as the feeling of being unwell and *disease* as the underlying cause of those feelings. In this sense, having a cold is an illness; acute viral rhinopharyngitis is the disease. Most people do not differentiate between *illness* and *disease* in this way. In Japanese, there is no such differentiation; *byōki* can be used in either sense.

Japanese names are given in the Western style of personal name first, family name last. People in Bethel use both first names (with the formal *-san* or more affectionate *-chan* or *-kun* honorific suffixes) and occasionally last names in talking about each other. Because there are three Mukaiyachi family members involved with Bethel, I refer to the husband as Mr. Mukaiyachi and the wife as Etsuko or as Mrs. Mukaiyachi. Their son, Noriaki, who works in the Bethel Tokyo office is not mentioned in this ethnography.

A Disability of the Soul

CHAPTER ONE

Arrivals

In May of 2005, I stepped off a small diesel train at the town of Urakawa with mixed feelings of hope and trepidation. Like thousands of people before me, I had traveled to this remote fishing village on the northern frontier of Japan in search of what was supposed to be the Holy Land for people with mental illness—a place where they could live, work, and prosper without fear or prejudice. It all sounded too good to be true, especially when contrasted with the utter desolation of the landscape that greeted me when I got off the train. All I could see were abandoned houses and storefronts. This couldn't possibly be the right place. But right outside the station, a young man with a mustache and glasses waved at me. He was my ride.

Bethel House (*Beteru no Ie*) was founded in the town of Urakawa in 1984 to help people with severe mental illnesses such as schizophrenia live in the community after being discharged from the long-term psychiatric ward of the Urakawa Red Cross Hospital. From its modest beginnings in a run-down church, Bethel House has grown over the past three decades to become a major nonprofit with over 150 members and supporters and several million yen in annual revenue. Every year, several thousand of "psychotourists" (my coinage) visit Bethel from all across Japan, many to attend the annual Bethel Festival and its Hallucinations and Delusions Grand Prix. In addition, Bethel members, many with quite severe symptoms of schizophrenia and other mental illnesses, lecture all across Japan, talking about their lives and how they have dealt with illness and recovery. They sell not only themselves but also a wide range of products, from books and videos about their lives to T-shirts and aprons festooned with comic representations of their hallucinations and delusions to seaweed and noodles packaged by members in their in-house workshops.

Getting to Bethel

I had been on trains for almost fourteen hours when I arrived at Urakawa Station. I had woken up before dawn to take the first bullet train heading north from Tokyo Station, traveling several hundred kilometers past the city of Sendai to the town of Hachinohe on the outskirts of Aomori. There I changed to a regional express train that took me underneath the ocean, through the Seikan Tunnel, to the island of Hokkaido—Japan's northern frontier. Once back on firm land, the express took me past the regional capital of Sapporo to the small port city of Tomakomai. At this point I changed trains for the final time, catching the Hidaka Main Line, which skirts the southeast coast of the island.

Despite its impressive name, the trains on the Hidaka Main Line are only a single diesel car in length, more a glorified tram than a train, and run just a few times each day. The train ride is both exhilarating and

Figure 1.1 Map of Japan.

terrifying, as it runs along the very edge of the ocean and occasionally has to screech to a halt for deer, humans, and other creatures that wander onto the tracks. It was a long three hours on the Hidaka line before I reached the town of Urakawa, located on the southeastern edge of Hokkaido, almost the last stop. Because I had caught the first train in the morning in Tokyo, I was able to catch the last train into Urakawa in the evening; otherwise it would have been a multi-day journey.

There are other ways to get to Urakawa. You can catch an airplane to Sapporo and then an intercity bus to Urakawa. Some people also take the car ferry from the mainland to Tomakomai and then drive to Urakawa. But I prefer to take the train. It is peaceful watching the landscape change from the sprawling urban metropolis of Tokyo to the golden rice fields and farmlands of Tochigi and Fukushima and then to the green forests of Aomori. When the train dives beneath the ocean and passes under the Tsugaru Strait though the Seikan Tunnel, the longest and deepest tunnel in the world, it feels as though one is passing through a liminal space, only to reenter an unfamiliar world.

About the same size as Ireland, the island prefecture of Hokkaido feels very different from mainland Japan. The air is cleaner, the sky is bigger, and there are far fewer buildings and people. Hokkaido still feels like the colonial frontier that it once was. Everywhere there are legacies of the original Ainu people, who were pushed out, colonized, and killed. The place names still mark many of the cities and towns: *Sapporo,* the dry great river; *Otaru,* the river between the sand banks; *Tomakomai,* the river above the swamps; and *Urakawa,* the river of fog. Museums dedicated to Ainu culture dot the landscape, keeping time frozen behind glass, even as the descendants of the Ainu people try to sustain their culture and language in the present.

Encountering Bethel

I first learned about Bethel in 2004 when I was doing research on disability protest movements in Tokyo. At the time, several national organizations of people with disabilities in Japan were staging large-scale demonstrations against the government. This fascinated me, as it seemed quite contrary to the image of Japan as the nation where the nail that sticks up is hammered down. Bullhorns and protest banners were out in force in front of the Ministry of Health and Labor. Since the early 1900s, people in Japan with severe physical, intellectual, or psychiatric disabilities had been warehoused in nursing homes and other institutions for their entire adult lives. At the protests, I watched as various grassroots organizations representing people with physical and psychiatric disabilities lobbied for greater funds to allow for more deinstitutionalization—the ability for people with disabilities to live independently in the community rather than in hospitals, nursing homes, and other long-term care facilities. The activists wanted better funding of independent living centers and guarantees for full-time personal care attendant coverage and other support mechanisms.

I was puzzled, though, by the absence of groups representing people with psychiatric disabilities. Encoded into Japanese law is an understanding of three types of disability: physical, intellectual, and psychiatric. Given the visibility of deinstitutionalization and patients' rights movements in the United States and Europe for people with mental illnesses, I was curious whether there were any organizations of people with psychiatric disabilities that were organizing politically in Japan.

I went to several nonprofit organizations for people with psychiatric disabilities in Tokyo and Osaka, but for the most part they were operating as halfway houses, group homes, or sheltered workshops for people who had just come out of psychiatric hospitals.[1] In one of these sheltered workshops, former patients folded cardboard boxes for *bentō* box lunches in silence. When I asked whether there was a place where people with psychiatric disabilities were more active, I was told about a small group named "Bethel" up on the island of Hokkaido.

I put off going to Bethel for the longest time. When I looked at a map, the town of Urakawa was a just tiny speck on the southern edge of nowhere. It would take me a good two days to get there and back, and I had little expectation that it would prove any different from the other places I had seen. But I blocked off a week in my research schedule and decided to pay it a visit.

Visiting Bethel House

The man with the moustache who greeted me at the train station in May 2005 was a minister in the United Church of Christ in Japan. Reverend Hamada was in his early forties and had just been assigned to the small church in Urakawa. He had not known much about the local church and its special relationship with Bethel House before he arrived, but he had since become a full-fledged supporter, continuing in the tradition of the previous minister, Reverend Miyajima.

Packing me into his beaten-up SUV, Hamada-san gave me a quick tour of the town. This was easily accomplished, as the town of Urakawa has only one main street about two miles long, which hugs the contour of the ocean. New Bethel (the name for the office headquarters of Bethel) and the train station are on one end, the Urakawa Red Cross Hospital is on the other. In the middle is the town hall, the library, and Bethel's main store, Yonbura. It was late at night, and all of the stores were closed, so I peered into the darkness as we drove by.

Hamada-san had kindly agreed to put me up in the church rectory. He asked me if it was all right if I shared the space with a college student who was also visiting Bethel. We drove up to the church, which was nestled in a side street behind the station. It was a modern, two-story white concrete building, quite in contrast to the dilapidated wooden houses and shacks that lined the street in front of it.

My new roommate and I were staying on the first floor of the church, which was originally designed as a small apartment for the resident minister's family but was now used as guest accommodations for Bethel visitors who could not afford to stay in one of the inns in the area. Staying in the church was free, but Bethel charged ¥1,000 (US$9) a night for the use of futons and blankets.

As I walked across the room to greet my roommate, the floor felt strangely soft. In some places it seemed as though my foot might go straight through. Despite the modern exterior of the church, it turned out that the floor was rotten in places, especially near the bathroom. I had to be careful to tread on the main beams only. Later on, I heard that the modern architecture of the building, with its spires and jutting edges, was entirely inappropriate for the long, cold Hokkaido winters, as the building had many leaks and cracks.

My roommate was a young college student from the mainland. She lived with her parents at home, worked during the day, and went to classes in the evening. A petite girl, she later confessed that she had been suffering from depression and, after reading a book about Bethel, had decided to come up to see what it was all about and to take a break from things. This was her first visit.

She had arrived the day before, and Hamada-san asked her to show me around while he dug out some laundered sheets for me. There was a huge pile of futons and mattresses in the corner. Before the minister left, my roommate asked him about the hot water, as the water heater in the bathroom apparently wasn't working properly. The previous night, she had taken a sponge bath by heating water in a kettle on the stove. Hamada-san managed to turn on the small propane water heater for the bathroom so that we could take a quick shower in the chilly room, but the one in the kitchen remained broken for our entire visit.

The room itself was heated by the aforementioned large kerosene stove. Despite it being mid-May or early summer in Hokkaido, the evening air was quite chilly, and we needed the stove to stay warm. It was very efficient at this task, but we reluctantly turned it off at night since neither of us trusted it not to kill us with carbon monoxide poisoning, even with all the drafts in the room. Every year in Japan, several people die of carbon monoxide poisoning from indoor space heaters, so this wasn't an entirely unfounded fear. We put extra futon blankets on top of ourselves in an attempt to keep warm at night. Lying in the dark with several heavy blankets pressing down on my chest, I wondered what I had gotten myself into.[2]

Morning Meetings

The next morning I woke up and found that I could see my breath in the air. My roommate had risen before me and had made a small breakfast for us. As we ate, we talked about what we would do that day. The first event on Wednesday mornings was the Morning Meeting at New Bethel at 9:30. We folded our futon mattresses and blankets and made our way out of the church.

The building called New Bethel was a twenty-minute walk from the church. We made our way down the hill and crossed the train tracks over to the main road. We walked along it, past the small train station, for another ten minutes until we reached New Bethel, on the westernmost edge of town.

New Bethel was a squat two-story office building. It had housed a printing company that had gone out of business, and Bethel had seized the opportunity a few years ago to buy it. Until then, Bethel had been run out of an old wooden building (now named *Original Bethel*, or just *Bethel House*) next to the church where I had spent the night. The first floor of New Bethel was a relatively open space with a small television and a smoking room on the side. Workshops, events, and seaweed packaging were done on the first floor. The main office space on the second floor was divided in two. One third of the room had a set of desks organized just like any Japanese office, but the remaining two thirds of the floor space was left open. When we arrived, the space had been arranged for a group meeting by placing a folding table in the front and organizing chairs around it in a semicircle.

Three people were sitting at the folding table in front. The woman on the far left was wearing an apron, and the other two were more informally dressed. The older woman on the right was wearing a soft cap and had a very dour look to her. It took me a moment to realize that these three women were the Bethel members in charge of the meeting.

The meeting began. I looked around; there were about thirty people sitting or standing in a wide circle. The women at the table started by asking people how they were feeling physically and psychologically and how many hours they planned to be working today. Someone responded, "Physically feeling a bit lethargic today; psychologically a bit depressed; I'll work three hours." Since each person had to report in, it took a fair bit of time. The staff were asked the same questions. Since no one wore uniforms or had ID cards, it was impossible to tell who was a registered Bethel member (and thus someone with a diagnosed mental illness) and who was one of the paid staff (who often joked that they merely had *undiagnosed* mental illnesses).

After the individual physical and psychological declarations, there was a detailed report from each of Bethel's business sections. The mail order department read through each and every order that had been placed, reading the name and address of each customers and what they were purchasing. The packaging department gave meticulous statistics on how many units of seaweed they had packaged the previous day. The morning meeting was mind-numbingly boring.

Just as I was nodding off, the dour-looking lady and two other women came up to me. The older woman asked me if I knew the song "Welcome to Bethel." I shook my head and said that I didn't. Suddenly, she and the two other women began singing and dancing.

♪ Welcome to Bethel, everybody! (PAPAYA)
♪ We're the face of Bethel, how are you?
♪ Whatever you learn here, please don't be surprised.

♪ Isn't schizophrenia terrible? (PAPAYA)
♪ With its hallucinations, voices, and delusions?
♪ You just can't stand not doing anything,
♪ So you end up cutting yourself.

♪ Zun zun-zun zun-doko Kana-chan

♪ Isn't insomnia terrible? (PAPAYA)
♪ Making noise at all hours of the night.

𝅘𝅥𝅮 You keep all of your family up.
𝅘𝅥𝅮 No one in the neighborhood slept all night!

𝅘𝅥𝅮 Zun zun-zun zun-doko Tomo-chan

𝅘𝅥𝅮 Isn't alcoholism terrible? (PAPAYA)
𝅘𝅥𝅮 Drinking morning, noon, and night
𝅘𝅥𝅮 Smashed all day,
𝅘𝅥𝅮 To top it off, you run a tab at the bar.

𝅘𝅥𝅮 Zun zun-zun zun-doko Masa-chan

𝅘𝅥𝅮 Isn't mental illness terrible? (PAPAYA)
𝅘𝅥𝅮 It's our gift from God.
𝅘𝅥𝅮 Even if we're different from normal people,
𝅘𝅥𝅮 We're all first-class sickos.
Thank you very much!

Orientation

After the morning meeting and my disorienting welcome from the Welcoming Committee, a young woman named Rika Shimizu started my official orientation. One of the three women who had led the morning meeting, Rika-san wore glasses, an apron, and a fleece sweater. She gave me my Bethel orientation handbook, which detailed the history and purpose of Bethel and had humorous vignettes of the members in cartoon form. A core Bethel member, Rika herself appeared many times in the orientation book (as well as other Bethel publications). While she was describing Bethel to me, Rika kept on getting interrupted and then had to go off to run a meeting, so another member finished my orientation and went over the schedule of the week's various events.

After the orientation, I went downstairs to find Rika in the television room, where about fifteen people were watching the latest video that Bethel had produced. It featured a young woman named Asami Matsubara. In the section I watched, she was in a personal conference with about half a dozen other people. I'm not sure who was leading the discussion. She had about seven dolls (Winnie the Pooh, Piglet, and so on) piled up in front of her. One of the people in the video was saying how the stuffed animals represented her "Gencho-san voices," which were her auditory hallucinations of people talking to her. At first, they were in a pile, but Asami-san later arranged them in a circle. Another person asked her if they were still her Gencho-san voices, and she said no, they now represented the circle of friends who supported her. Each one corresponded to a real person in the physical world.

After the video ended, Rika-san asked the audience for their comments. Each person responded. Several said that Asami-chan had improved a great deal since she had become friends with Kaku-san.[3] Another added that it was clear from the video just how much she had improved. One of the staff said it seemed like the medications she was taking were helping her mental state.

In the afternoon, I visited the Bethel Yonbura store, which was located in the middle of the shopping area in downtown Urakawa. Calling it a "shopping area" might be a little grand, since most of the twenty or so stores on the main road were shuttered. The Yonbura building itself used to house a bookstore on the first floor, and the bookstore owners used to live above it. If you looked at the store's three-story facade closely, you could still see a faint shadow of "BOOKS" where the store sign used to be. The owners apparently ran off in the middle of the night, leaving their house, the store, and creditors behind. As with many other properties in town, Bethel snapped it up. They turned the first floor into a storefront for Bethel products and the two upper floors into women's-only residential units.

I browsed around the store and bought some of the books about Bethel that the members had written as well as some seaweed that they had packaged. After paying for the merchandise, I joined several of the members and staff who were in a planning meeting for the Bethel Festival, which was scheduled to be held a month later, in June. The Bethel Festival, which apparently attracted several hundred people to the town, was their biggest yearly event. It was a good occasion for Bethel to improve its relationship with the townspeople, who benefited from the influx of tourist money, somewhat tempering their usual gripes about Bethel.

The Town of Urakawa

Urakawa is a town of fewer than fifteen thousand residents, about half of whom are involved in the fishing and seaweed industry, the other half in horse breeding. Actually that statistic is misleading, as fully a third of the people in the town are retired, a proportion that is only increasing as young people leave for the prefectural capital of Sapporo or the mainland, and only the old people remain behind.

The region surrounding Urakawa used to be the breeding grounds for the imperial horses before World War II. After the war and the concomitant reduction of the emperor to human status, the ranches started breeding thoroughbred racehorses. More recently, however, globalization has meant that owners in the Japan Racing Association can get their stallions directly from the United States, so the horse industry in Hokkaido is slowly dying. The local fishing industry is also collapsing, the result of long-range fishing boats, refrigeration, global competition, and overfishing.

With the local economy doing so poorly, the town of Urakawa is dying of old age. Young people move to the cities in search of jobs, and all that remain are old men and old women. Who can blame the youth for leaving? Like so many other rural towns in Japan, Urakawa has nothing to offer them. There are no jobs, and there's nothing else for them to do.

It's a vicious cycle. With so few customers these days, local shops cannot sustain themselves economically. The main thoroughfare has become one long "street of closed shutters." The downtown supermarket has closed. The bookstore has closed. Even some of the ever-popular pachinko gambling parlors have gone out of business. The Urakawa Red Cross Hospital, which is the largest private employer in town, looks rundown and vanquished. There are only two businesses in Urakawa that seem to be thriving: the funeral parlor and Bethel House.

The Church

In the evening, I went back to the church, where I found the minister, Hamada-san, getting ready for the Wednesday evening Bible study group. There were about ten people at the study group, most of them Bethel members. They met in the main chapel on the second floor of the church, right above where I had spent the night. Each week, the study group usually read a section of the Bible, but this week (and for the next three weeks) Hamada-san was showing the 1956 Cecil B. DeMille film *The Ten Commandments* on his laptop. After about an hour of Charlton Heston railing against the Egyptians in dubbed Japanese, Hamada-san turned off the computer and asked the group for their impressions. We had about half an hour of conversation about the film and ended with a prayer for the health of the members. After the close of the meeting, we had some tea and sweet potato snacks.

As we were cleaning up the chapel, Hamada-san came in to look for some tools. Apparently he was locked out of the kitchen. He grabbed some cutlery and went to jimmy the recalcitrant door latch. A few minutes later, one of the members came in and said that Hamada-san had now locked himself *in* the kitchen. We went over to have a look, and it turned out that the latch was broken. It took me a while to spring the lock. By the time I opened the door, Hamada-san had his foot outside the window with a large butcher's knife in one hand and a fork in the other, looking for all the world like a cat burglar.

SSTs and Personal Conferences

The second day of my stay began just like the first—with an incredibly stultifying morning meeting at New Bethel where everyone reported their physical and psychological condition and how many hours they'd work that day; then each of the various divisions of Bethel reported on what had happened the previous day. One of Bethel's core principles apparently was "Meeting is more important than eating"—indeed, it seemed like most of the day at Bethel was taken up with meetings or conferences of one sort or another. Lots of information was being shared, but none of it was very interesting for an outsider.

After the morning meeting, I had a conversation with Hamada-san about religion and the church. I commented how the meeting last night was remarkable in its flexibility of interpretation. He said that this was one of the highlights of the church, and perhaps of Bethel. The church thought informed Bethel, he said, and Bethel practice informed the church thought. One of the significant things was that before the arrival of his predecessor, Reverend Miyajima, in 1983, there was a period of about eight years where there was no minister at all in the Urakawa church. The members just met on their own to pray. They were used to doing things their own way.

We looked up to see people arranging chairs. Thursdays at 11 a.m. was the time for the social skills training (SST) meeting. About thirty people began to seat themselves in a large semicircle on the second floor of New Bethel. Someone pulled out a whiteboard, and the meeting started. Everyone in the audience was asked to introduce himself or herself and describe his or her physical and psychological condition. Several people who had been given homework from the last SST meeting were asked to present their results and let the group know whether the feedback and suggestions they had received had helped them. They were then asked what could they work on further. After the homework presentations, the main SST session started, with several people asking for help with various social situations that were coming up in their lives. The group worked on each issue in turn. This took about an hour and then we broke for lunch. Most people had brought their own homemade *bentō* box lunches or had purchased riceballs from the convenience store; others poured hot water on instant ramen noodles; while just a few had enough money to afford real ramen noodles at the restaurant across the street. I went across the street.

Right after lunch was a personal conference. This was also held on the second floor of New Bethel, but this time two folding tables were placed together in the middle of the room. A young woman was sitting at the table, along with a nurse from the hospital. The young woman seemed quiet. I noticed that she had scratches on her forearms and a deep scar on her chin. She had a nice manicure but her hair was unkempt, and her blouse had some food stains.

The conference was run by Etsuko Mukaiyachi, the wife of the social worker who had originally helped found Bethel. Etsuko had worked as a nurse for the hospital but was now one of the paid staff on Bethel's salary and the de facto administrative manager. Etsuko had a detailed notebook with notes from previous personal conferences for this member. This woman had been doing the Bethel self-directed research regimen and had made a drawing of herself split in two with little Gencho-sans (or voices) to her left and right. At Bethel, the Gencho-sans were represented by little Pac-Man–like stick figures. In her drawing, there were also Gencho-sans in her head and in her stomach.

Mr. Mukaiyachi later explained to me that at Bethel, hallucinations were called Gencho-sans ("honorable voices"), as he wanted the members to be able to externalize the voices and treat them as separate from themselves. The Gencho-san Pac-Mans ended up becoming a major brand icon for Bethel, festooning their seaweed products and their books. Gencho-sans were distinguished from Okyaku-sans (or "honorable visitors"), which was the Bethel lingo for negative self-thoughts, and which were recognized as coming from inside yourself. Everyone had Okyaku-san visitors from time to time, but only people with schizophrenia had Gencho-san voices.

Etsuko verbally reviewed the member's personal conference report from the last time they met and then asked her how she was now. Apparently the young woman was doing very poorly. Her mental condition was deteriorating, and she wasn't coming to Bethel these days to work. Her

Figure 1.2 A hallucinatory Gencho-san (honorable voice) chasing after Kiyoshi Hayasaka on a Bethel notecard. The text on the top reads, "We are Bethel People!" Photo by the author.

physical condition also wasn't good. She lived in a group home at the top of a steep hill. While she could make it down to the supermarket, she had to take a taxi back up. She took a breath and continued. Her Gencho-sans were also getting worse; they would call out from her television set telling her that she was a bad person. The morning news anchor had made a special report saying that she didn't eat breakfast. In the past, watching television was one method she could use to quiet her hallucinations, but now the Gencho-sans were appearing on the television. The Gencho-sans also forced her to go repeatedly to the vending machine to buy juice, so between that and the taxi charges, she was always short of money.

Staring straight down at the table, the young woman went on to talk about other issues. She was unhappy about her living conditions. One of the elderly men that she lived with in the group home made her take care of his dirty diapers, along with other menial tasks. She was filled with Okyaku-san visitors, negative self-thoughts that this man was taking advantage of her. Compounding the other issues, one of her other housemates was going out with a boy that she liked, and seeing them together rubbed her the wrong way.

The goal of the personal conference was to see what could be done. Etsuko said that it was important that she come to Bethel each day, since it provided her with additional income. Right now her workload was too much and it was stressing her out, so Etsuko suggested ways that she could reduce her work. There was talk about her medications. There wasn't any talk about moving group homes, however. Still, the woman seemed relatively satisfied that at least some of her concerns were being recognized and addressed, and with that the meeting ended.

The Hospital

After the personal conference, Etsuko Mukaiyachi took me and some of the other visitors, including a nurse from Sapporo, for a lightning tour of the town. We first stopped by the Mukaiyachis' house to pick up her youngest daughter, who was still in high school. The Mukaiyachis lived on a bluff overlooking the entire town of Urakawa and the bay below. Etsuko joked that their three children were raised by Bethel members, who had babysat them when they were young. Etsuko's husband, Mr. Mukaiyachi himself was no longer working at Bethel or at the hospital. He had gotten a job teaching social work at a Hokkaido Health Sciences University in Sapporo. He only came back to Urakawa two or three days a week.

While we were up at the Mukaiyachis' house, we visited one of Bethel's group homes, Rika House, which was literally located in the Mukaiyachis' backyard. Named after one of its early residents, Rika House

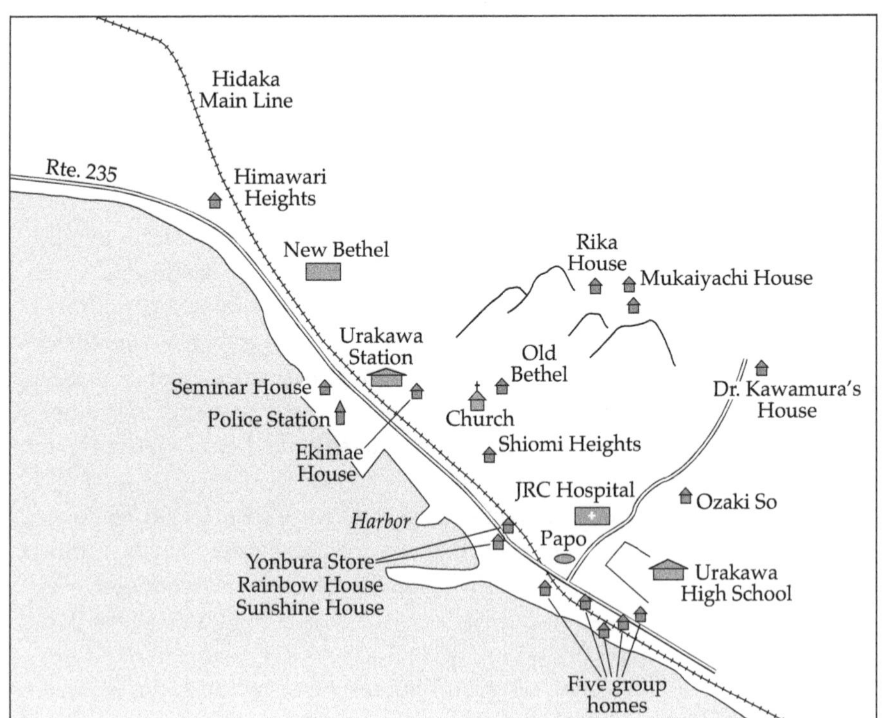

Figure 1.3 Map of Urakawa

was gorgeous. A newly built Western-style house, it had six individual rooms. There was a large living area that was well illuminated by two skylights. Everything was bright and airy. The rooms themselves were huge. Everything was on one level, and there was even a wheelchair ramp to get in the front door.

We went inside Rika House, where we found Asami Matsubara, the young woman who had appeared in the video with the stuffed animals the previous day. She was there with two visiting nurses from the hospital. Asami-chan at first seemed normal when she greeted us, but she quickly became excited and started giggling at stories that only made sense to herself. At times she laughed uncontrollably. It was clear that Asami was in her own world—and thoroughly enjoying it.

After leaving Rika House, Etsuko drove us down to the hospital. We entered the hospital through the rear staff entrance. Etsuko showed us the psychiatric day care unit. There were several rooms with different purposes: a smoking room, a music room, a computer room, and so on. We visited the shop that Bethel had in the hospital, selling various personal care items like adult diapers that the hospital didn't provide. One of the young male members, Shimono-kun, was there. Bored out of his mind, he was bouncing a ball against the wall when we walked in. We visited the hospital's laundry and dishwashing facilities, which were run by Bethel.

We then went to the closed psychiatric ward on the top floor of the hospital. The entrance to the ward was blocked by a windowless steel door. Etsuko pressed the intercom button and asked for us to be buzzed in. We walked past the nurses station, which was staffed by five or six nurses, all of whom seemed to be in their twenties. The Red Cross Hospital had an attached nursing school, which helped greatly in keeping their staffing levels up, although turnover was high, as many nurses left as soon as they could find jobs in more glamorous climes.

Etsuko grabbed one of the patients, who agreed to show us around the closed psychiatric ward. The young man's name was Gen'ichi Nakayama, and he gave us a grand tour of the main lobby of the ward, the dining hall, the smoking room, and the television corner. Then he took us down the male and female wings of the ward.

The ward held around sixty patients in total. Many of the men in the closed psychiatric ward seemed quite old, in their sixties and seventies. Some had been in the hospital for several years. Later I would learn that the longest resident had been there since the 1970s. One of the patients seemed quite disturbed, while others shuffled around like zombies. Others were dressed in light *yukata* pajamas; they looked like they had just taken a bath and were out for a stroll. Some were asleep in their rooms, while a few were watching a sumo wrestling tournament on the television in the main lobby. There seemed to be a huge contrast between the lethargy of the psychiatric ward residents and the frenetic energy of the Bethel members on the outside.

At our prompting, Gen told us about himself. He was actually in the process of checking himself out to leave the next day for his hometown of Mito, on the mainland, to talk about psychiatric disabilities and to give a viewing of some of the paintings and sketches that he had done as a ward resident. We thanked Gen for showing us around and left the hospital. Etsuko drove me back to the church. I had to get up early the next morning in order to catch the first train in order to get back to Tokyo the same day. It had been a very strange two days in Urakawa. I knew I had to come back if I wanted a deeper understanding of what was going on.

About Me

I am a cultural and visual anthropologist. That means that I live in *foreign* cultures, study them, and write books and make films about them. I place the word *foreign* in italics because although both of my parents are Japanese, I was born and raised abroad. So going to Japan is always an odd experience for me; I am neither fully Japanese nor fully not Japanese. My blood is Japanese, my heart is American, and my body is Australian. I often feel like a chimera, the creature from Greek mythology with the head of a lion, the body of a goat, and a tail of a snake.

My specialty as an anthropologist is minority groups in Japan, especially people with disabilities. As noted before, Japanese law defines three types of disability: physical (for instance, being deaf or blind or having mobility issues), intellectual (developmental or learning disabilities), and psychiatric (mental and psychiatric disorders, including epilepsy and dementia). My first book, *Deaf in Japan,* was about deaf culture, sign language, and the politics of identity in contemporary Japan. This book is about the possibilities of recreating society to better accommodate people with psychiatric disabilities.

In Japanese, the term for psychiatric disability is *seishin shōgai.* The word *seishin* means spirit, mind, or soul; *shōgai* means disability. In the early 2000s, GlaxoSmithKline Pharmaceuticals ran print and television advertisements in Japan suggesting that their drugs might be able to cure "colds of the heart" (*kokoro no kaze*)—in other words, mild depression

(Vickery 2005, 345; Kitanaka 2012, 14). I've taken some liberty with the title of this book to gloss *seishin shōgai* as a "disability of the soul," but the spiritual connotations that I'm trying to draw should become more apparent later in this book when I address the role of Christianity in the formation of Bethel.

At the time that I started this project, what I knew about psychiatric disability in Japan was rather bleak. There is an incredible amount of shame surrounding mental illness in Japan. In addition, Japan has some of the longest hospitalization/institutionalization rates in the developed world as well as the highest rates of pharmaceutical use. In simpler terms, people with mental illness are warehoused in hospitals for long stretches of time and take a lot of medication. Those who aren't in hospitals are often secluded in their own homes, prevented by their families from going outside and bringing shame to the family name.

I wanted to find some alternative models to this system. I was especially interested in groups run by people with disabilities themselves. Although I ran into some "centers for independent living" run by and for people with psychiatric disabilities in Tokyo and Osaka, there was very little that seemed noticeably progressive. But many people mentioned the community of Bethel, up on the northern island of Hokkaido, as something different.

The majority of the hundred or so Bethel members had been diagnosed with some form of schizophrenia.[4] This condition is characterized predominantly by the presence of hallucinations (voices, sensations, or images that aren't real) and delusional thought. It's also characterized by the absence or flattening of emotions. But there was also a panoply of diagnosed and undiagnosed conditions at Bethel: bipolar disorder (formerly known as manic depression), borderline personality disorders, epilepsy, mental retardation, post-traumatic stress disorders, depression, alcoholism, and so forth.

I am not a medical doctor or a social worker, so my intent in going into the Bethel community was not to diagnose anyone or to build case histories. I am also not interested in what Arthur Kleinman (1977) rightly criticizes as the ethnocentric "category fallacy" of trying to determine whether people with the Japanese medical diagnosis of *tōgōshicchōshō* have what we in the United States would call *schizophrenia*. This is not a comparative medical analysis or a treatise on what used to be called "culture-bound syndromes." Rather, I want to understand how the social model of disability works at Bethel as a possible model for thinking about accommodating psychiatric disabilities more fully in society.

We are now accustomed to the types of physical and social accommodation that are necessary for people with physical disabilities to participate fully in society: wheelchair ramps on buildings, Braille letters on ATMs, or sign language interpreters in public. At schools and universities, we make accommodations for people with learning disabilities by providing tutors and alternate testing methods. But we know very little about what it would take for people with severe mental illnesses to live and work in the community successfully. As an intentional community designed around the needs of people with psychiatric disabilities, Bethel seemed to promise some of the answers to these questions—while raising a host of others.

I wrote this book in order to facilitate a more open and frank discussion about mental illness. I do not think that Bethel is a perfect example of the social model of living in the community. Like anything else, it has its good points and bad points. I hope that understanding how Bethel works can shed light on different ways of doing things and help us think of new models for incorporating people with mental illness more fully into the community.

Like my roommate in the church and the many thousands of other Bethel visitors, I read some books about Bethel and was inspired to make a pilgrimage up there. And like those others, after my initial short stay I was convinced that there was something special here, something that required living there long-term to understand.

This book is the result of those explorations.

Visual Anthropology/Textual Ethnography

Enclosed with this book are my two ethnographic films about life and death in Urakawa—*Bethel: Community and Schizophrenia in Northern Japan* and *A Japanese Funeral*. You can also stream the films at http://www.disabilityofthesoul.org. From the very beginning, I intended this project to have both a visual and a written component. Mental illness is so far from most people's normal experience and yet so laden with prejudice that I felt it critical to use both visual and textual modalities.

This is because each ethnographic modality has its own strengths and weaknesses, what one might call "complementary incompetence," to steal a phrase from another author.[5] Ethnographic film can bring to life—quite literally—what it means to live in another culture. It shows the texture of life and the quality of interactions in a community. But for all of its strengths, one of the weaknesses of ethnographic film is the difficulty in providing historical or social context and analytical depth. Ethnographic writing, on the other hand, can supply theoretical richness and analytical depth at the expense of the ease in which inference, polyvocality, juxtaposition, and montage can be used in its visual counterpart.[6]

Because the film *Bethel* provides a vivid introduction to life in Urakawa, you should watch it in its entirety before reading much further in this book. After viewing *Bethel,* many viewers have remarked that the people in Urakawa seem very different from their own stereotypical image of people with mental illness—usually gleaned from media reports, Hollywood films, or the mentally ill homeless that they might encounter on the street. But most people don't know how typical or atypical the people at Bethel are, or what their backstories might be, or the larger picture of mental health care in Urakawa, or in Japan.

This is where the text of this book complements the film. The first section of the book consists of a history of mental illness and psychiatric care in Japan, from medieval times up to the present moment. I follow that with some background on the settling of Hokkaido and the reasons that the Christian church was so predominant there. In the second section of the book, I shift to the founding of Bethel by a social worker and the early relationship Bethel had with the Urakawa Church of Christ. I introduce the chief psychiatrist of the Urakawa Red Cross Hospital and his philosophy on the treatment of people with mental illness and how that has affected the relationship between the hospital and its patients. The third section of the book consists of an ethnography of everyday life at Bethel, including an analysis of the various meetings and workshops. Here again, I invite you to watch some of the shorter visual vignettes in order to provide another layer of understanding beyond that which can be conveyed by text alone.

Woven into the three sections are the stories of five Bethel members. These key interstitial chapters are designed to give you insight into the individual lives of members, the way that they found themselves at Bethel, and how they are living lives of recovery in Urakawa. They are also designed to illustrate various themes within Bethel: the role of memory, through Kiyoshi Hayasaka's autobiographical narrative; the importance of being needed, in Rika Shimizu's narrative; the social function of mass delusions, in Kohei Yamane's tale; why people may choose to be institutionalized for thirty-seven years, in Yuzuru Yokoyama's narrative; and the meaning of a good life, in Gen Nakayama's story. After reading Gen's chapter, you should watch *A Japanese Funeral,* as it depicts the events portrayed there.

Kohei Yamane's UFO story is a good example of the different strengths of film and text. In the film, the story is woven together by Rika Shimizu, Shio Hayasaka, and Kohei himself. In this book, I delve further into Kohei's history before coming to Bethel and the significance of the UFO incident to the community. The text is not merely the backstory to the film; my goal was to use each medium so that readers could see the incident from different angles, a textual-visual *Rashomon.*

In the closing chapters of this book, I note that Bethel has changed significantly since its early days and will likely change yet again, due to many internal and external forces. And I return to the query that initiated this research project in the first place—what does Bethel, as a closed intentional community, tell us about the possibilities and potentiality for people with psychiatric disabilities to live full and productive lives in the community? Bethel provides no easy solutions to these difficult questions, but it does provide potential directions. The goal of anthropology is to illustrate the broad diversity of human existence and to show that another way of living is possible. This book and the films were designed with that in mind; I hope that is the message that you, as the conscientious viewer and reader, take with you.

Ethics and Representation

All of the names used in this book and the accompanying films are real names and not pseudonyms. There are no composite or fictional characters. In addition, Urakawa is the name of the actual town, and Bethel House is a very real organization. I made the decision to use real names after very carefully considering the possible benefit and harm this could do to my research informants—the people in the Bethel community.

There are many ways that an anthropologist can harm his or her informants—even by just asking questions. For example, we can be grossly insensitive or cause secondary trauma by indelicately probing areas of their past that are best left alone. We can cause or exacerbate tensions within a community by revealing to another person information told to us in confidence.

Second and far more dangerous is the anthropologist's ability to harm a community by what we write about it. For example, we can depict a group as more violent or less competent than they actually are. We can reveal ritual secrets to the uninitiated, upending decades or even centuries of tradition. We can make it easier for state oppression to occur by diagramming internal power structures or allow ethnic misunderstandings to fester and breed. Anthropologists have done all of these things, and sometimes much worse.

To protect their informants, many contemporary anthropologists obfuscate the exact place where they did their fieldwork, and use pseudonyms or vaguely drawn maps. Most institutional review or university ethics boards will specifically ask how confidentiality and privacy will be maintained. However, it is often possible to use deductive methods to find out where the fieldwork happened and who the various informants are.

In my case, Bethel's unique qualities ruled out the option of attempting to anonymize the community. Bethel is very well known in Japan, having been featured on numerous television programs as well as in over a dozen books. It is also a unique organization—whether in its Christian origins, its location in northern Japan, or the striking personalities of its various members.

Most importantly, though, the reason I decided to use real names is that my informants asked me to. In their public lectures across Japan, Bethel members use their real names as they talk about their lives. Part of their motivation for their openness are various steps in the Urakawa Schizophrenics Anonymous process that encourage them to accept themselves as they are and to communicate with others the lessons learned from their experiences with psychiatric disabilities. Shame is one of the key barriers facing honest discussion of mental illness across the globe, but particularly in Japan. The use of real names helps dissipate that cloud of shame.

That is not to say that this is a tell-all book. I have tried to exercise discretion in using information that is not public or that was obtained in private interactions with individuals. I have used my fieldwork data only when I thought it was clear that I was acting in my public role as researcher (through the obvious markers such as my field notebook, audio recorder, film gear, and so on) and not as my private roles as their friend or comrade in disability. While in Urakawa, I did not look or ask to look at any medical files or charts, nor did I inquire about the medical diagnoses of patients or members. These protocols were approved by my university's human subjects review committee.

Because self-disclosure is such an important part of Bethel culture, I was open in telling Bethel members my own history of mental illness, and I feel the same responsibility to you, the reader, so that you know how I conducted myself in the field and obtained the trust of my field informants. Since at least my late teens, I have been through several periods of depression. I have been given different diagnoses over the years: dysthymia, adjustment disorder, and depression. In the past twenty years, I have had two episodes of major depression. The more recent of these occurrences overlapped with my stay in Urakawa, although I should note that I was never under the medical care of the Urakawa Red Cross Hospital or Dr. Kawamura. In fact, even though I was open about my depression with Bethel members, Dr. Kawamura himself did not know of my condition until well into my fieldwork, as (I am embarrassed to admit) I was ashamed of my own disability. Anthropologist, heal thyself, indeed.

In writing this book, I want to honor the spirit of Bethel and its members in promulgating an open discussion of mental illness. Like the rest of us, many Bethel members don't want their lives to have been wasted, and fostering open discussion of mental illness is part of their life work. In allowing me to witness their life stories, they also placed a great deal of trust in me. This responsibility to my informants weighed on me most of all as I wrote this book, and I hope that I have done their lives justice.

Memory and Catharsis: Kiyoshi's Story

> I've told this story so many times before. . . .
> When I talk about it, my body all goes "Bwaaah"
> As long as you understand, Karen-san, it's OK.
>
> —Kiyoshi Hayasaka

Kiyoshi Hayasaka is one of Bethel's founding members. Over the past three decades, he has served as the president of Bethel and its sales manager, among several formal and informal titles. Many people in the town of Urakawa joke that Kiyoshi is Bethel's mascot. He's certainly the best known of all of the members, and cartoon drawings of him are blazoned on Bethel T-shirts, posters, books, and calendars. His centrality is not unwarranted. Kiyoshi has the uncanny ability to help people in times of crisis, knowing just what to say at the appropriate moment. But that insight and kindness comes from many years of struggling with his own demons.

When I asked Kiyoshi-san to tell me his story for *Bethel,* he heaved a long sigh and told me that he had told this story so many times before—no doubt to every researcher, psychotourist, and film crew that had passed through Urakawa as well as during the many talks he's given for Bethel across Japan. And every time he told the story, he would feel physical and psychic pain afterwards with the aftershocks of the memory.

Autobiography as Catharsis?

In the West, we have the notion of self-narration as catharsis, as a freeing of pent-up emotions. We feel a compulsion to tell the stories of our lives to our therapists, to our priests, to our neighbors, to strangers on the bus.

Figure 1.4 Kiyoshi Hayasaka at a Bethel cookout, July 6, 2007. Photo by the author.

In a way, self-narration is self-discovery—we find out who we are by telling the story of who we are.

But when is this not true?

I was surprised when I found out that Bethel does not encourage much delving in the past. Both Dr. Kawamura and Mr. Mukaiyachi felt that there wasn't much use in carrying around too many things in what they called the "trash can of the soul" (*kokoro no gomibako*). Using a computer metaphor, people were regularly encouraged to empty their mental trashcans so that they can open up more room for other things in order to get on with their lives. Through gentle suasion, the various self-study and SST sessions (see chapter 6) held in Urakawa covered not the past but the present.

Time at Bethel was treated as cyclical, not linear. That is, you looked into the past to understand the patterns in your life that kept repeating, rather than to unwind it in a straight line. What are the things that happened before you ended up being hospitalized? Could you detect any patterns to your emotional states? What always happened before flare-ups or shutdowns? In their self-directed research presentations (more on this in chapter 6), members would talk about their past in the context of these types of self-diagnosis.

Other than giving clues to the future, the past had no agency in the present. Causality was not explored. People were discouraged from thinking that they had become schizophrenic because of something their parents had done or because they had been bullied at work or other past traumas. Past events were simply the context in which people's illnesses first manifested and the pattern started or became clear.

I didn't know this at first when I came to Bethel to make my film and do the fieldwork for this book. I thought that I could get the life stories of members simply by pointing my video camera or microphone at them and asking them to start talking. That is what I had done in my previous projects, and I thought it would work at Bethel as well.

Instead, what I encountered was an inability or unwillingness to delve into the past.[1] Kiyoshi Hayasaka is one of the main figures at Bethel, but as you can see in *Bethel,* he doesn't want to talk about his past. He tells me that he's already talked about it before and that every time he talks about it, his body freezes up. The same happens when I ask Yamane-san to talk about his UFO story; he can't go into some of the details of key moments because, in his words, "other painful things would come up."

What should I have done? In the film, I ignorantly tried to push Kiyoshi a little further and got some basic details . . . he was born on . . . in the neighboring town of Samani-cho. When he was in middle school, he had his first hallucination . . . then he tells me it is too difficult to continue and that as long as I understand, it's okay.

What does it mean to understand, though?

I wondered: Aren't autobiographical narratives a core component of good ethnography? Don't readers want to know the life stories of the people that the author has encountered or that shaped the organization that they are studying? I agree that sometimes anthropologists go too far and that some social histories are written entirely in terms of the pivotal figures without whom things would have never been the same. I try my best to avoid this all-too-hagiographical tradition in my work, as it tends to put too much attention on certain (usually male) figures while downplaying the roles that other people, social institutions, or cultural and historical forces might also have played.

In Kiyoshi's case, his role in forming Bethel really was central, although like any good narrative it weaves in a whole cast of characters (the social worker Mr. Mukaiyachi, Dr. Kawamura, and the Reverend Miyajima and his wife) who will be fleshed out later in this book. I later found out that, with the help of some of the staff and other members, Kiyoshi wrote a short biography for a 1992 edited volume put out by Bethel. I've translated that in its entirety here. If I had truly listened to Kiyoshi and read what he would have "written on a card," as he told me in the film, this might have been what he would have penned.

Walking Together with Bethel

Kiyoshi Hayasaka

I was born on January 13, 1956, in the Utabetsu hamlet of Erimo, Hokkaido [a couple towns east of Urakawa]. My family consisted of my parents and my little brother, who is four years younger than me. In truth, I had a little sister too, but her heart was weak, and she died when she was only a few months old. When I was old enough to remember things, we were living in the Tomiuchi area of Hobetsu [a remote mountain village located about a 120 kilometers southeast of Sapporo].

My father worked at the Hobetsu sawmill along with my mother. My father loved to drink and was always getting into fights with my mother. I remember running away once with my mother and my little brother. My father didn't only have a drinking problem, he also fooled around with women a lot and that resulted in a lot of fights with my mom as well. Well, that was my dad, but I also remember him having a kinder side too, taking me fishing or playing ball with me. In any case, my parents divorced when I was in fifth grade. My mother, my little brother, and I moved to the village of Samani [just a few kilometers east of Urakawa] after the divorce. My father quickly remarried.[2]

I didn't study much in school but instead played with my *menko* cards and marbles.[3] My mother was angry that I was bad at my studies and played all the time, so she used to beat me with the long metal chopsticks that she used to tend the charcoal brazier.

When I was entered middle school, I was put in Group G [the special-ed group]. Because I had a lazy eye, the kids used to call me "cross-eyes," and my friends used to make fun of me by making the letter *g* with their hands. I couldn't do anything about it but stuff my feelings inside me.

Around that time, my mother started drinking even in the morning. She'd often yell at me things like, "Someone like you is just going to be worthless in society." Even though I was naive of the world, I started to hate myself. I was bitter about the fact that everyone made fun of me.

When I was in 8th grade, my mother started to get ill a lot. Now that I think of it, that must have been around when the cancer got in her. In the September of my 9th grade year, I suddenly became filled with this anxiety that my mother was going to die. I started hallucinating. When I was trying to sleep, I'd see police handcuffs nailed to the wall of the room. I became absolutely neurotic.

One of my teachers from the school took me to the psychiatrist at the Urakawa Red Cross Hospital, and I was hospitalized. They told me that I had schizophrenia. These days, they wouldn't call it schizophrenia, they'd call it a hysterical attack.[4]

I was in the [psychiatric ward of the] hospital until July of the next year. They gave me my [middle-school] graduation diploma at the hospital.[5]

After I was discharged from the hospital, I was given an introduction to a job as a projectionist at a small cinema in the small town of Eniwa, south of Sapporo. The owners provided me with a room in the movie theatre to live in.

Soon after that, I heard about the death of my mother. Surprisingly, no tears came from my eyes. My brother, who was still in seventh grade, cried. He went to live with our father.

I lived in Eniwa for eight years. While I was in Eniwa, I had a couple of seizure attacks where my body would freeze up and I'd fall over, but I only had to be hospitalized once. I was only being paid a pittance there [at the cinema], so one day I decided to just up and quit and leave.

I returned back to the town of Samani and worked at a ranch, but the bosses didn't follow up on their promises. They never paid me, and they yelled at me all the time. Once again, I began to lose my sense of myself, and in a dreamlike state, I somehow found myself hospitalized at the Red Cross Hospital.

After I got better, I left the hospital and returned to the ranch but ended up fighting with the boss again and soon found myself homeless and alone by myself in the rain. I asked to be admitted to the hospital again.

I was 24 years old at the time. It was the start of yet another stretch of life in the hospital. I was there for a year and eight months. One of my fellow patients in the psychiatric ward was a fellow named Fujii-san. He invited me come with him to the Urakawa Church, and I went to my first service there. Because of that, I got to know the housewives at the church. They helped me a lot.

Even though I was a patient in the hospital, I tried to do little things for the church like chop the firewood and stack it. Even though it wasn't much, I tried to do my bit to contribute. At first, the sermons during the services were too difficult for me to really understand. But when I sang hymns with others, it felt like the fog that had enveloped me was lifting.

After consulting with Dr. Kawamura and Mr. Mukaiyachi, on April 9, 1983, I discharged myself from the Red Cross Hospital and moved into the old Urakawa church [which is now called Bethel House]. I lived there with Minoru Sasaki and Watanuki-san.

I think if I hadn't met Dr. Kawamura, I would have most likely spent the rest of my life in a hospital or institution. I could have been discharged earlier, but I had no home to go to and so I had no choice but to stay in the hospital. When I was in the hospital, I was really miserable.

With [divine] guidance, I was baptized in December of 1983. I didn't have many friends before, so I was really happy to make friends through the church. After I was discharged, I tried to help the best I could around the church.

But even then, I would get anxious and have seizure attacks. I would lash out badly at times. I got into a lot of fights. I'd get an attack and would run around and then freeze up and fall over. I'd get really angry and scream out loud. There were a lot of episodes like that.

In the winter, I would help the missus at the church [Mrs. Michiko Miyajima] with the seaweed packaging piecework. In the spring, I'd go till the fields or pull up some weeds. In the summer, I'd help haul in the seaweed from the oceans.

When I was in the hospital, I thought that there was no way that I could cook for myself. But after I was discharged, I gave it a try and was surprised that I could. I began to gain some confidence in myself.

In the hospital, all I did was eat and sleep. I felt like I was losing myself. Now, I receive social security and a disability pension, and together with the income from Bethel, I'm able to make a living. I'm not really good with my money—I quickly lose track of how much I have—but I try hard to not waste any money.

I always go to church for Sunday service and for prayer meetings. I enjoy praying and talking with the other people there. Ever since I started to put my trust in God, my feelings of anxiety have gone down, and I feel more self-confident.

I try to serve the church as best I can. I lead some of the Sunday services and some of the prayer meetings; on Sundays when the minister isn't here, I give testimony. And I'm also a teacher at Sunday school. Before I came to the church, I had never been asked to stand in front of people and do things [requiring responsibility], but at church I've been asked to do many things.

Since living at Bethel, there have been many times when I really struggled. In May of 1988, Reverend Miyajima and his family were called back to minister in Takikawa [on the mainland]. My anxieties built up, and I had a seizure attack and froze up. I couldn't go to sleep, and even the littlest things started to bother me. Even my housemate, Mr. Okamoto, got sick.

In November, our seaweed packing side business ran into problems. One of our members got into a fight with the boss at the seaweed plant, and he stopped sending us orders. Since we couldn't fill any orders for them, we decided to start up on our own and package and sell seaweed by ourselves.

[When I was a child,] my mother would try her best, but I wasn't able to stick to any job for more than three days. My parents didn't think much of me. I have this fear of my parents. My family would make fun of me. Even then, I thought, "I should be able to be good at something" or "I'm not stupid." I was angriest when everyone called me an idiot. It only made my feelings of inferiority worse.

But when I started packing seaweed, I started to feel some confidence that I could do this job. Right now, we not only package and sell seaweed, we also sell disposable diapers. We take orders over the phone and deliver them. Through a computer service called MUG; we're also networking with people from around the area.

Shimizu-san [one of our supporters] sent us a music box all the way from Niigata. As this book shows, I've made many friends over the years.

But still, many of my peers are still in the hospital. In order to get them to be able to return to society, we need to try our best.

Even now, I still worry about too many things, get depressed, trip all over myself, flail around, seize up, and fall down. That's my everyday life. Someone who doesn't know me might be afraid of me at first, but if we have a true meeting of our souls, that person might come to understand me. If we can increase the number of those people who can understand even one or two at a time, then maybe my friends in the hospital might become less worried and [gain the confidence to] get discharged.

I hope to increase the circle of humanity through my work selling seaweed.

Kiyoshi wrote that biography in 1991, when he was 35. I first met him in 2005, when he was 49. Not much had changed in his daily routine from his early days, although the years had not been kind to his body. Like many people who have taken antipsychotics for a very long time, he has lost his teeth. One of the side effects of many first-generation antipsychotics is dry mouth, and without saliva it's easy for teeth to rot out of their sockets. The national health system provided him with dentures, but they didn't fit well. In the many scenes in *Bethel* where Kiyoshi appears to slobber or spit, it's because his dentures were causing problems.

Kiyoshi still lives in the old Bethel House, which has been expanded over the years to hold eight people. He still freezes up from time to time

Figure 1.5 Kiyoshi talks with Mrs. Miyajima at the occasion of Gen's death, June 30, 2007

and checks into the hospital for a few days to rest up, get loose again. He likes to joke with Dr. Kawamura about placing a reservation for his usual room on the ward. One of the things that continues to worry Kiyoshi is his lack of a life partner. He wants to get married, but every time he meets an eligible woman (due to his prominence at Bethel, he gets many marriage offers) he starts to become anxious about all the responsibilities that marriage entails, freezes up, and has to check back into the hospital.

Kiyoshi's Budget

One of the things that Kiyoshi no longer worries about is money, as he goes to see a financial manager from the town hall about once a week. She is part of a national program called the Civil Rights Protection program (*Kenri Yōgo*). It has a lofty title, but at root it provides financial management for the elderly, the cognitively impaired, and others with money management problems. Since the 2000s, the news media had begun reporting on elderly people all across the nation falling prey to a host of scams, while people with intellectual and psychosocial disabilities were also proving susceptible to being cheated, occasionally by their own family members. Run by local city or town halls, Civil Rights Protection programs were designed to make sure that one of the most neglected of basic civil rights, financial security, was protected.

In Urakawa, the Civil Rights Protection financial manager met her clients once a week. They went over their income and expenditures, making sure that they had enough money to pay their rent or buy food, had saved up money for special occasions, and so on. It was entirely voluntary, and her clients retained possession of their own ATM cards and bank passbooks. The program was popular among Bethel members, as they saw that people in the program had more spare money than people outside of it—especially at the end of the month when everyone was dirt poor, as the welfare checks only got deposited once a month.

I filmed Kiyoshi meeting with his financial manager (the vignette is included in the bonus clips section of the DVD). After the meeting, I asked him if we could go over his budget along with his financial manager. Kiyoshi receives income from three sources: (1) he had a certified moderate physical disability and receives ¥66,000 a month (about US$600) in disability pension (*shōgaisha nenkin*); (2) he receives another

¥44,000 a month (about US$400) from social security (*seikatsu hogo*); and (3) he works at Bethel. That month he hadn't put in too many hours, so he received only ¥3,480 (about US$32) from Bethel. (It is worth pointing out that the wages at Bethel were very low, only ¥220 an hour—about US$2—when I was there.)[6] In total, he earned around ¥110,000 a month (about US$1,000).[7]

His expenses were very modest. He budgeted ¥24,000 (about US$220) in rent to live at Bethel House; ¥16,740 for meal services (about US$152); and ¥9,390 for utilities (about US$85). In addition, he tithed ¥3,900 a month (about US$35) to the Urakawa church, and he gave back ¥5,000 (about US$45) a month to the "Bethel Bank" in order to pay off a small loan. His total expenses were just over ¥51,000 (about US$450).

Subtracting his expenses from his income, he had ¥59,000 or around US$500 left over each month, which, even with cigarettes and the occasional meal out, meant that he could start saving a little. He was very proud of his financial independence—rightly so, considering that few people with severe mental illnesses are able to achieve this.

Most Bethel members receive some kind of public assistance, although not all to the same extent as Kiyoshi. Only a few receive the disability pension for physical, psychiatric, or intellectual disabilities because of the strict diagnostic requirements involved. On the other hand, about two thirds of them are on social welfare (*seikatsu hogo)*, which guarantees a basic income and makes them eligible for public housing or subsidized rent. Bethel staff work with the town social welfare office on the public assistance applications; I never heard of anyone from Bethel being denied welfare benefits by the town of Urakawa—in contrast to other towns in Japan where social welfare offices are notably stingy. Finally, everyone with a diagnosis receives free medical care—physical and psychiatric—through the national health system's provisions for people with severe mental illnesses.

Even though none of the members are wealthy, the combination of social welfare checks and their work through Bethel means that all of the Bethel members are housed, have three meals a day, have free access to medical care, and are usually able to save up enough money so that they can enjoy their free time. While some members look (and smell) like they are homeless, they have homes to go back to and baths and laundry facilities that they can use—or refuse to use, as the case may be. Others are dressed quite well and would be indistinguishable from any other townsperson or college student in Urakawa.

Kiyoshi's Feelings on Mental Illness

Bethel ends with Kiyoshi Hayasaka and some of his friends outside the Red Cross Hospital in the evening. While snow falls around him, Kiyoshi looks directly at the camera and says:

> When this video or film or whatever it is gets to audiences abroad. . . . When people overseas watch it, I want them to know that people with psychiatric disabilities aren't abnormal.
>
> If someone is . . . if your mother gives birth to you . . . if you . . . if you have psychiatric disabilities or are ill right now, please live life with all your energy.
>
> Living life is important. Life is something that God has given us, and even if you are ill right now, please live life with all your energy.
>
> Just because you are ill is no reason to close your soul to the outside world.
>
> People with psychiatric disabilities or people with physical disabilities, for people who are about to begin life, or for people who are at the end of their life, I think the most important thing is to live now.
>
> Thank you very much.

In the next chapter, I will go over the history of psychiatric care in Japan. You might already have noticed several things—the very long hospital stays that Kiyoshi had in the past. Or that he was in a private hospital run by the Red Cross and not a public institution. The history of psychiatric care in Japan is short by Western standards, only about 150 years long, but with various twists and turns is as equally shameful and fascinating.

CHAPTER TWO

Psychiatry in Japan

Mental illness is a disease of modernity. This is true in at least three senses. The first is that the regimentation of daily life and increased stressors of modernity have led to a rise in various types of mental illness, just as changing diet has led to an increase in diabetes.[1] This is what you might call a biomedical or epidemiological perspective. Second, we can chart the ways by which psychiatry has come to understand and define mental illness, especially in terms of its modernist fascination with the neurochemical underpinnings of schizophrenia and depression. We might call this a history of science or social constructionist perspective.[2]

Finally, we can also try to recognize the complex interactions among individuals, their illnesses, and the larger social contexts in which these are all embedded. Behaviors and ideas that might have been tolerated in rural environments where the predominant form of social existence was the extended family or clan—these become seen as aberrant and dangerous through the mediating lenses of psychiatry and in the communities of strangers found in modern society. This is what I would call a biopsychosocial perspective, as it incorporates an acknowledgment of the interplay among the biological, psychiatric, and the social or cultural. My own intellectual attraction to the biopsychosocial perspective is that it opens up the possibility for societies to change in ways that can accommodate or include more people with psychiatric disabilities while denying neither the underlying biomedical aspects of mental illness nor the socially constructed and culturally mediated aspects of psychiatry.

In emphasizing the possibilities raised by the social context of psychiatric disabilities, I do not want to engage in the romanticization of the past or of "primitive" cultures that some authors fall into.[3] It is all too easy to imagine that in days past or in distant cultures, people with mental illness were honored as shamans and given positions of esteem within their community. This is a common theme in antipsychiatry literature, which ignores the reality that such people were just as likely to be abandoned or killed by their families or by intolerant others.

This romanticization of the past also elides very real features of mental illness. Depression, schizophrenia, and bipolar disorders can all be very physically and psychically painful and can also lead to significant self-harming behavior. No discussion of mental illness in a cross-cultural or transhistorical context can be made without stating that being mentally ill can lead to considerable suffering if not properly treated.

That being said, social accommodation of mental illness is both possible and necessary for recovery. Scholars and activists in the field of Disability Studies use historical and transcultural studies of disability to show how perspectives on illness and disability have changed over time. Part of the goal of this chapter is to show how the history of psychiatry in Japan and how the contemporary mental health system in Japan developed. This forms the backdrop for succeeding chapters, where I talk about Bethel's place in the larger context of Japan.

Overview

We can divide the history of psychiatry and mental health care in Japan into three periods. The first was when home confinement of people with mental illness was the predominant form of care. This existed from at least the 1800s to the 1950s. Starting in the 1950s, there was a shift toward mass institutionalization of mentally ill patients, leading to a rapid growth of private psychiatric hospitals. Finally, in the 1980s there was a move toward greater expansion of patient's rights and toward the development of independent living facilities.

One driving force in the shift from home confinement to mass institutionalization in the postwar period was the development of first-generation antipsychotics, which greatly lowered the cost of hospitalization by reducing the physical infrastructure, particularly the number of nurses and orderlies, required to run a psychiatric ward. Increased demand for psychiatric hospitals was driven by the demographic shift to cities in the postwar period (urbanization) and the move to nuclear families (two parents and children), which reduced the availability of spare family members (and physical space) to care for family members with mental illness. Finally, government policies in the postwar period granted low-interest loans for the construction of psychiatric hospitals and authorized the long-term institutionalization of people with mental illness at state cost.

The recent shift from mass institutionalization to independent living has been driven by the development of second-generation antipsychotics, which allow many more people with severe mental illness to live outside of closed hospital wards. It is also being motivated by government cutbacks on the reimbursement of long-term care for people with mental illnesses as well as revelations of scandals at several psychiatric hospitals discussed later in this chapter that have turned the climate against long-term institutionalization.

I should note that I initially expected Japanese psychiatrists to see Japanese psychiatry as distinct from Western medicine, but based on my interviews with psychiatrists and reading of published histories of Japanese psychiatry, it is clear that contemporary Japanese psychiatrists do not see themselves as participating in a tradition separate from Western psychiatrists and psychiatry (see Omata 2005; Kitanaka 2012). In their view, Japanese mental illnesses are for the most part the same as American or French mental illnesses. Most Japanese psychiatrists now use either the American DSM system of diagnosing and classifying mental illnesses or the more prevalent International Classification of Diseases (ICD) published by the World Health Organization.

These psychiatrists might acknowledge that there are some cultural differences that might cause some Japanese people to express symptoms differently or to be more susceptible to some forms of mental illness than others, but on the whole Japanese biomedicine is seen as the same as Western biomedicine. They see the Japanese brain as the same as the Western brain. And because the Japanese brain is seen as the same, the psychiatric mediations that are used in Japan are those that are manufactured by major international pharmaceutical corporations, such as Janssen, Pfizer, and Eli Lilly, and have brand names that would be familiar to any American pharmacist: Risperdal, Zyprexa, Paxil, or Zoloft.

Phase I: Home Confinement

Before the Dawn

In the ancient capital of Kyoto, there is a Buddhist temple called Daiunji that was built over a thousand years ago, in the year 971 (Daiunji 2011a). In his extensive history of psychiatry, Waichiro Omata notes that the daughter of Emperor Go-Sanjo was said to have suffered from mental illness. When the imperial princess visited the temple in 1072, she sat and meditated under its waterfall (Omata 2005, 65). Her cure inspired other people to visit the temple, which even today advertises on its website that it is said to be able help those with "diseases of the brain" and "diseases of the soul" (Daiunji 2011b).

At the time, it was thought that people went mad because they were possessed by supernatural spirits. The name for the spirits and ghosts in the Shinto traditions was *mononoke,* a name now associated with the popular animated movie *Princess Mononoke,* about a young girl who fights to protect the spirits of the land. People might also be driven mad by foxes, which according to Japanese legend are able to shape-shift and deceive people, or by a broad variety of creatures drawn from local traditions and from the Buddhist pantheon.[4] The best cures for possession were to physically drive the spirits out by hydrotherapy (sitting under a waterfall), by taking vile-tasting Chinese herbs, or by making the spirits so bored through quiet rest and meditation that they would leave for more exciting hosts.

According to Omata, around the Daiunji temple were numerous lodging houses that accommodated the pilgrims while they were visiting. Over the centuries, these inns specialized to take care of more of their needs; in the nineteenth century, at least two of them became private mental hospitals: the Iwakura Mental Hospital and the Kitayama Hospital (Omata 2005, 65; Mandiberg 1996, 416).

While there were temples such as Daiunji that served as pilgrimage sites for people with mental illness, by far the predominant form of mental health "care" in the Japanese middle ages was home restraint or home confinement. Under the ritsuryō legal system of the time, those who were *tenkyō* (insane, lunatic) were not considered liable for their own actions. However, their families *were* responsible for compensating any damages and otherwise making sure that their afflicted family members did not cause a public nuisance.

This placement of responsibility on families was not unusual. In premodern Japan, social control was decentralized. Neighborhood blocks,

Figure 2.1 Iwakura Daiunji Temple. From the *Miyako Meisho Zukai* (1780/1786). Courtesy of the East Asia Library, Yale University Library.

family clans, and rural hamlets were responsible for maintaining local control of their own members, with harsh punishment meted out to all if social harmony was disturbed. This system of social control at the grassroots level continued through the Edo period up through the end of the Pacific War. Many might argue that it still continues now, although in a greatly ameliorated form.

There is a particularly moving example of home confinement in Tōson Shimazaki's epic historical novel *Before the Dawn*. Written in 1929, the story is set in the tumultuous years from 1853, when the American naval commodore Matthew Perry broke Japan's two and a half centuries of hermitage, to 1868, when imperial loyalists seized power from the crumbling shogunate and restored the Meiji emperor as the ruler of Japan. The "dawn" of the title is the dawn of Japanese modernity.

Shimazaki's novel follows the travails of Hanzo Aoyama, the headman of the remote town of Magome and the surrounding hamlets, through the 1850s and 1860s as he struggles through the changes that are happening at the national and local level as Japan's feudal government crumbles and modernity sets in.[5] By the end of the book, the now-aging Hanzo begins to act out in strange ways:

> That Hanzo, the patriarch of the village, should have tried to set fire to the village temple had aroused the most intense horror and revulsion among the residents. They decided to get an immediate opinion from . . . the physician from the Yamaguchi village. Hanzo's behavior . . . was exhaustively discussed. The consensus was that the master had at last become insane.
>
> Some said that this outrage [the burning of the temple] had been perpetrated in broad daylight and if it was not certified to be the act of a madman not responsible for his actions, they themselves would strangle him for it. Others observed that although the fire had not caused any serious damage, there would certainly be a great deal of trouble if it came to the attention of the district police office. If the Aoyama [family] intended to dispose of the matter within the family, then they had better move the master to a safe place quickly, place a strict guard over him, and take appropriate measures to ensure that the people of the village could once again sleep soundly.
>
> Hanzo's cousin Eikichi carried the greatest weight in the family council. When talk in the village reached this pitch, he felt that they had no choice but to place Hanzo in confinement. The next morning he ordered Sakichi to clean up part of the woodshed and make preparations for Hanzo to be kept there. Then he called the village carpenter over to install windows high up on the wall, put in a floor to ward off the damp, and build a room next to this one where an attendant could sleep, all to be done soundly and in good order. . . . Since the place was to be used to confine Hanzo . . . who was quite

> strong, it was decided that heavy bars should be placed outside all the *shōji* windows. (Shimazaki 1987, 737–739)[6]

While locked in the woodshed, many of Hanzo's former disciples visit him. While he has some lucid moments, it is clear that he is also deteriorating. In a famous scene, he writes in beautiful calligraphy the Chinese character for *bear*, bursting out in maniacal laughter when he shows it to his daughter. By the end, his condition is frightful. Like a caged bear, he is found disheveled and flinging his feces at visitors. He dies soon after that, right before the dawn of a new Japanese era.

The Dawn of Modernity

The reasons for the collapse of the Tokugawa shogunate in 1868 are complex. Japan was under intense pressure from Western nations to open its closed borders for trade and commerce. The shogunate itself was under numerous internal pressures, and the old social order could not hold. When the shogunate was overthrown and the Meiji government was installed, the goals of the new national leaders were to modernize and industrialize the country so that it could better protect itself from what it saw as ravenous Western colonial powers. The nation's new leadership, seeing that it needed to catch up to the West, made a concerted effort to bring in the best industrial, military, colonial, political, and medical technologies to Japan.

Japan was in need of new medical technologies to treat mental illness. Omata notes that in 1868, there were some thirty institutions for the insane in Japan. Of these, eighteen were run by esoteric Buddhist sects that used hydrotherapy (sitting under a waterfall or in hot springs, being dunked in cold water, or drinking holy water); four were run by Pure Land Buddhist sects which used Chinese medicinal herbs; five were run by Nichiren Buddhists who believed that chanting sutras would cure you; two were clinics that specialized in Chinese medicinal herbs; and one was a custodial institution based on detention and confinement (Omata 2005, 117).

In 1869, the second year of the Meiji Restoration, the nation's leaders debated which medical tradition they would follow—the British one or the German one (see Totsuka 1990, 193). In the end, they chose the German tradition; indeed, until just a few decades ago, medical doctors were trained in Japan to use German rather than Japanese, English, or Latin. For example, I noticed that the notes that Dr. Kawamura at the Urakawa Red Cross Hospital wrote in a patient's *karte* (medical chart) were in German, although his younger colleagues used English or Japanese.

In 1873, the Ministry of Education established a Medical Affairs Bureau, which was responsible for training and licensing doctors.[7] The next year, the Medical Affairs Bureau published its first regulations, including ones that called for the establishment of asylums for the insane or lunatics (*tenkyōin*). The first one was built the following year in Kyoto on the temple grounds of Nanzenji temple. This hospital was known as the Kyoto Prefectural Asylum for the Epileptics and the Insane.[8] A similar asylum for the insane was established in Tokyo a few years after that.

Unfortunately, the reality was that at the time there was very little treatment for these types of mental illness except for rest and seclusion, and the only available medications were Chinese herbal medicines or sedatives such as opium extracts.

Western Medical Technologies

Western biomedicine had seeped in slowly during the Tokugawa Period (1603–1868), but the trickle became a flood once the Meiji Restoration opened up Japan fully in 1868. The first Japanese professor of psychiatry, Hajime Sakaki, was appointed to the Tokyo Imperial University after four years of study in Germany. Sakaki served as the consulting psychiatrist at the Tokyo Asylum for the Insane (Totsuka 1990, 194).

Many of the medical and psychiatric textbooks at the time were from Germany. The German psychiatrist Emil Kraepelin (1856–1926) later became extremely influential in this regard. Having traveled to Southeast Asia in 1904 to engage in cross-cultural psychiatric fieldwork, Kraepelin believed most mental illnesses to have an organic or biological cause, much like any physical illness (Metzl 2009; Jilek 1995). He focused on two forms of mental illness in particular: schizophrenia (what he called *dementia praecox*) and manic depression.

Some western treatments were introduced into Japan in the early twentieth century. Electroshock therapy and insulin shock therapy were both developed in the 1930s and were common by the 1940s. These treatments were designed to "shock" the mind, in the hope that it would somehow quieten the raging monster of schizophrenia. Leucotomy and lobotomy surgeries were also developed in the 1930s. Both shock therapy and psychosurgery fell in popularity (although didn't entirely disappear) when the first generation of true antipsychotic medications appeared after the war.

What all of these early psychiatric therapies had in common was that they were labor-intensive. Running a psychiatric hospital was expensive, as you needed a great number of nurses and orderlies in order to help hold down patients, treat them with the various procedures, or otherwise make sure that they didn't harm themselves. You also needed electroshock machines, ice water baths, and other capital-intensive infrastructure. No wonder only the rich could afford private psychiatric hospital treatment in Japan. While the destitute could find some succor in the few public hospitals for the insane, the vast majority of the middle class had few options in between (Russell 1998). Meanwhile, the Japanese criminal justice system was not interested in becoming a warehouse for the insane.

Family Responsibility

In 1900, the Law for the Confinement and Protection of the Mentally Ill was passed by the Japanese national government.[9] This was the first national law in Japan that explicitly dealt with people with mental illness. While the law used the modern term *mental illness* (*seishinbyō*) rather than "lunacy and insanity," the law did not actually go into any detail as to what *mental illness* was in the actual text of the legislation.

In any case, the primary thrust of the law was to make the "guardian, spouse, parent, head of household, or relative-to-the-fourth-degree" responsible for the confinement and protection (*kango*) of their mentally ill wards.[10] The confinement and protection requirement led to the construction of prison cells within homes, colloquially called "bird cages."[11] As can be seen in the earlier example of Hanzo Aoyama, this was merely the formalization of prior practice, rather than the creation of a new custom. One scholar notes that "mental illness was treated in the same manner as infectious disease . . . a regime of fear shame and secrecy—images of mental illness that were to last long into the decades to come" (Kitanaka 2012, 43).

According to a survey done at the time by the police, there were approximately twenty thousand people with mental illness who fell under the Confinement Act (see Sugimoto 2001, 19). Unfortunately only two thousand beds were available in psychiatric units in the entirety of Japan, about half of those were located in the Tokyo area (Nakatani 2000, 590). There was no way that the law could compel hospitalization, as the beds just didn't exist.

Under the Confinement Act, people with mental illness were considered a police and public safety issue only when they became a public nuisance, but few provisions were made for any type of public assistance or medical or mental health services for them or their families.

Mental Hospital Law of 1919

Citing the "inhumane detention" of people with mental illness in their homes, physicians started to advocate the repeal of the Confinement Act of 1900. Tokyo University psychiatrist Shuzo Kure, himself a disciple of Emil Kraepelin, was one of the leaders within this movement.[12] In one of his most famous statements, Kure wrote: "For the tens of thousands of mentally ill in our country not only have to suffer the unhappy fate of their illness, but they also have to suffer the unhappy fate of having being born in this country" (Kure 1918). A survey that he conducted in 1917 suggested that there were sixty-five thousand people with mental illness. As a result, the government enacted the Mental Hospital Law of 1919, which authorized the construction of public mental hospitals and the subsequent confinement of people with mental illness to them. The law also subsidized half the cost of institutionalization in public hospitals and one-sixth of the cost in private hospitals.[13]

Still, there was not much growth in the number of mental hospitals in the early half of the twentieth century due to a general lack of funding and a lack of political interest in the situation. Until after the end of World War II, the vast majority of middle-class people with mental illness were still being "treated" in their family homes (Mandiberg 1996, 420).

Etsuro Totsuka writes about the attitudes toward people with mental illness in early-twentieth-century Japan:

> Mental illness was regarded as genetic, incurable, impossible to understand and dangerous, namely one of the worst diseases. As a result, the mentally ill were thought to be a disgrace to the family. The Japanese did not want to talk about them, did not want to see them, to hear about them, to get married to them, and did not want to employ them. Japanese families hid these mentally ill relatives in a cell at home or in a mental hospital. Even conscientious doctors and families thought mental patients would be happier in remote asylums rather than in the community. Thus, concern about public safety took precedence over patients' rights. This historic attitude towards the mentally ill has had its effect on subsequent and current approaches to psychiatry in Japan. (Totsuka 1990: 194)

Native Japanese Psychotherapies

There are two forms of psychotherapy that were developed in Japan, both of them in the prewar period: Morita therapy and Naikan therapy. Both have reached a certain level of support in Japan, but neither can be said to be widespread or even generally accepted as clinically efficacious in the treatment of general mental health problems.[14] While it is not difficult to find a Morita therapist or Naikan practitioner, especially if you are willing to travel, neither would be the first thing most contemporary Japanese patients or their families would think of in terms of clinical psychotherapy.

Morita therapy was developed in 1919 by Dr. Shoma Morita (1874–1938), a psychiatrist at the Jikei University School of Medicine, to treat neurasthenia, neurosis, and anxiety by cultivating a sense of mindfulness of self. Morita therapy is different from Western-style "talk therapy" as it relies on a good amount of solitary isolation and introspection of the patient. In the first phase of the treatment, the patient is supposed to rest quietly in a hospital bed without moving or talking. The only movement allowable is during meals and bathroom visits. This period of rest is followed by light work, solitary journal writing, and one-on-one clinical interaction with the Morita therapist. Later, more active phases involve intensive work therapy, where the emphasis is on physical labor in order to clear and focus the mind. A full span of Morita therapy can take several weeks to several months.

An important aspect of Morita therapy is its emphasis on the notion of *arugamama,* which can be translated as "how things are/as things are." That is, it is impossible to change the world around us, so we should accept it *as it is* and try to adapt ourselves to it rather than trying to force change. This finds similarities in Bethel's own core philosophical statements of *sono mama ga iimitai* ("things are better left alone") and *soredejunchō* ("things are going well as they are"), although Bethel members and staff would draw the connection from Alcoholics Anonymous and Christian belief to Bethel, rather than from Morita therapy.

Some other aspects of Morita work therapy are similar to Bethel's workgroups, but this is largely on a superficial level, as Bethel's work program is designed to encourage social participation and interaction ("move your lips, not your hands"), whereas the purpose of Morita work therapy is to focus the patient's thoughts.

Naikan therapy was developed in the 1940s by Ishin Yoshimoto (1916–1988) as a secular version of some of the ascetic meditation practices of Pure Land Buddhism. In Naikan therapy, the patients are expected to sit in solitary, mindful meditation and think about the social relations in which they are enmeshed. Once a day, the Naikan practitioner may enter their room and ask them the three central questions of Naikan practice:

What have people around you done for you? What have you done for them in return? What troubles have you caused them? Through thinking about social relations, Naikan attempts to reintegrate people back into society. Naikan has reached some level of support in the treatment of prisoners and alcoholics but is otherwise not well known outside of those circles.

Phase II: Mass Institutionalization

In 1945, Japan suffered a crushing defeat by the Allied forces and was occupied for the next seven years. Historian John Dower has written about the deep psychological impact this had on the Japanese populace and the widespread feeling of neurasthenia (*shinkei suijaku*)—a weakening of the nervous system that leads to fatigue and apathy. This general sentiment of malaise was compounded by the return of tens of thousands defeated soldiers from the front lines, at a time when unemployment was high and food and other resources were scarce.

In 1950, the Mental Hygiene Law was passed.[15] This law was notable in that it defined "people with psychiatric disabilities" for the first time, including within this group people with substance addictions, mental retardation, and mental illness.[16] It outlawed the forced home confinement of people with mental illness and as a result sponsored the creation of public and private psychiatric hospitals to fill a need that had previously been the responsibility of families. Despite the use of the term *psychiatric disability* (*seishin shōgai*), it should be emphasized that this was a medical law and not one with any significant social welfare provisions except one: finances.

In order to address the issue of the lack of medical facilities for the mentally ill, the Mental Hygiene Law directed every prefecture to construct a public psychiatric hospital and guaranteed 50 percent of the funding from national coffers (Article 6). It also directed the public health centers that had been installed in most major towns and cities in 1947 for the control of epidemic diseases to establish mental health consultation offices as well.[17] These consultation offices were not only to advise local administrations on matters of mental health and disseminate information but also to direct mental health care in their jurisdictions.

Furthermore, the law also mandated government responsibility for up to 95 percent of the medical bills for outpatient psychiatric care. This included consultations, medication, and outpatient day care services at both private and public clinics. With only a five percent copay, psychiatry and psychiatric services became affordable for a broad spectrum of the population for the first time. Many municipalities even covered the remaining 5 percent, making treatment entirely free in those areas. Every single person I know of that that I met in Japan who was using outpatient psychiatric services used the provisions of Article 32 (as it was called) to pay for their psychiatric care.[18]

One of the darker aspects of the Mental Hygiene Law was that it established that a person with a psychiatric disability could be assigned a legal guardian who would be authorized to admit him or her into psychiatric wards, even without the patient's consent.[19] This would normally be a spouse or parent (even if the patient was an adult). Homeless people would become wards of the mayors of the towns or cities in which they resided. Legal guardians were responsible for making sure that their wards received medical care as well as ensuring that they could not cause harm to themselves or others. In reality, this meant that parents and siblings could dump their mentally ill kin without their consent into mental hospitals.

Furthermore, the law allowed for prefectural governors, on the basis of medical advice, to place people into protective medical custody without the consent of the individual or his or her relatives if they posed a risk of harm to themselves or to others.[20] In those cases, the entire cost of medical care would be assumed by the government.[21]

Like the Confinement Act that preceded it, the Mental Hygiene Law of 1950 ran roughshod over the civil rights of people with mental illness. It allowed state agents and family members such as spouses or parents to institutionalize people against their will. By shifting the burden of payment almost entirely to the government, it also reduced the barriers to long-term institutionalization, allowing families to give up relatives who would then be warehoused in psychiatric hospitals. To be fair, though, one could debate whether it was better to be imprisoned in a cage at home or in a hospital bed in a psychiatric ward. The image of frying pans and fire comes to mind.

In its first annual white paper on the state of the Japanese populace published in 1956, the Ministry of Welfare used the term *shūyō* to refer to mental patients in psychiatric hospitals.[22] This word is usually translated as "to imprison or to detain" (as in *shūyōjo,* a detention center or internment camp), although in this context the English word *institutionalize* is normally used. The term *nyūin* (hospitalization) is otherwise used in the government document when referring to patients in regular hospitals and even those in tuberculosis isolation wards. It is clear that the intent was not to treat and release psychiatric patients but to hold them indefinitely.

The Rapid Growth of Private Psychiatric Hospitals in the Postwar Period

Through the early 1950s, the Japanese economy was still trying to emerge from the rubble of war, but things began to turn around by the late 1950s and the nation began to take its first steps toward what would become the rapid economic growth period that started in the 1960s. At the time, the government realized that there was demand for broader access to medical care. Many hospitals and clinics had been devastated by the war and needed to be rebuilt. Unfortunately, banks were hesitant to loan money for the creation of hospitals, which were seen as having a low rate of return.

Psychiatric hospitals in particular were very cramped. Data from a 1960 Ministry of Welfare report shows that in 1954, occupancy at psychiatric hospitals was at 112 percent (36,969 patients for 32,834 beds). Each year, there was an increase of almost ten thousand beds, to a total of 76,133 beds by 1959, but this decreased occupancy only slightly, to a still staggering 105.6 percent. Patients in psychiatric hospitals were being crammed into every available nook and cranny. Despite the growth in the number of

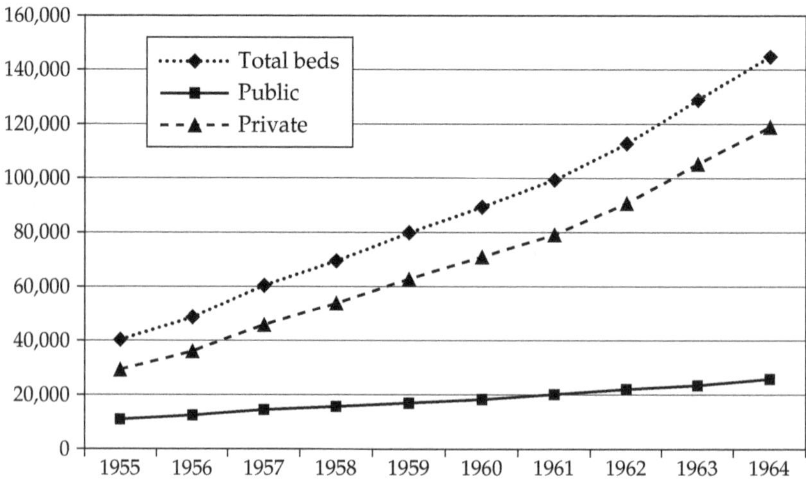

Figure 2.2 Number of beds in psychiatric hospitals, 1955–1965.
Source: Ministry of Health, Labor, and Welfare (1964).

beds, the government still felt that the nation as a whole was lagging behind the rest of the world. The same government report indicated that Japan had only 8.3 psychiatric beds available for every 10,000 people in the population, far behind other "leaders" such as America (43.3 beds per 10,000) and England (36.2) and New Zealand (45.4). Clearly greater numbers of insane people needed to be hospitalized.

Even at the time, Japan differed from most other industrialized nations in that most of the psychiatric hospitals were privately run. In the 1960s, around four-fifths of the beds for psychiatric patients in Japan were in private psychiatric hospitals, most of them very small facilities. Figure 2.2 above shows the rapid growth in the number of beds and the overwhelming percentage of private hospitals from the 1950s to the 1960s.[23]

The Chlorpromazine Revolution

In 1952, chlorpromazine (brand name: Thorazine) was developed in France and quickly caught the attention of the worldwide psychiatric care community. It was accepted for clinical use in Japan in 1955, and by the late 1950s, it was in widespread use to treat people with schizophrenia (Osawa 2010). The drug had the remarkable ability to calm agitated people, to make them seem indifferent and calm. From the perspectives of doctors, nurses, and family members, it was a wonder drug: it quieted "mad" patients, making them docile and manageable. Psychiatric wards could now look like proper hospital wards, with rows of patients happily sleeping in their beds. They no longer needed any restraining devices or straitjackets, ice water baths or icepicks, or large groups of muscular psychiatric nurses and orderlies. A simple pill or injection did it all. And a hospital could make considerable profits by prescribing chlorpromazine to their patients.

From the perspective of the patients, chlorpromazine and the other first-generation antipsychotics (such as Haloperidol and Sulpiride, released in Japan in 1966 and 1979, respectively) were double-edged swords. For many, especially in the West (for better or for worse, the United States and Italy were notable pioneers in deinstitutionalization), these miraculous new drugs quieted the voices, stifled delusional thoughts, and allowed many to leave the mental asylums and live independently. But on the down side, for others the high doses of chlorpromazine and other first-generation antipsychotics fogged their minds, made them simultaneously restless but also unable to move quickly. Patients shuffled aimlessly in psychiatric wards, back and forth. The high doses also made their hands shake, their faces grimace, and their mouths drool. Much of what the general public now associates with the external manifestations of mental illness are actually the unfortunate side effects of the early antipsychotics.

Financing the Growth of Private Psychiatric Hospitals

In July of 1960 a law was passed creating a special government agency, the Medical Care Facilities Finance Corporation.[24] This quasi-bank was designed to finance the building of private hospitals and clinics in Japan through the use of government-backed loans with very low interest rates. This led to a rapid expansion of private hospitals and clinics, including those dealing with mental health.

Doctors and other medical entrepreneurs realized that there was money to be made in the mental health field. The government allowed mental hospitals to have one-third the number of doctors and only two-thirds the number of nursing staff that regular wards were required to have (see Ito and Sederer 1999, 209; Tomita 2000, 111). Psychiatric hospitals could petition to have even those lax regulations waived, so in many cases, the true ratio of staff to patients was much lower. For example, reporter Kazuo Okuma noted that in the hospital he investigated, there were only fifteen to twenty registered nurses for the four hundred patients there, with very high turnover of nursing staff due to the lack of training and low pay.

A 1961 revision to the law established that people who were involuntarily institutionalized or received care in either private or public psychiatric hospitals would receive free care. The national government increased its payment for people who were forcibly institutionalized from 50 percent to 80 percent, with the prefectural government making up the remainder. This led to a near doubling of the expenditures on people with mental illness from 1962 to 1966.[25]

Doctors followed the money, and the number of hospital beds for psychiatric units exploded. In 1956, there were only around 50,000 beds, but by 1966, there were 190,000 beds, almost a fourfold increase. About a third of these (65,000) were forced institutionalizations. The government noted that of the 1.24 million people with psychiatric disabilities in 1966, an estimated 280,000 required hospitalization, data that encouraged them to try even harder (and spend even more money) to increase the number of beds.[26]

In his self-described "explosive" memoir, psychiatrist Yasushi Nagaoka explains that running a psychiatric hospital in the postwar period was easy money.[27] You could easily get a loan from the government at very low interest rates. You didn't need any special equipment, and you didn't have to hire nearly as many nurses as other hospitals. You could keep the patients sedated on high doses of antipsychotics (for which the government would reimburse your in-house pharmacy). It's no wonder that the head of the Japanese Medical Association, Dr. Taro Takemi, said, "The practice of psychiatric medicine is like livestock farming" (Nagaoka 2008, 143).

Nagaoka remembers his father (also a psychiatrist) telling him, "Psychiatry is the field that doctors choose when they can't make it in any other specialty." When he asked his friends in medical school why they chose psychiatry, they told him, "Psychiatry seemed like it was the easiest field. And you can make a good amount of money doing it." (Nagaoka 2008, 17–18).

Eugenic Sterilization

This is not to say that the Japanese government was not concerned with the growing number of mentally ill citizens. One way to reduce costs is to prevent people with mental illness from propagating. Eugenics was popular in many western countries during the early twentieth century (including in the United States); anthropologist Jennifer Robertson notes that in the prewar period, British and American eugenics texts were eagerly read by Japanese political and social leaders who were trying to argue for the purity of the Japanese race. Early Japanese feminists such as Raicho Hiratsuka also supported eugenics laws, which they saw as part of their goal of strengthening the Japanese nation (Matsubara 1998).

In particular, Robertson notes a debate between two leading Japanese eugenicists in the 1920s and 1930s as to whether "positive" or "negative" eugenics was a better solution to improving the population:

> Positive eugenics, promoted by Ikeda Shigenori, refers to the improvement of circumstances of sexual reproduction and thus incorporates advances in sanitation, nutrition, and physical education into strategies to shape the reproductive choices and decisions of individuals and families. The effects of biology (genetics) and environment are conflated. In this connection, "eugenic" was often used in the early twentieth-century Japanese literature as both an adjective meaning, and a euphemism for, "hygienic" and "scientific." Negative eugenics, enthusiastically advocated by Nagai Hisomu, involves the prevention of sexual reproduction, through induced abortion or sterilization, among people deemed unfit. "Unfit" was an ambiguous term that included alcoholics, "lepers," the mentally ill, the criminal, the

> physically disabled, and the sexually alternative among other categories of people. (2002: 196)

In 1940, the Japanese government passed its first eugenics law, based on the 1933 Law for the Prevention of Genetically Diseased Offspring in Nazi Germany.[28] The law called for the prevention of the number of people with "pernicious hereditary diseases." Heading the top of the list of categories authorized for eugenic surgery was "hereditary mental illnesses."[29] While only 454 eugenic surgeries were performed between 1941 and 1945, the spirit of the law still managed to make it clear that mentally ill persons were a drain on national resources.[30] One scholar notes that the number of people in psychiatric hospitals plummeted in its aftermath and that the mortality rate at the Matsuzawa Hospital for the mentally ill in Tokyo was 40 percent in 1945, mostly due to starvation (Russell 1988, 49).

Even after its defeat in 1945, the ardor for protecting the purity of the race continued unabated. In 1948, the Japanese government passed the Eugenic Protection Law with this stated purpose: "This law attempts to prevent the birth of defective offspring from the perspective of eugenics as well as protect the health and life of mothers."[31] While there were a few positive eugenic elements (focus on sanitation, nutrition, or education), the law was overwhelmingly oriented toward "negative eugenics"—that is, the sterilization of certain types of people and the prevention of the birth of "unfits."

For example, the law listed the conditions under which eugenic surgery and abortion were permitted.[32] The law normally allowed for eugenic surgery (that is, sterilization) and abortion only with the permission of the patient and their spouse (if applicable), but this consent could be waived if the person was a minor, mentally ill, or mentally retarded. In these cases, the patient's legal guardian or, in the absence of a legal guardian, the governor of a prefecture could request the Prefectural Eugenic Protection Committee to authorize the eugenic surgery or abortion without the patient's consent (Kimura 1991, 159–160).

In a 1965 white paper, the Ministry of Welfare noted:

> The Eugenics Protection Law goal is to prevent the birth of inferior offspring from the perspective of eugenic sciences. Eugenic surgery [sterilization] can be authorized if the person or his/her spouse has a genetic mental illness, genetic physical abnormality, or genetic mental retardation; or, if any of the relatives in the 4th degree of the person or his/her spouse has a genetic mental illness, genetic physical abnormality, or genetic mental

> retardation. In these cases, if the prefectural committee finds that this is in the public interest, the entire cost will be borne at public expense.

Under the Eugenics Protection Law, the following (among others) were considered hereditary conditions: "schizophrenia, manic depression, epilepsy . . . pronounced genetic psychiatric types [such as] pronounced sexual psychopathology and pronounced inclination towards crime . . . pronounced genetic physical conditions such as . . . total blindness, retinitis pigmentosa, genetic deafness or hearing impairment, hemophilia. . . ."

According to Takashi Tsuchiya (1997), from 1949 to 1994 there were 16,520 sterilizations performed without the patient's consent, usually under the category of hereditary diseases. The majority of the surgeries—68 percent—were on women. In my own research with people who were deaf or hard of hearing in Japan, I came across many elderly deaf women who had had hysterectomies when they were young girls. Other Japanese researchers have reported on eugenic sterilization of people with physical disabilities when they were institutionalized.

The Reischauer Incident and the Clark Report

On March 24, 1964, U.S. Ambassador to Japan Edwin Reischauer was leaving his office in Tokyo when a young Japanese man stabbed him with a knife. The assailant was later found to have had a history of mental illness. While Reischauer survived the incident, it was a huge shock to U.S.-Japan relations, as Reischauer was well known as a friend to Japan. Furthermore, Reischauer was given substandard treatment at a local Japanese hospital, receiving a blood transfusion tainted with the hepatitis virus, leading to further national embarrassment.

The "Reischauer incident," as it was known in Japan, became the impetus for sweeping changes to mental health laws the following year that gave more authority to local governments to force the institutionalization of people with mental illness, required mandatory reporting of the hospitalization of people with mental illness, and guaranteed free mental health care (including clinical and pharmaceutical coverage) to people with mental illness through the national health insurance system.

Two years after the Reischauer incident, the Japanese government asked noted British psychiatrist David Clark to conduct research on Japanese mental health care facilities. His report was issued in 1968 through the World Health Organization.[33] Many of the aspects of the report are things that were covered earlier in this chapter, such as the large number of private psychiatric hospitals and the relatively small size of psychiatric hospitals in Japan. Clark noted that while the psychiatric hospitals he came across were newly built, that did not mean that the conditions were any better than the asylums he knew in England or the United States:

> Japanese mental hospitals differ from those in Europe and the United States of America in that they are small, recently built (few older than twenty years) and mostly privately operated. There are however many similarities: the patients are mostly schizophrenics; many are long-stay residents; many are apathetic, withdrawn and tend to regression; the wards are overcrowded.
>
> Too many wards were locked unnecessarily. There was too much use of methods of restraint, seclusion rooms, cells and security blocks. Patients were locked in solitary confinement, many clearly for long periods. In two hospitals the newest buildings were security blocks with elaborate devices such as steel bars, closed circuit television, etc., all of which lead to harmful isolation and regression.

In explaining the trend for institutionalization, Clark noted that the financial incentives made inpatient treatment much more lucrative than outpatient visitations:

> The payments for inpatient treatment are well worked out and relatively generous. A doctor can make a good living treating inpatients and hospitals flourish economically. Outpatient psychiatric treatment is poorly paid and a flat rate is paid for each visit regardless of its length or the quality or intensity of the treatment given. This means that doctors are discouraged from spending any length of time with individual patients and have a positive incentive to see very many patients frequently for very brief interviews. The writer has been told that it is not possible for a doctor to make a living practising psychotherapy, or seeing patients for planned and lengthy interviews. There is no payment to psychiatrists for time they may spend advising courts, child guidance clinics, prefectural governments, etc. This means that there is a positive inducement for a psychiatrist to spend his time exclusively on individual treatment, especially physical treatment of inpatients and to turn his back on work for community mental health services. This must inevitably cripple development and impoverish such services.

Clark was critical of the training of psychiatrists. There was no special training for doctors who wished to be psychiatrists. Anyone who had graduated from medical school and had passed the general medical board examination could practice as a psychiatrist. Surprisingly, fifty years after his report, this system is still in place: Any general practitioner can practice as a psychiatrist.

> Psychiatric instruction consists usually of a few formal lectures and demonstrations of patients, though some universities include a period of attachment to the department of psychiatry where some patients are examined.
>
> There is little specialization within psychiatry; every psychiatrist expects to handle psychosis, inpatient and outpatient psychogenic reactions (depressions and psychoneurosis), disturbed children, subnormal persons, epileptics and psychotherapy.

In his conclusion, Clark warned that Japan might be following in the same footsteps as England or the United States in the creation of long-term institutionalized patients:

> Certain trends in the population of the mental hospitals were noted. During the last, fifteen years many new places in Japanese mental hospitals have been made available and filled with schizophrenics. In the hospitals visited there was already a tendency for a chronic population to accumulate. The number of patients who had stayed more than five years was increasing and most of these were people in early adult life aged 25–35. With a normal life span they may live another thirty years in the hospitals.
>
> It appears that Japan is in grave danger of suffering the same experience as Europe. There schizophrenics were gathered into hospitals, cared for physically and locked up in idleness. They lived long lives and the inpatient population accumulated until the hospitals filled with vast numbers of idle, hopeless, "institutionalized" people. Only recently, by the rigorous application of social psychiatry, of active therapy and rehabilitation has this trend been reversed.

As we will see, Clark was much too optimistic about the future of psychiatric treatment in Japan. Despite his report, long-term institutionalization of psychiatric patients became the norm, with some patients hospitalized for decades.

Deinstitutionalization in the West

Despite Clark's warnings, there was no subsequent national movement to deinstitutionalize psychiatric patients in Japan into community-based programs, although there were local efforts.[34] Running private psychiatric hospitals was much too lucrative for the psychiatrists to complain, and there was no fiscal pressure on politicians or bureaucrats to take on the logistical headache of deinstitutionalization, what with the economy booming and the government flush with cash through much of the 1970s and 1980s. The money kept flowing; except for the patients in the psychiatric hospitals, everyone was happy.

In contrast, large-scale deinstitutionalization in the United States had already begun in 1963 with the Mental Retardation Facilities and Community Mental Health Centers Construction Act. One of this bill's supporters was President John F. Kennedy, whose younger sister Rosemary was said to have a mental illness; she was lobotomized and then permanently institutionalized by her family (Leamer 1994). The bill had two goals: the release of patients who were warehoused in psychiatric institutions (most of which were large state-run hospitals) and the creation of local community-based mental health care centers.

The American public was already primed to view the large state-run mental asylums with distrust. Sociologist Erving Goffman's 1961 book *Asylums*, a bestseller, criticized the mechanisms by which such "total institutions" created the very type of patients and symptoms they were allegedly trying to treat. The following year, Ken Kesey's novel *One Flew Over the Cuckoo's Nest*, which focused on the institutionalization of mental patients, came out. In 1965, Senator Robert Kennedy visited the Willowbrook State School for the Mentally Retarded and issued a scathing summary of the deplorable conditions there.[35]

Deinstitutionalization was aided by the aforementioned development of first-generation antipsychotic medications in the 1950s and 1960s. Many patients with formerly unmanageable psychoses were now able to control their symptoms enough to be able to live independently or with their families. The first stage of deinstitutionalization occurred in America during the mid- to late 1960s, and a great number of institutionalized patients were released. Unfortunately, due to political infighting and budgetary constraints, the second stage, the creation of local community-based mental health care organizations, never happened in the United States. A large number of former psychiatric hospital patients who were not able to live with their families or to live independently instead became homeless or ended up in prison.

Meanwhile, life in Japanese psychiatric hospitals continued much as Clark had found them. The development of those new antipsychotic medications had made psychiatric patients easy to manage but it did not result in deinstitutionalization, nor did it result in the development of a national policy for the creation of community-based mental health services (Ito and Sederer 1999, 209).

The public did not know what was going on in Japanese psychiatric hospitals until the 1970s and 1980s, when a series of scandals rocked the mental health care world. This in turn helped push Japan toward new models.

Revelations at Japanese Psychiatric Hospitals

In 1970, a young man by the name of Kazuo Okuma was carried by his wife and a friend to a private psychiatric hospital. Kazuo smelled of cheap alcohol and was nursing a bad hangover. The chief psychiatrist (and owner of the hospital) looked into his eyes with a penlight and talked to him for a few minutes before declaring him a chronic alcoholic and admitting him to the hospital's psychiatric ward. At the time, alcoholics were seen as having a severe mental illness and many psychiatric wards were filled with alcoholic patients. Okuma was placed into solitary confinement and given a strong sedative. When he woke up a couple of days later, he was put in with the general psychiatric population in a locked ward.

In reality, Okuma was not an alcoholic but a reporter for *Asahi Shimbun,* one of the leading national dailies. Although he had planned to spend fourteen days in the psychiatric hospital, he made it through only eleven before he gave the secret "help!" signal to his wife during one of her visits; she managed to have him discharged, much to the vehement disagreement of the chief psychiatrist that had labeled him an alcoholic. Kazuo wrote about his experiences in a series of articles in *Asahi Shimbun.* These later became a bestselling book called *Report—Psychiatric Hospitals* (1973).

The private hospital that Okuma described was absolutely horrible. There was unimaginable overcrowding. Even when he was in "solitary" confinement, Okuma had to share his cell with a teenager, whom he befriended. Understaffing was chronic, and patients were forced to do many of the jobs that the law required nursing staff to handle. Many of the patients had been there for many years and had given up any hope of ever leaving. The psychiatrist only saw them for a few minutes each week on his rounds. Elderly patients with dementia were crammed into a room that the staff labeled the "filth room," in which patients would lie in their own excrement. In the winter, there was no heat except for a single kerosene stove for the entire ward.

The hospital chief ruled over this domain like a feudal lord of yore. In one of the most incredible parts of Okuma's story, the hospital chief decided to run in a local election. He forced his patients to become part of his campaign: they wrote addresses on thousands of campaign postcards and glued campaign posters onto canvassing boards. Adding insult to injury, on the day of the election, he had his staff round up the few patients who still had voting rights and drove them to the balloting booth—but not before checking several times that they knew how to write the chief's name on the ballot form. Fortunately, the chief lost the election.

Despite the significant attention Okuma's reportage briefly received in the early 1970s, there was almost no visible change in the management of psychiatric hospitals in Japan in its aftermath. In the 1980s, another scandal emerged that was even more appalling.

1983—The Utsunomiya Hospital Incident

In 1983, two psychiatric inpatients died in separate incidents at the Hotokukai Utsunomiya Hospital, a private psychiatric hospital located in a large city about an hour north of Tokyo. No one took note of their deaths at the time. The details unfolded first in a newspaper article that was published on March 14, 1984. The newspaper article led to a police raid of the facilities; the arrest of the hospital director and four staff members on charges of murder, assault, and fraud; and finally, domestic and international attention on the treatment of patients at Japanese psychiatric hospitals.

Utsunomiya Hospital was run by a Dr. Bunnoshin Ishikawa. Born in 1925, Dr. Ishikawa had graduated in 1949 from Osaka University Medical School; a few years later he set up his own small clinician's office. In the course of another few years, he was able to expand it into a hospital and then into a hospital group. He wanted to open up a psychiatric hospital, but he had practiced in internal medicine his entire life and had no experience in psychiatry, so he enrolled as a research student at the Tokyo University Medical School Department of Psychiatry. This was not the norm, as one did not require special training other than a medical degree to practice psychiatry; perhaps it was a sign of Ishikawa's eagerness to enter his new field of study.

Dr. Ishikawa's supervisor at Tokyo University was Dr. Nobuyoshi Takemura in the Brain Research Group. Although Dr. Takemura had no psychiatric clinical experience himself, he became Dr. Ishikawa's link to

Tokyo University, which, as the leading university in Japan, was a source of much prestige.

Utsunomiya Hospital opened its doors as a private psychiatric hospital in 1961. Over the years, the hospital quickly expanded from a modest 57 beds to 852 a decade later. The hospital became famous for accepting patients who had been refused by other psychiatric hospitals. The hospital was nicknamed the "North Kanto Prison" by those who knew its reputation for staff brutality, locked wards, and generally dismal conditions.[36]

By 1983, the hospital had 920 beds and 948 psychiatric inpatients. Only three doctors saw all of the patients, Dr. Ishikawa and two others. Staffing was kept at minimal levels, with senior patients serving as nursing aides in many cases. (This was not unusual; Okuma reported that patients served in staff positions at the hospital he investigated as well.) What was unusual was that at Utsunomiya Hospital, senior patients and untrained orderlies conducted clinical procedures such as taking X-rays and administering EEGs.

On December 30, 1983, one of the patients was granted a rare visitation privilege. He had been admitted as an alcoholic and had been in the hospital for five months. He told his visitor about the horrendous conditions at Utsunomiya, but the conversation was overheard by a staff member. After the visit ended, five staff members took him aside and beat him with a metal bat and other implements. He later died the same day. As in earlier incidents at the hospital, the true cause of death was covered up by the clinical staff.

On March 15 the next year, an *Asahi Shimbun* article, "A 'Death Lynch' of Two Patients," chronicled the death of the man in December as well as another patient earlier in the year. The police moved in and on March 29, 1984, the director and four hospital staff were arrested on charges of inflicting bodily injuries. As the investigation proceeded, more charges were added: medical fraud (for using unlicensed staff in clinical procedures) and bodily injury resulting in death. Many of the patients at the hospital were also found to have been detained illegally under the Mental Hygiene Law.

The criminal investigation revealed that through Dr. Takemura, Tokyo University Medical School had had a very close relationship with the hospital. They were running numerous clinical experiments on the patients. Tape recordings of clinical interviews would later come to light showing that the Tokyo University researchers knew full well what was going on at the hospital. The head of one of the clinical research teams, Dr. Yoichi Saito, had a database of patients in which it was noted that in the three years preceding the investigation, 222 patients had died.[37] Unfortunately, forensic investigation into the cause of death of most of those patients could not be done, as the bodies had already been cremated according to Japanese custom (Totsuka 1990, 197).

The police investigation nevertheless revealed that illegal autopsies had been done on the patients who had died, with untrained orderlies and, in some situations, senior patients themselves conducting the autopsies on their dead comrades. The principal goal of the autopsies was the removal of the brains, which were sent to Dr. Takemura's Brain Research Group at Tokyo University.

At the twenty-fifth anniversary celebration of Utsunomiya Hospital, Dr. Takemura was reported to have said, "Thanks to the central efforts of Dr. Takajiro Hirahata and Dr. Bunnoshin, like a fish in water, we [at Tokyo University] have maintained a close relationship with this hospital. As a result of this, in the realm of psychiatry as well as in our lives, we have been able to reap a bountiful harvest [*tadai na shūkaku wo etsutsu arimasu*]."[38] In the context of his collection of brains harvested from the dead bodies of former patients, Dr. Takemura's warm sentiments about his relationship at Utsunomiya Hospital remind me of the earlier statement by the head of the Japanese Medical Association, that "the practice of psychiatric medicine is like livestock farming" (Nagaoka 2008, 143).

The hospital chief, Dr. Ishikawa, was given a one-year sentence, which he appealed. The remaining staff members were given sentences ranging from eighteen months to four years on the charges of bodily injury resulting in death. As a result of the scandal, Dr. Takemura was forced to resign from Tokyo University, but he was immediately hired by Utsunomiya Hospital and was never criminally prosecuted. Dr. Ishikawa himself resigned from his position as head of Utsunomiya Hospital.

Phase III: Growth of Patient's Rights and Independent Living

The shift from mass institutionalization to independent living in the 1980s and 1990s was driven by the development of second-generation antipsychotics, which allowed many more people with severe mental illness to live outside of the closed hospital wards. This was in turn also forced by government cutbacks on the reimbursement of long-term care for people with mental illness as well as revelations of scandals at several psychiatric hospitals, which turned the climate against long-term institutionalization.

Early Steps toward Independent Living

The Utsunomiya incident was not an isolated one. There were many similar incidents at other private psychiatric hospitals. But the uproar caused by the Utsunomiya incident managed to bring international scrutiny to the situation. The International Court of Justice as well as the United Nations Sub-Commission on Prevention of Discrimination and Protection of Minorities held hearings on the issue (Mandiberg 1996, 413). This caused the government, finally, to propose legislation that protected the civil rights of people with psychiatric disabilities. This was quickly met with intense criticism from the Japanese Private Mental Hospital Association. In the past, this lobbying would have worked to prevent further scrutiny, but this time the domestic and international pressure was too much for inaction.

In 1987, changes were made to the Mental Hygiene Law that allowed for the creation of independent living facilities and sheltered workshops. The independent living facilities were designed to help people with mental illness in their rehabilitation to daily life. The sheltered workshops were designed to provide training and jobs for people with mental illness. The legislation emphasized that consent of the patient was of upmost importance, and it also allowed for smoother discharge procedures. Various hospitals across Japan had already been experimenting for some years with the deinstitutionalization into the community of some of their patients, and the new amendments gave their efforts extra support.

As I mentioned earlier, the 1950 Mental Hygiene Law referred to "people with psychiatric disabilities" (*seishin shōgaisha*), but there were no provisions in it that treated mental illness as a disability. In contrast, the Welfare Law for the Physically Disabled (1949) and the Welfare Law for the Mentally Retarded (1960) had both allocated significant welfare benefits for people with physical or intellectual disabilities. To add insult to injury, when the Fundamental Law for People with Disabilities was enacted in 1970, only physical and intellectual disabilities were included. It wasn't until 1993 that the Fundamental Law for People with Disabilities was changed to include people with psychiatric disabilities, granting them many but not all of the benefits that people with other disabilities had, including access to a disability pension, reduced taxes, reduced medical care costs, and free or lower fees on public transportation and public facilities such as museums.

According to 2008 Japanese government statistics (Mental White Book 2008: 198), there were 2,868,000 people with psychiatric disabilities in

Japan, about 2.2 percent of the entire population. Of that number, 323,000 were in institutional care, and the rest (approximately 2.5 million) were outpatients.

The Ministry of Health and Social Welfare defines psychiatric disabilities in terms of seven categories:

- Vascular and other forms of dementia;
- Emotional and behavioral problems caused by psychotropic substance abuse;
- Schizophrenia and schizophreniform disorders;
- Emotional disorders (including bipolar disorder);
- Neuroses, stress-related disorders, and other somatoform disorders;
- Other types of mental and behavioral disorders;
- Epilepsy[39]

People with schizophrenia and schizophreniform disorders are just a small part of the total number of people with mental illness in Japan (558,000 of the 2.9 million), but they represent an overwhelming majority of the people institutionalized in mental hospitals and psychiatric wards. Almost two hundred thousand people are in full-time institutional care with schizophrenia—this represents almost two thirds of the total number of people in institutional care with mental illness in Japan.

Psychiatry in Japan Today

If you were hospitalized in Japan with a serious mental illness such as schizophrenia, you could expect several things. First, you would most likely be staying in a private psychiatric hospital rather than a public one. You would likely have been admitted with your voluntary consent, although in some cases your family could involuntarily admit you or, in much rarer cases, you could be temporarily hospitalized against your will by a psychiatrist or by the government psychiatric review board.

Once in a psychiatric hospital, you could expect to stay there a fairly long time, even several years. The big difference from the past is that technically, you could voluntarily discharge yourself at any time. But even if you were discharged, you might just end up being admitted again. This is especially the case if your family did not want you back home or there were no community-based programs in your area.

While in the hospital, you could expect to take several different antipsychotics at a time in rather high doses, perhaps along with antidepressants and other medications. These would fuzz up your brain, making it hard at times to think straight. You would likely gain weight because of the side effects of the drugs. Still, the hospital is a modern facility with lots of windows (with bars) and is nice, bright, and sunny. They run a few day programs such as simple work therapy, or you might watch television all day long. If you are at a progressive facility, you might spend the day at their day care facility, where you might bake bread or be a waiter in their café.

In short, your stay would be in a private psychiatric hospital, the likely length of your stay would be long, you would be subjected to high doses of multiple medications, and there would be an absence of talk therapy and of community-based mental health care.

Predominance of Private Psychiatric Hospitals In 2008, 82 percent of the 1,667 psychiatric hospitals in Japan were privately run. If we go by the number of beds rather than by the number of hospitals, the private-to-public margin is even larger. Of the 350,353 total beds in psychiatric units, 90 percent were in private hands.[40] The average size of a private psychiatric hospital is around 250 beds, which is moderately large. Most of these private hospitals are independent enterprises (that is, not part of hospital chains) and are run by their psychiatrist-directors.[41]

The overwhelming predominance of private psychiatric hospitals means that it is very difficult for the government to change psychiatric mental health policy without strong lobbying pushback from the Japan Private Mental Hospital Association or the problem of potentially releasing thousands of mentally ill patients into communities that are not prepared for them. The government is aware of the American experience with deinstitutionalization and there are many stakeholders, so change has been very slow. There are other important issues besides private care that the government has been working on, such as the length of stay, the comparatively greater use of pharmaceuticals, and absence of community-based care. The rest of the chapter will examine these.

Long Average Length of Stays In 2007, the average length of stay in a Japanese psychiatric hospital was 318 days, much longer than in any other industrialized country.[42] In contrast, in the United States the average length of stay was just seven days, although this figure is artificially low due to the lack of national health insurance and laws preventing extended involuntary admission.[43] In Canada, the average length of stay in a psychiatric ward was 16 days, and in the United Kingdom it was 54 days. The closest to Japan was another Asian neighbor, Korea, where it was 105 days.[44]

Emphasis on the metric of "average length of stay" hides some startling details. Many patients with minor issues such as an anxiety attack are hospitalized for only a few days, which means that others with more serious conditions stay much longer. In a 2004 study of East Asian counties, researchers found that the median stay for patients with schizophrenia in Japan was 3,783 days—more than ten years![45]

To be fair, the average length of stay at Japanese psychiatric hospitals has been steadily decreasing since the 1990s.[46] And Japanese psychiatric hospitals should not bear the entire brunt of the criticism for long hospital stays. Especially since the post-1987 legislative reforms, most psychiatric patients technically are in hospitals of their own volition. They *could* discharge themselves if they wanted to. But there are very few community-based programs to which the hospitals could release these patients and so the patients themselves are reluctant to leave.

Family members are known to put pressure on hospitals to keep their relatives safely warehoused away. Ito and Sederer note that 39.9 percent of families of hospitalized psychiatric patients said that they did not want

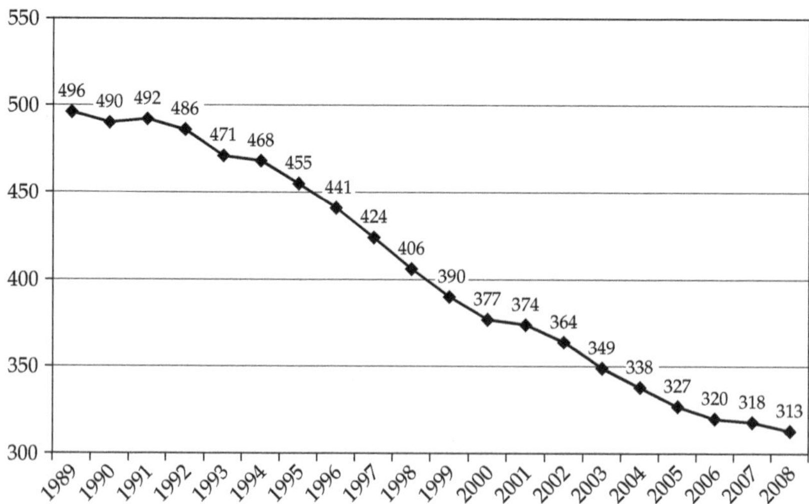

Figure 2.3 Average length of stay in psychiatric hospitals, 1989–2008
Source: Ministry of Health, Labor, and Welfare (2010)

them to come back home; of those that did, 29.5 percent said that it would cause difficulties if they did (Ito and Sederer 1999, 212). In Japan this is referred to as "hospital admission for social reasons" (*shakaiteki nyūin*) rather than for medical reasons.

Patients are well aware that they have nowhere else to go. The government ran a comprehensive survey of patients in psychiatric wards and asked them the question, "If the conditions were right for [social] integration, would you discharge yourself from the hospital?" Of the 103,100 patients who had been hospitalized for less than a year, almost a quarter of them said yes. This represented 25,300 patients. Of the 44,100 patients who had been hospitalized for more than twenty years, a fifth said that they would want to be discharged under those circumstances.[47]

Of course, if all of the patients who said yes were actually discharged—all 75,700 of them—the government would need to make sure the conditions were right for social integration, or they might end up homeless or in prison, as in many Western countries.[48]

Polypharmacy and High Dosing *Polypharmacy* refers to the use of multiple medications at the same time. With the exception of rare cases where drug "cocktail" regimens have been clinically verified (for example, in cancer drugs or anti-HIV retrovirals), the medical standard of care in the United States is usually to prescribe only one type of each class of a drug. This helps to avoid drug interactions that might happen if you were to give two different antidepressants that acted on the same neural pathways, for example.

In contrast, polypharmacy is the norm in Japan. In a 2002 study reported in *The Lancet,* Nori Takei and others found that of the 2,405 patients with schizophrenia surveyed at

> 16 national psychiatric hospitals, 50% were receiving three or more antipsychotics concomitantly; 18% were receiving four or more. Among the 457 patients taking risperidone, 59% received two or more types of antipsychotics. New drugs seem to be simply added to current ones. Moreover, along with multiple antipsychotics, two or more types of anticholinergic drugs and hypnotics are generally given to schizophrenic patients for many years or even decades. Consequently, secondary negative symptoms and extrapyramidal side-effects are highly likely and cannot be overlooked.

The authors of the article explain that polypharmacy in Japan may have its roots in the herbal medications of China, where it is very common for the herbal practitioner to mix his or her own special blend of herbs in the appropriate proportion for each patient. The authors further argue that "this situation is reflected symbolically in a compound that consists of chlorpromazine, promethazine, and phenobarbital, which is still used as a hypnotic, especially for patients with schizophrenia. The notion of multi-acting receptor-targeted antipsychotic agents (MARTA) for atypical antipsychotics should not be used as the justification for administering multiple neuroleptics." In simple English—mixing herbs is one thing, mixing antipsychotics is something entirely else, and has not proven to be clinically beneficial.

In addition to polypharmacy, Japanese psychiatric patients also receive higher doses of medication than in other countries. The figure often used to compare medication dosing across countries—given that there is a broad range of psychiatric medications available—is in chlorpromazine equivalent units (CPZ mg).

The Research on East Asia Psychotropic Prescription (REAP) study compared dosing for schizophrenia in different countries in East Asia. They found that in 2001, Japanese patients were receiving 1004 CPZ mg per day, while their Hong Kong peers were receiving 512 CPZ mg and Koreans were getting 763 CPZ mg.

In response to this report, the general trend changed in the direction of reducing dosages, and the 2004 REAP study showed a considerable drop. Japan fell by just a little less than 50 percent, to 524 CPZ mg per day. The other countries also fell, but by much less pronounced amounts.[49]

This is still high. Created by the World Health Organization, the Defined Daily Dose (DDD) is the assumed average maintenance dose of a drug if used for its main purpose. For schizophrenia, the DDD is 300 mg of chlorpromazine per day. Looked at this way, schizophrenic patients in Japan in 2001 were receiving over three times the defined daily dose of antipsychotics each day; even in 2004 they were still receiving one and a half times as much as recommended.[50]

Absence of Talk Therapy

In his classic works *The History of Sexuality Vol. 1* and *The Birth of the Clinic,* French philosopher Michel Foucault connected the Christian religious rite of confession to psychotherapy as forms of self-articulation. The weekly therapy session has become both ritualized performance and sacred rite. Foucault has written much on the archaeology and history of psychiatry (1963, 1964, 1973), questioning everything from the form and structure of mental hospitals to the practices of psychiatry and psychotherapy.

It is too bad that Foucault never wrote about psychiatry in Japan, because it can be characterized as notably *not* talk therapy. There has never been a moment when a form of talk therapy has been predominant in Japan, whether Freudian or post-Freudian psychoanalysis or psychodynamic psychotherapy.[51] Perhaps this is because, unlike Christianity, the Buddhist and Shinto traditions have no notion of the narrative confession of sins.[52] It's not impossible to find a purely psychodynamic therapist in Japan, especially in the metropolises of Osaka or Tokyo. But it is relatively rare, and it is not covered by the national health care system, so it is very expensive.

If you are diagnosed with a mood disorder (such as depression or bipolar disorder) or a personality disorder and don't need hospitalization, you might see a psychiatrist or a general practitioner on an outpatient basis. Your conversation with that doctor will likely be 15 to 30 minutes at first and then 1 to 10 minutes each time after that. Your doctor might suggest that you see a psychiatric social worker who might help you with everyday coping skills or assign you to a variety of group or individual therapies at the outpatient psychiatric day care unit, such as cognitive behavioral therapy, social skills training, work therapy, or even psychodrama therapy. It would be relatively rare for you to have scheduled, weekly, one-on-one intensive sessions with someone where you talked about your past and present fears, anxieties, and concerns.

This comparison with the United States as the mecca of talk therapy may soon be an anachronism, as America is itself moving away from individualized talk therapy toward psychopharmaceutical therapy. In this case, however, the impetus of change is coming from American private insurance companies who are loath to reimburse fees relating to talk therapy and only too happy to pay for much cheaper medication instead.

The Sick Role in Japan

Sociologist Talcott Parsons talked about something he called the "sick role," which he understood as a period during which you are exempted from your normal social duties and responsibilities but in turn are obligated to try to get better and to cooperate with your doctors and nurses to the best of your ability (Parsons 1951, 452–460). Patients in Japan are very much expected to play the sick role in hospitals, giving up their outside responsibilities and becoming a passive, compliant, and . . . patient.

Meanwhile, on the outside, life goes on. Your friends graduate and get jobs. They get married and have children. This is the negative side of the sick role. You are no longer a social being but are stuck in a period of what anthropologists call "liminality" and what sociologists used to call "social deviance." Life cannot continue until you get better, but psychiatry has not yet cured mental illnesses, only found medications that dampen some of the symptoms for a time.

This makes mental illness profoundly disabling in Japan. If you are *ill*, you are expected to do everything you can to become better before returning back to society. In many ways, the push to have mental illness understood as a psychiatric *disability* is an insistence that social participation can happen even without the underlying impairment being fully cured.

Absence of Community-Based Mental Health Programs

Unfortunately, returning to society is not easy. The 1965 Clark Report noted the lack of community-based mental health care programs that could serve to help integrate people with mental illness into their local communities. This situation continued well into the 1980s. In her doctoral dissertation on community-based living in Japan, anthropologist Mamiya Ikuko noted that in the 1960s, the national organization of psychiatric social workers in Japan had expressed the fear that "psychiatric disability (schizophrenia) was at risk of becoming chronic, so hospital-based therapy needs to focus on the rehabilitation of social skills" (Mamiya 2005, 23). The early efforts of psychiatric social workers were focused on changing the practices inside hospitals and public health centers. It was only later that they began to realize that they needed to create programs outside of hospitals that could help receive deinstitutionalized patients.

Perhaps the most successful of the early community mental health care programs was the Yadokari no Sato group in Saitama City, located just north of Tokyo. The name Yadokari no Sato means "home for hermit crabs." The group was started in 1970 by a pioneering group of social workers that was trying to help a man with schizophrenia discharge himself from the closed psychiatric ward of a mental hospital. Their first problem was finding any public or private housing that would accept a former mental patient. Once housing was secured, then questions of social reintegration, employment support, and other issues arose—as well as an increase in the number of people who wanted their help in leaving their hospitals (cf. Mamiya 2005; Yanaka 1993).

The 1987 revisions to the Mental Hygiene Law helped spur the creation of some sheltered workshops and day care units, but the real change finally came in 2005 with the Independent Living Support Act of 2005, which made the shift to independent living and deinstitutionalization a priority for people with all disabilities—physical, intellectual, and psychiatric. The passage of this law led to a boom in the creation of independent living centers for people with psychiatric disabilities as well as various day programs that are open to outpatients. For the first time, the number of people hospitalized in psychiatric units decreased from the previous year. This represented a significant change.

In 2003, the government surveyed the living situation of people with registered psychiatric disabilities who were living outside of hospitals. They found that 76.8 percent of them were living with family, 17.9 percent were living alone, 1.3 percent were living in welfare homes, 1.7 percent in group homes, 0.5 percent in elderly nursing homes, and 1.8 percent were none of the above.[53] The data indicates that there needs to be a greater push toward both independent living and small group home facilities.

Of those with a job, about a third had full-time jobs, just over a third were working in sheltered workshops and other welfare programs, and about 8 percent were working in family businesses.[54] Most people with schizophrenia were depending on a government disability pension or other social welfare programs for their income. Only 13.8 percent of those who were working said that they could rely on their wages.[55]

AFTER spending some time in Bethel, I decided to go to Saitama City to see Yadokari no Sato. Forty years later, the home for hermit crabs still exists, helping some three hundred people with psychiatric disabilities live in the community. I visited their sheltered workshops and shops and remarked on the parallels with Bethel's organizational structure. Their social workers have published a number of books and pamphlets about the Yadokari system. But despite its relative size, Yadokari remains a very local organization, unlike Bethel, which has garnered national attention and support.

I left after my short visit to Yadokari mulling over several questions. What was it about Bethel that allowed it to become the national leader in the conversation about the role of mental patients in society? Why weren't there more community-based independent living programs? What would it take for deinstitutionalization to take root in Japan?

To answer some of these questions, we have to look at the roots of Bethel House.

Coming of Age in Japan: Rika's Story

I loved Sundays in Urakawa. If I woke up early enough, I'd go to Sunday services at the Urakawa church.[1] Waking up early is a relative term since church service began at 10:30. The rather late start time was perfect for Bethel members (and people like myself) who had trouble dragging themselves out of bed in the morning.

Riding the doctor's "Porsche" (the little pickup truck), it took me about ten minutes to get from the hospital where I was living to the church, since they were nearly on the opposite sides of town. I would have to drive along the main road of Urakawa, past the ocean, past the Yonbura store, past the new pachinko parlor, past the supermarket that went out of business, past the many shuttered shops, past the harbor, and then a right turn at the *bentō* box store, over the train tracks, up the hill, and to the church. The chapel was on the second floor. The spare apartment where I stayed that very first night was on the first floor.

After Reverend Hamada moved back to Hiroshima, the Urakawa church didn't have a regular pastor. They were supposed to be getting one soon, but the United Church of Christ in Japan was not doing well economically, so one hadn't been assigned yet. A visiting pastor came once or twice a month, but the other times the members held services themselves.

Leading the service was supposed to rotate among the church members, but for some reason Kiyoshi was often the head of services when I sporadically attended. He would often dash into room at 10:40, unshaven and his hair unkempt, his shirt half dangling out of his pants. But he was also the best meeting leader for the simple reason that his faith was so direct and sincere.

On days that Masako Yoshino came to Sunday service, she'd play the keyboard for us. But on other days, or for songs that she didn't know how to play, there was a small, ancient-looking music box. Someone would type in the three-digit hymn number on the keypad, and eventually a thin reedy tone would come out of it.

Services were always simple. Songs dominated most of the time. There was a real spirit of unity when everyone sang together. If the visiting pastor was present, he would give us a sermon, but he often had to tone down the complexity to make it understandable to the parishioners, the majority of whom were Bethel members. Around a dozen people usually showed regularly.

We'd hold the service for about an hour, followed by tea and snacks. Everyone cleared off the tables in the chapel, and then we reorganized them so that we could eat. The former pastor's wife, Mrs. Miyajima, always made something delicious, usually Okinawan-style food, as her daughter was living there now. In the winter, we'd have a stew or miso soup going on the kerosene stove; in the summer people would break out the cold tea and rice balls.

We'd all sit and talk and enjoy the food. After a while, people would start cleaning up, and there would be a flurry of activity as people took away the plates and washed them, wiped down the tables, mopped the floors, and cleaned the hallway of the church. And then we'd slowly trickle away. Mrs. Miyajima would get a ride from someone back to her home on top of the hill.

Sunshine House

On Sundays after church, or if I had slept in and skipped church, I'd go to Rainbow House. If I hadn't eaten or hadn't eaten enough at church, I'd stop at the small convenience store across the street from Rainbow House and pick up some tea and rice balls for lunch. I'd park the Porsche in the lot behind Rainbow House, right by the sea wall, and I would walk up to the third floor using the rear stairway.

Centrally located on the main shopping street, the building used to have a bookstore on the first floor, and the owners lived on the second and third floors. With the bad economy and increasing debts, the owners fled from their creditors in the middle of the night, so Bethel was also able to pick up the building for a song (much like the New Bethel facility in the first chapter). The first floor became the Yonbura Bethel store and the second and third floors became shared residences for women.

Several of my closest friends at Bethel, such as Rika and Megumi, lived on the third floor of Rainbow House; they had nicknamed the top floor Sunshine House (*Hidamari Sō*). This name was quite fitting, as the top floor got an incredible amount of afternoon sunlight through the large windows in the living room. My favorite place in Sunshine House was the *koagari* in the living room. This was a small raised tatami space where the women always kept some fleece blankets and pillows. It was perfect for taking an afternoon nap. The sunlight would stream into the third-floor windows, and the house was usually very quiet. I'd lie back and watch the clouds float by in the sky outside the window or listen to the waves crash against the concrete sea wall. At night, I would look out of the windows at the pitch-black ocean, occasionally making out the lights of the fishing boats returning back to port.

WA Meetings at Sunshine House

Sunday afternoons meant the weekly Women's Anonymous (WA) meeting. WA was a spinoff of the Schizophrenics Anonymous (SA) meetings that met each week at the hospital. Some of the women in Bethel felt that the SA meetings didn't address enough women's issues and that the presence of men made some topics difficult to bring up, so they created their own WA group at Sunshine House.[2]

About six to eight women would attend WA each week. We used the same manual and format as the SA meetings, with a few differences: all of the meetings were closed; the meetings were held at Sunshine House; and of course, only women were there. The SA at Urakawa had never been picky about requiring schizophrenia to be a prerequisite of attending, and neither was WA.

In both SA and WA meetings, we'd begin by introducing ourselves along with the name we gave our own conditions, along with the usual physical and psychological report. So, for example: "Hi, I'm Karen and I have a disability of hope. My bones hurt a bit, and I'm feeling dull-minded today."

We each had our own SA/WA Manual, which consisted of a clear file folder with photocopies of the rules, goals, and steps as well as some other material collected over the years. After the introductions, we would then read out loud the rules and goals of SA/WA and read through the eight steps and the associated keywords:[3]

1 **I acknowledge.** I acknowledge that I need the help of my peers, my family, and specialists. I cannot recover by myself.
Keywords: *The power of peers. Family support. Using specialists. Accepting weakness. Getting help.*
2 **I believe.** I believe that there is a great power within myself.[4] I believe in the ability of the power to help me and my peers.
Keywords: *To believe. My own power. My potential. Helping myself. Helping my peers.*
3 **I accept.** I accept that because of different unpleasant symptoms and the occasional undesirable actions, I have no choice but to express my feelings. In addition, I believe in the possibilities created when I share and can mutually understand the nature of these deep emotions with my peers.
Keywords: *Unpleasant symptoms. Undesirable behaviors. To express myself. To be aware of my own emotions. The importance of sharing stories. Living with myself. Knowing myself.*
4 **I choose.** I choose to recover and I choose to try to become happy. I acknowledge the responsibility needed to make such a choice. From the bottom of my heart, I understand that this choice is necessary in order to have purpose in my everyday life.
Keywords: *Choosing to recover. To become happy. To choose oneself. To accept responsibility.*
5 **I forgive.** I forgive myself for the mistakes of my past and accept my weaknesses. At the same time, I forgive the people who have hurt or harmed me in any way in the past. I free myself from being a prisoner of those feelings.
Keywords: *To forgive. To accept my weaknesses. To be imprisoned. To be free.*
6 **I understand.** I understand that it was my own mistaken thoughts or self-destructive thoughts that have caused me to fail, to be afraid, or to be unhappy. I am prepared to change the patterns of my life from the very bottom up. By doing so, my life will change.
Keywords: *Mistaken thoughts. Self-destructive thoughts. Previous patterns of my life.*
7 **I resolve.** I resolve to entrust my life to a power that is greater than myself. I entrust all of myself as I am. Furthermore, I ask to be changed from deep within.

Keywords: *A power greater than myself. To entrust. To put in others hands. As I am. Change from deep within.*

8 **I will disseminate.** I will learn from the rich experiences that I have had as a person with psychiatric disabilities. I will disseminate this message to my peers, my family, and to society.
Keywords: *What I have learned as a person with psychiatric disabilities. The importance of getting out the message.*

After we read through the Eight Steps, the meeting chairperson would choose one of the themes for people to respond to. As we went around the circle, not everyone would use that prompt (either the step itself or one of the keywords), but it was handy if you didn't have anything in particular to talk about that week. There was almost never any interruption as people talked, nor were there any responses after a person finished. When we weren't speaking, our role in the group was to be witnesses to the monologues of our peers rather than to engage in dialogue.

After everyone had finished or skipped her turn, the chairperson would close the meeting. A jar would be passed around for contributions for space rental or buying snacks. Said snacks and tea would then be taken out and shared. The whole meeting usually took between an hour to two hours, depending on how many people came and how garrulous they were feeling.

Dinners at Sunshine House

After WA, some women would usually hang around for the entire afternoon at Sunshine House. Other women would drop by as well. There were very rarely any Bethel events scheduled on Sundays. In the winter, we would have *oden* stew or *yakiniku* barbecue beef parties. Four or five of us would bundle into Rika's little car[5] and head over to the supermarket on the far side of town to buy groceries for dinner. When we got back, we'd haul everything up to the third floor, cursing that Rainbow House didn't have an elevator.

We would take the bottles of beer or soda and put them outside on the window ledge by the living room. In the frigid weather of Hokkaido, the cold air and snow would quickly chill them. The dining table at Sunshine House usually only seated four, but if you pulled it over to the *koagari*, then four people could sit on the tatami portion and another six could sit on chairs.

Figure 2.4 New Year's Dinner 2008 at Sunshine House. I am in the middle, in an incredibly ugly Christmas sweater. Photo by the author.

If we were all too tired to cook, we would order out for pizza. I don't know how she did it, but if Rika-san and I started talking about maybe ordering pizza for dinner, within three minutes Nozomi Chidaka would come up the stairs from the second floor and join the discussion of what to get.[6] Japanese pizza is quite different from American pizza. The crust is soft and chewy, and the toppings are as delicious as they are bizarre: squid and octopus, teriyaki chicken with mayonnaise, potato slices, tuna and mayonnaise, cream cheese, Korean bulgogi barbecued beef, and curry sauce are just a few of the options. I still remember those pizza dinners with fondness as we fought over the slices. There's a saying that "at Bethel, the meek will starve." These group dinners proved the point.

At the end of each meal, we would divide up the cost of the meal, and each of us would pay an equal share. Sometimes, the meals would be very inexpensive, especially if one of the other members who was on public welfare made it. The meals that Rika-san or I would cook tended to be a bit more expensive, since we used meat, maybe ¥300 to ¥400 per person (about $5). The pizzas would be the most expensive, maybe ¥700 each, or $9 a head.

Nozomi usually didn't have enough money to pay her share, so she would have to borrow from the bank, meaning the Bank of Rika. She apparently did pay Rika-san back, judging from how often Rika-san loaned her money and how often Nozomi was reminded exactly what her balance was. Rika took good care of Nozomi; in fact she took good care of us all.

Rika's Story

Rika Shimizu was my closest friend at Bethel, and she remains a close friend to this day. We are about the same age, in our mid-thirties when we first met in 2005; we entered our forties together at the tail end of my research. She came to visit me in the United States after my fieldwork had finished. Rika figures in *Bethel*, where she and a staff worker talk about Yamane-san and his UFO adventures. She also plays a central role in Bethel operations, where until recently she was the facilities manager, which meant that she had been responsible for all of the Bethel buildings. Unfortunately, her Gencho-sans (in her case, auditory

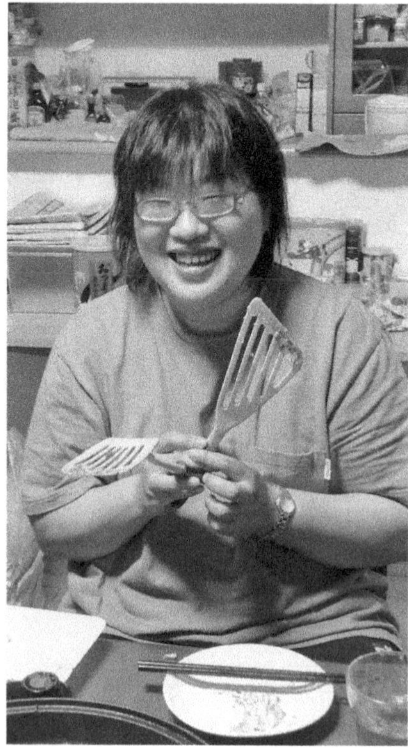

Figure 2.5 Rika Shimizu at Sunshine House. Photo by the author.

hallucinations) had been getting stronger, and she had to withdraw from Bethel management. She currently works on the Bethel staff in a non-management position.

Rika grew up in Utsunomiya, a mid-sized industrial city north of Tokyo. She was well loved by her parents and lived in a comfortable middle-class home. After graduation from college, she started work as a full-time staff member for a supermarket chain. It was then that she started to feel different from other people. She became very worried what other people were thinking about her. She thought that other people were able to read her emotions.

In her self-directed research report (see chapter 6), Rika wrote:

> I spent most of my twenties in anguish because I didn't understand that the feelings of persecution[7] caused by my schizophrenia were the real reason that my life was so difficult. Now that I know that my illness is why I feel this way, I'm slowly getting the knack of how to avoid feeling so miserable.
>
> I'm extremely ashamed of talking about my illness. However, it would be pointless for me to avoid the subject, so I began this self-research with the intent of trying to remember back to when I was having the hardest time, organizing my memories of what I was thinking about after I became schizophrenic[8] and thinking about how I was dealing with my feelings of persecution at that time. . . .
>
> For me, the first, clear indication of my illness came just after I had started a full-time job at a large supermarket chain. One day, during the morning staff meeting, I suddenly had the sensation that everything that I was thinking was being transmitted to others around me. Everyone could instantly know what I was thinking, and a rumor quickly spread that I was telepathic.

Rika uses the Japanese word *satorare* to describe this feeling. *Satorare* means to sense or to become aware, much in the same way that a samurai might "sense" the eyes of a ninja stalking him. At first, I was confused. I thought that Rika was able to read the feelings of others, but it was exactly the opposite. For example, when she was in the bathroom, she felt that other people could watch her defecate and urinate. She thought that she had become transparent and that others were able to read her mind, her feelings. Her sense of self slipped away.

> People who had bullied me in years past appeared again as auditory hallucinations. My brain raced with thoughts as it was swept over by tension and fear. I couldn't stop thinking about these things, and if I tried, it felt as if I couldn't breathe, and I collapsed after hyperventilating. I heard a

> voice laughing at my situation. The result of all this was that I wasn't able to continue at that job and was forced to resign from it. For the next seven years after that, except for when I was asleep, from morning to evening I felt like the deepest parts of my soul were under constant surveillance by other people.
>
> My parents suggested one day that I go in for a checkup at the psychiatric ward of the hospital. Personally, I didn't think that I was ill or that it was anything that medication would make better, but I did want to have someone with whom I could talk about the situation that I found myself in. I couldn't think of any other place that might let me talk about my problems, and so I went for a consultation at the psychiatric ward.
>
> I decided to open up to the psychiatrist and told him, "I've become a telepath," but I don't think that he believed me. That caused me to give up hope.
>
> I said to my doctor, "I'm having a hard time because other people are able to read my mind (*kokoro*), is it possible for you to give me a medicine that will make me not think anything at all?" He replied, "There's no medication that will make all the thoughts go away, but there is a medicine that will dampen down those thoughts. Do you want to give that a go?" I really had no other choice.
>
> I wasn't able to believe in the medication that he gave me, so I secretly went and bought a book and looked up the different types of drugs and found out that the one he gave me was prescribed for schizophrenia. Of course, I didn't think that I had schizophrenia and thought that it was pointless for me to take it. The reality was that the medication really didn't have any effect on the problems that I was having.
>
> After that, I stopped telling my psychiatrist everything I was thinking, but I wasn't brave enough to stop taking the medication either. For the next seven years, I kept going regularly to the hospital until I reached a point where I was so afraid of the public eye that I couldn't take the train and ended up having to take a pretty long taxi ride each time I had to go.
>
> I stopped all contact with other people and became a shut-in. Humiliating phrases kept popping up in my head. If you are being bullied for a long time, somewhere along the line, a part of your soul gets used to being bullied.

In addition to her feelings of being read, she had also been hearing the voices of a family who was always commenting on what she was doing. It was if the family was living in her head, looking out their windows (her eyes) at her every moment. She talked about these feelings at a presentation she gave to Mr. Mukaiyachi's college students at Hokkaido Medical University in 2007:

> [I was 23 years old.] I panicked and wondered how I was supposed to keep on living. I was panicking and suffering. I was working at the time,

> and even when I got off work and came home, the voices would continue on in my head, and there was no time for my soul to rest. That suffering continued for several years.
>
> I went to a local university hospital's psychiatric unit, but I wasn't really aware of my condition and was worried that if I told the truth, they would force me to become hospitalized or they might try to make me take some drugs. So I wasn't able to tell the doctor that there were some voices that I continued to hear or this feeling of being read.

Unable to handle the sensation of other people always reading her every thought, Rika quit her job and shut herself into her room at home, becoming what Japanese call a *hikikomori,* or shut-in. She continued to see the psychiatrist, but she wasn't able to tell the doctor what was really going on:

> I was a shut-in all during the years that I was home and living with my illness. I didn't know of anyone else with the same condition. I wondered what other people with the same experiences might be thinking. But I never had an opportunity to interact with them, even though I went to the psychiatrist at the hospital for seven years. It was a large university hospital, so I'm sure that there was a social worker there, but I was never introduced to one. I didn't even know that there was such a thing as a medical social worker. Once a month I went to the hospital and got my medicine. That was all I did. . . .

In 2000, just after Rika turned 30, her mother snuck out of the house to go to a small Bethel event in Okayama, a city about five hours away from Tokyo. Impressed by the sense of community at the event, her mother bought a Bethel book and video to take home. Not wanting to directly force the issue onto her daughter, Rika's mother left the video and book lying around the house where her daughter might stumble on them.

At the time, Rika never left the house, because she was afraid of other people. Her feelings of *satorare* meant that she was constantly afraid that people were looking at her and talking about her. But because she never left the house, she was also bored out of her mind, and it didn't take her long to find the book and video about Bethel.

When she watched the video, she suddenly saw a glimmer of hope. Urakawa was a small town out in the middle of nowhere, but it had a hospital with a psychiatric unit. Perhaps, she thought, in that sparsely populated rural backwater she could achieve her goal of living independently while never having to interact with anyone.

Rika asked her mother if she could go with her to Urakawa. Her mother pretended to be surprised by the suggestion, and after making a show of thinking about it a little bit, agreed to go with her. They arrived on a Wednesday afternoon, and Rika saw Dr. Kawamura for the first time the next morning. Her mother left that afternoon to go back home to Utsunomiya City, but Rika decided to stay a few more days in her hotel in Urakawa.

At first, Rika was entirely uninterested in Bethel itself, as she didn't want anything to do with the community. She came to Urakawa precisely because it was in the middle of nowhere. But the hospital psychiatric outpatient clinic was closed on Friday and the weekend. So Rika instead talked with Mr. Mukaiyachi, who convinced her to interact with the other members.

On Monday morning, Rika went again to Dr. Kawamura at the psychiatric ward. They talked about what Rika wanted to do in the future, and Rika talked about her goals of living independently. Dr. Kawamura agreed to take on Rika as a patient. That afternoon, Rika checked out of the hotel and checked into Ward 7, the hospital's inpatient psychiatric ward. She stayed there for three months before moving into one of Bethel's group homes.

Rika was the reason that Schizophrenics Anonymous (SA) first started up at Bethel. The way that I heard it from Mr. Mukaiyachi was that when Rika was discharged from the Urakawa Red Cross Hospital after those initial three months as an inpatient, she was worried about not having any meetings on the outside where she could talk to other people about her problems. She had become social while in the ward. But unlike the present day, there weren't any spaces on the outside where people could talk freely with other people about their symptoms and what they were going through. Her desire for such a space for sociality and peer support prompted the birth of Urakawa Schizophrenics Anonymous.

When she first arrived in Urakawa, Mr. Mukaiyachi told me, Rika was the very image of someone with schizophrenia. She wasn't able to express herself or talk at length about anything. This surprised me because it was so different from the image of Rika that I had myself. But she herself credits meeting Mr. Mukaiyachi for most of the change in her outlook in life:

> I came to Urakawa in my thirties, and for me . . . [realizing that] working with other people might be just as important as medication was surprising to me, and I wondered why I wasn't able to realize this when I was in Tochigi.
>
> I never even had the opportunity to meet a social worker. I wish I had met one earlier in my life, maybe my life would have been different.

> When I was home in Tochigi, my symptoms were pretty bad, although even now my symptoms are much the same. Even if I don't say anything, I feel as though my thoughts leak out and enter other people—my *satorare* has increased in intensity, and it's very burdensome these days, but I still feel as though I can somehow live with it now, and so I'm very happy for that. . . .
>
> Even now, I still have this sense of being read, but it's now been eight years since I came to Urakawa, and slowly I've gotten the courage to be able to live on with my feelings of being read.

Rika says that it's precisely because she has *satorare,* this feeling that her thoughts leak out unconsciously, that she has learned the importance of being able to talk about herself with other people. If she doesn't do this, she realizes, her symptoms get much worse. Community is a fundamental part of her care.

Finding Communion

In Japan, you become an adult at the age of 20. You are considered a *shakaijin,* a full social being. You are no longer a child with no responsibilities but an integral part of the fabric of society. You can vote, you can drink, and you are expected to think about starting a career and having a family. That is, unless you are ill.

One of the defining conditions of serious mental illness for most people in most countries is isolation and loneliness. Either they are isolated at home, shut away from human contact, or they are in mental institutions where there is often very little sense of community. In her narrative, Rika talked how she spent eight years as a shut-in before coming to Urakawa and finding community. In many ways, although she had legally come of age, she was not a *shakaijin* or social person anymore.

Losing social contact in this way is particularly acute for people with schizophrenia. Even now, some medical and nursing manuals in Japan, as well as books directed at the families of people with schizophrenia, recommend that caregivers not engage in the hallucinations and delusions of the affected person. People with schizophrenia soon learn to refrain from telling anyone about their hallucinations and delusions, lest they be ignored or told that they are not in touch with reality. This causes them to withdraw into their own world and increases the feelings of social isolation.

Bethel's philosophy is the opposite. People are encouraged to talk about their hallucinations and delusions. Thus, hallucinations and delusions become communal property, something that everyone can talk about and deal with. Every year, Bethel holds an annual festival where the highlight of the festival is the Hallucinations and Delusions Grand Prix. Here, the best hallucination or delusion is celebrated. The twist is that "best" means the hallucination or delusion that brings together the most people or has the most community involvement.

The chief psychiatrist at the hospital, Dr. Kawamura, respects the voices that his patients hear. He says that too many doctors, when confronted with a patient who says that he or she is hearing voices, will just up the dosage of the medication without really listening to what the patient has to say. Eventually the patient learns to just shut up (or to not take the medications as prescribed). In his own practice, Dr. Kawamura tries to recognize that not all voices are negative, rather that the voices themselves are often indexes to other things that are going on. It was important to listen to the voices.

One day, I was sitting in the main office of New Bethel, and Shimono-kun was sitting next to me, mumbling, "Kill, kill, kill, kill. . . ." Surprised, I asked him about what he was saying. He said that occasionally those thoughts would bounce around his head, and the best way for him to deal with that was to express them. I said that I thought that was scary, and he said it would be scarier if he tried to keep the thoughts bundled up inside his head, under control. It was best to let them out so that he could deal with them. At Bethel, they call this the process of externalization (*gaizaika*), making things visible so that they can be shared and handled by other people rather than bundling them up inside of yourself.

Another time, I was out having lunch at a restaurant with some of the women from Sunshine House. We had just finished the meal and were relaxing. Megumi suddenly shivered and gave herself a little hug. I wouldn't have noticed it, but Rika did, and she asked Megumi if her boyfriend had just visited her. He had, said Megumi. Her boyfriend had died several years earlier. We then spent the next ten minutes talking about her boyfriend and what he meant to all of us, before he died several years ago. He still visits her from time to time. We made a plan to go visit the part of the countryside by a riverbed where Megumi had spread his ashes after his death.

Since I had the Porsche, I felt a responsibility to give people a lift whenever I could. The hospital was located at the far end of town and could be quite a walk from the center. I often asked Megumi if she wanted a ride, since she worked at the Bethel branch shop by the hospital. She always said no. She said that walking was one of the things that she enjoyed most. She said that it was the time when she could enjoy a good conversation with her voices. They would talk to her as she walked along.

Many people at Bethel told me that they would miss their voices if they were gone. Rika called her daily doses of Risperdal (a second-generation antipsychotic medication) her sleeping aid. She took it before she went to bed, and it quieted the voices (especially those of the often loud family in her head) enough so that she could go to sleep. But during the day, she didn't mind the various conversations that took place in her head, as long as they weren't being too hard on her.

This isn't to say that all the voices were positive. Some people, such as Nozomi, were plagued with critical voices that constantly criticized and belittled them. The SST sessions that Nozomi went to provided her with insights into how other people dealt with their negative voices, as well as giving everyone in the community a better understanding of what she was going through during the day. In Nozomi's case, the solution that people in the group came up with wasn't to increase her medications but to try to get her to recruit good voices, such as the prime minister or police officers, who could help counter the proliferation of negative voices in her head.

I should hasten to add that Nozomi was of course under Dr. Kawamura's care and that he certainly didn't believe that *only* cognitive behavioral therapy such as through SST or social support was enough. He would say that medications were a necessary component of recovery but—on their own—not a complete program of recovery. Social support and personal determination continued what the medications could not finish by themselves.

Love and Marriage

I spent Christmas Day of 2005 at Sunshine House. In the evening, my partner and I talked with the women about love and relationships. Finding love was a perennial problem at Bethel. There were some couples that were known to be going out together, but these relationships were often quite fraught, as both partners also had to deal with the ups and downs of their own emotional states. There were also several pregnancies and births at Bethel, causing the community to try to find support mechanisms to help the new parents take care of the children.[9]

In her late thirties when I was conducting my research, Rika-san thought from time to time about dating and marriage, but she did not want to get into a relationship with anyone at the Bethel community. She saw the many problems that her friends had with their relationships—alcohol abuse, domestic violence, codependence—and she didn't want that for herself. But that being said, she did not think that she could date outside of the community while she was there. And she did not foresee leaving.

We asked her if she ever thought of starting her own family:

> I'm 36 now, and it's about the time to start thinking about children. If you're over 40, it's difficult to have children. It's getting to the point where I won't be able to have a family. If I think about that . . . I think about the type of happiness that that would provide. . . .
>
> But when I'm here, living here with all of you . . . that becomes a substitute for having a family. I think. . . . But still sometimes, I think about those other things.
>
> Family. . . . Perhaps in a while, I'll start to think that this is my family again.

Rika remembers back to when she first moved to Urakawa and was living in Rika House (the group home was named after her). There was a young 15-year-old living in Rika House. She was the foster child of the Mukaiyachis, who had rescued her from an abusive family. This young woman had many psychological problems of her own when she first arrived in Urakawa. Rika recalls what it was like moving in with her:

> I came here when I was 31 years old. It was like I suddenly had a kid who was 15. . . . As well as a 66-year-old grandma named Kurano-san. And I was in the middle. I was a shut-in, but I still had to go out to buy groceries and to cook, and I really struggled to make something that both a 15-year-old and a 66-year-old granny could eat. I was exhausted just making dinner—and the human relationships, and I wondered if this was what it would be like to have a family.

That 15-year-old was now sitting at the table in Sunshine House, eating along with us. Now in her twenties, she was a full, active member of Bethel and a bit embarrassed about all of the talk about her as a young brat back in the old days.

In the intervening decade since Rika's arrival, other couples at Bethel have had children, so all of the women are aware of the difficulties of raising children. Many of the children born into Bethel are in foster care or in institutional care, or they are with their grandparents. Bethel runs a group called Condom-Sha (which in its original Japanese, *Kondo-umusha,* carries the double entendre of "Let's Give Birth Sometime" and "The Condom Company") to promote birth control among the couples.

None of the women in Sunshine House was going out with anyone during the time I was there. Rika often joked that Sunshine House was a nunnery (*shudōin*) or one of the *kakekomi dera* Buddhist temples that provided sanctuary for women fleeing from abusive husbands. The other women jokingly called her Mother Superior in turn. And she did act like a mother to the rest of us, especially to Nozomi, whose condition would often deteriorate. Nozomi had Rika on her speed dial on her phone, calling her (or Mr. Mukaiyachi or the doctor) dozens of times each day.

When I left the field in 2008, Rika was doing data entry at New Bethel. Her new medication left her very tired all the time, and she had trouble getting out of bed, so she always ended up going to work late, sometimes not being able to show up until around eleven a.m. or so. As a result, she was constantly being scolded by Etsuko-san or the other office staff. She ended up being hospitalized; after her release, she stepped down from her position as facilities manager.

I worried often about Rika. She was the glue that held the Sunshine House together. Although she had originally gone to Urakawa to escape society, she had found communion with others and had become a social being again at Bethel. This was now one of her reasons for living (*ikigai*). Rika was well enough to be able to work full-time (or close to it) at Bethel and was one of the few individuals who owns a car at Bethel, so many of the other members depended on her for rides to the grocery store or for the occasional escapes out of town. She took all that responsibility and buried it deep in herself.

CHAPTER THREE

Hokkaido and Christianity

Bethel House

Bethel's name derives from the Old Testament (*Beth El* = "house of God") because it was founded by a group of Christian Japanese. Why one of Japan's most innovative community-based mental health care experiments was being run by Christians on the northern edge of nowhere is the topic of this chapter, which blends the history of Christianity in Japan, the colonial ambitions of the imperial government, the dire treatment of the native Ainu people, and mental illness.

Christianity and Japan

Less than 1 percent of the Japanese population identifies as Christian. The vast majority engages in a mixture of Buddhist and Shinto beliefs and practices.

Francis Xavier is usually credited with being the first Christian missionary to Japan. Arriving in 1549 along with other Portuguese Catholics, he established a strong presence in the city of Nagasaki, on the western edge of the island of Kyushu. At first these Christians were tolerated, especially because they traded in goods and technologies that various military lords wanted, such as medical texts and firearms.

This honeymoon period did not last long. The Catholic missionaries were perhaps too successful in converting people to Christianity, and when the warlord Toyotomi Hideyoshi came to power in 1585, he was not happy that the new converts were pledging allegiance to Christ and the Pope and not to himself. It was estimated that at the end of the sixteenth century there were around three hundred thousand Christians in Japan. In a show of force to try to quell the appeal of the new religion, Toyotomi publicly crucified twenty-six Christians near Nagasaki in 1597.[1]

After Tokugawa Ieyasu overthrew the Toyotomi clan to become shogun in 1603, he and his son continued the persecution of Christians in Japan. In 1637, there was another rebellion of Christians, peasants, and landless samurai near Nagasaki. The Tokugawa shogunate sent 125,000 troops and called in Dutch naval support to quell the rebels who had occupied the castle at Shimabara. While it took several months for the siege of the castle to succeed, in the end the rebels never had a chance. The shogunate made a deliberate show of beheading everyone—the rebels, their supporters, even the townspeople and peasants who had taken shelter in the castle—an estimated forty thousand people in all.[2]

In 1639, the shogunate started enforcing very strict maritime restrictions on who could enter and leave Japan. In particular, the shogunate was not fond of the Portuguese Catholics, whom they saw as troublemakers. In reward for helping with the Shimabara rebels, they allowed Dutch traders (who were Protestant and not possessed of the same missionary zeal as their Catholic Portuguese counterparts) to engage in commerce in a few, limited ports. For the next two hundred years, Christianity in Japan was effectively driven underground, cut off from outside sources of contact.[3]

The Return of Christianity

Christian missionaries began returning to Japan after it was forcibly opened to outside trade in 1854 by Commodore Matthew Perry. There was a brief efflorescence of missionary activity in the late 1800s and 1900s, and several key figures in Japan's early modern history were Christian.[4] Throughout this period, the city of Nagasaki on the southwestern edge of the nation grew to become one of the strongest areas of Christian influence in Japan. There were also significant missionary activities by Russians in the north, in the island of Ezo (today Hokkaido), as I will describe in more detail later on.

Starting in the 1930s, as the country moved deeper into militarization, Christians in Japan faced more active persecution by the state. Foreign missionaries were expelled, and all of the various protestant Christian denominations were amalgamated in 1941 under a single organization, the United Church of Christ in Japan.[5]

After the end of World War II, the Allied forces reestablished freedom of religion in the new constitution of Japan. Christians could once again practice openly and freely, although they have always been a very small minority and have mostly been concentrated in western Japan. In order to understand why Christianity also found a foothold in the northern territory of Hokkaido, we need to go back again to the early nineteenth century and the nascent history of colonialism and imperialism in Japan.

A Short History of Hokkaido

Up until the 1800s, the island that is now known as Hokkaido was not part of Japan. It was called Ezochi, which means "land of the Ezo people." The Ezo are what we now know as the Ainu people, the native peoples of northern Japan.[6] From an archaeological and cultural perspective, the Ainu people are extremely different from what are now known as the Yamato Japanese. The archaeological evidence shows that the Ainu's distant forebears, the Jōmon people, had existed on the Japanese mainland for over ten thousand years. These people wore different clothes, spoke a different language, practiced a different religious system, made different forms of pottery, and most significantly, were hunter-gatherers and fishers and did not practice farming.[7]

In contrast, the Yamato people (the ethnic group to which I belong) are thought to have come over from the Asian mainland around fifteen hundred years ago. Unlike the native people, the Yamato newcomers practiced wet-rice agriculture and other sedentary farming techniques. The Yamato people made their initial base in central Japan and then pushed north and west, pushing the native peoples out. By the 1600s, Japan proper consisted of the islands of Honshu, Kyushu, and Shikoku.

Although there were some military and trading outposts in Ezochi by the 1800s, the main portion of the island was still largely Ainu territory. The shogunate was not strong enough to annex the large island entirely, and several efforts to do so were rebuffed by Ainu forces. In the eighteenth century, there were attempts by Russian missionaries to convert the Ainu to Christianity. The Russians started at the northern end of the Kuril Islands and were making their way south down the archipelago. The shogunate was alarmed, with one advisor stating in 1795:

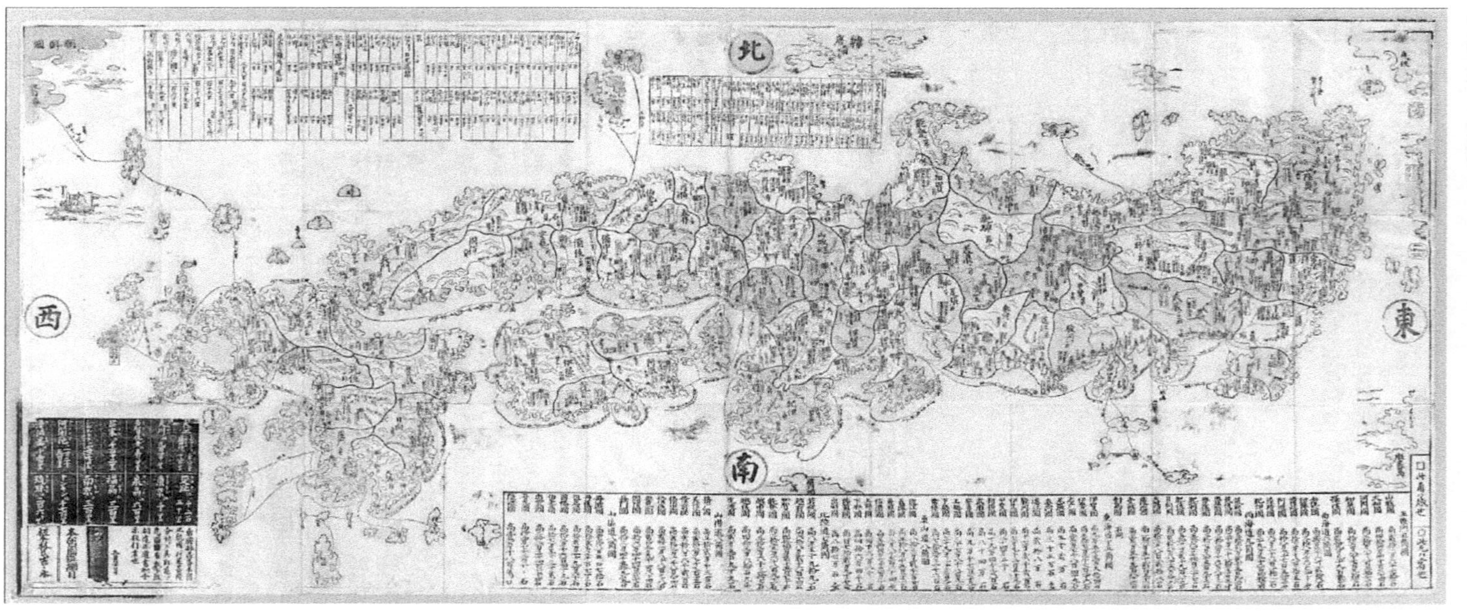

Figure 3.1 Map of Japan in 1630. Courtesy of the C.V. Starr East Asian Library, University of California, Berkeley, available at http://luna.davidrumsey.com:8380/luna/servlet/s/0kfy18.

> If the present situation continues to prevail, it is said that the Russians will bring images of Christ to be worshipped by the natives saying that worship of these images will bring fulfillment of wishes as quick as lightning and they will teach the words of prayer to the Ezo. This prayer is that of Christianity which is strictly forbidden in our country and the image of Christ to be sent to the Ezo of Etorofu for worship is similar to that image used on a copper plate in Nagasaki on which people trod during the investigations of Christianity. The contradiction would be too great were the Ezo left free to worship this same. (Shinichirō and Harrison 1960, 73)

The advisor recommended treating the encroaching Russians as an invading force. Although they weren't able to seize the entirety of Ezo and the Kuril Islands, the mainland Japanese troops managed to encroach on coastal settlements, where they drove away the Russians and confiscated images of Christ and crucifixes from the Ezo villagers. The shogunate then set up Buddhist temples in various villages in Ezo in order to introduce a proper "Japanese" religion to the "natives" (Shinichirō and Harrison 1960, 73).

In 1868, the ailing Tokugawa shogunate was overthrown, and the emperor was restored as the head of Japan. The new Meiji government wanted to modernize the nation aggressively in order to protect it against Western powers. The island of Ezo was a high priority for several reasons. First, it was very abundant in natural resources—its forests and soil produced great quantities of lumber and coal. Second, it formed a physical bulwark against the encroachment of the Russian empire, which was seeking a warm water port on its eastern frontier. Third, Ezo was a convenient location to resettle tens of thousands of rebellious peasants and other malcontents who were frustrated by the new government's high taxes and poor agrarian policies.

But perhaps the foremost reason is revealed in its new name: Hokkaido, "the road North." Hokkaido would be the first stepping stone to the expansion of the Great Japanese Empire. In 1869, the imperial government officially annexed Ezochi, renamed it Hokkaido, and started to engage in a massive colonization process, driving out the native Ainu people and settling mainlanders there in masses.

The colonization of Hokkaido was done with American assistance. The capital city of Sapporo was laid out in the same grid pattern as an American city. The head of the Massachusetts Agricultural College, William S. Clark, was hired in 1875 to help set up the Sapporo Agricultural College. The American taught his Japanese students the value of hard work and Christian prayer. Clark's statue stands on a bluff overlooking the city, commanding its denizens, "Boys, be ambitious!"

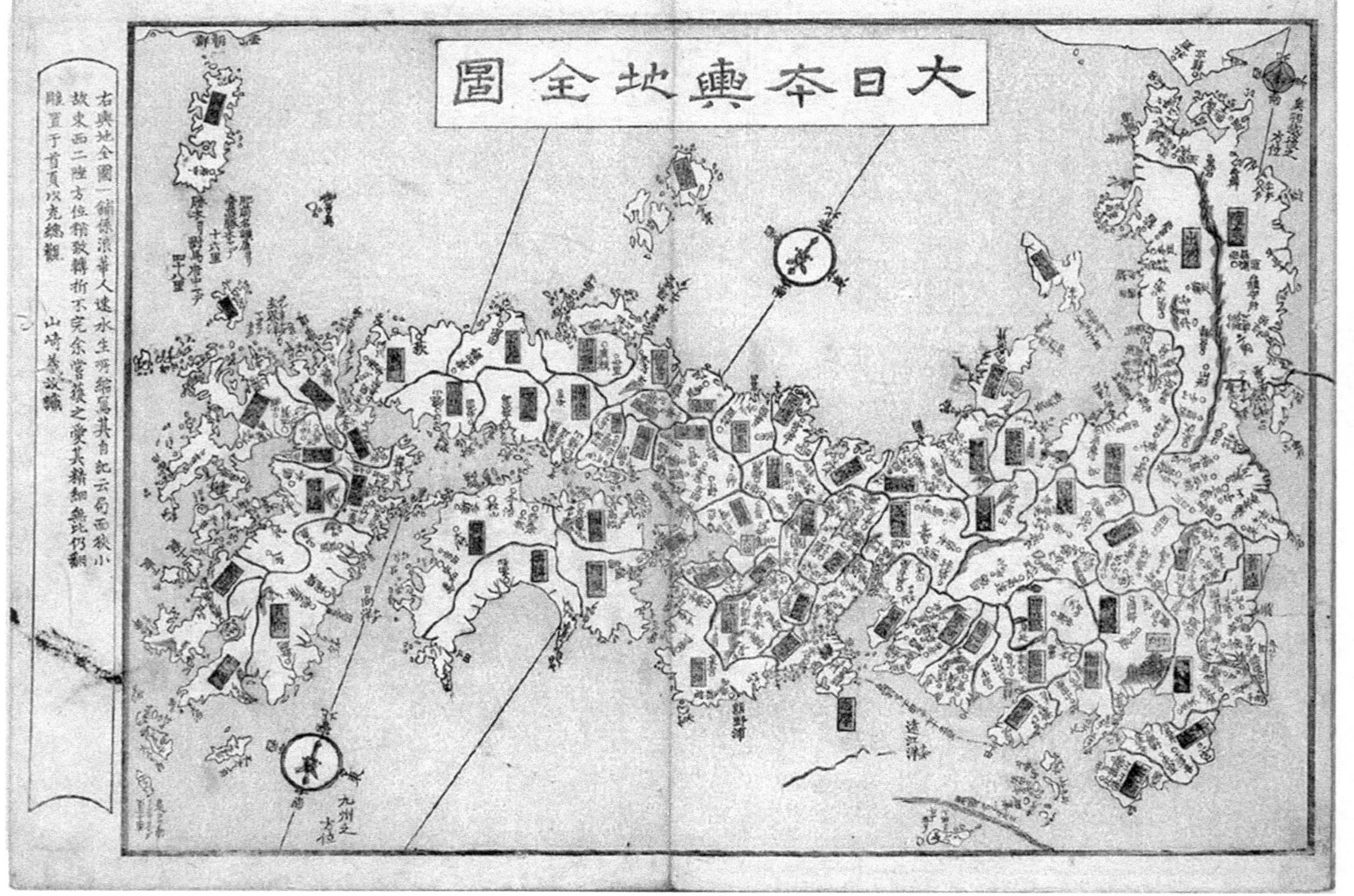

Figure 3.2 Map of Japan in 1834, still showing just a few outposts in Ezo in the upper right corner. Courtesy of the C.V. Starr East Asian Library, University of California, Berkeley, available athttp://luna.davidrumsey.com:8380/luna/servlet/s/09910e.

Figure 3.3 The Moto-Urakawa Church built in 1894. Courtesy of Sekishinsha. Copyright © Sekishinsha Group.

The Sapporo Beer Company was founded in 1876 to slake everyone's thirst after a long day of work.

The central government encouraged the colonization and development of Hokkaido by mainlanders, especially those marginalized by mainstream Japanese society. A group of Christians from Kobe got together in 1879 to form a development company that they named Sekishinsha (literally, Red Soul Group). Over the next two years, they established a colonial outpost of 130 farmers in the town of Urakawa, on the southeastern edge of the island. The surrounding region, known as Hidaka, was called the "Ainu capital" of Hokkaido, as more than a third of all of the Hokkaido Ainu resided there (Cornell 1964, 292). The land and the oceans were rich and fertile, and the weather was pleasant and hospitable.

By 1886, Reverend Tasuke Tanaka and thirteen other parishioners were able to build a small wooden church. Using the church—one of the first churches in Hokkaido established by Japanese mainlanders from the south and not Russians from the north—as its base, the Sekishinsha group engaged in missionary activities in the surrounding area. They built a larger church building in 1894 and ran a school there that later became the formal public school for the area children (Pettee 1895).

A QUEER PEOPLE

They Live in the Kuriles and Northern Japan.

BY ROMEYN HITCHCOCK.

HE who in distant lands leaves the beaten paths and seeks for adventure or discovery, may often find either nearer than he thinks. The far East is not all unknown, yet it teems with unstudied problems of the deepest interest to those who will but think of them and pass but a few steps beyond the narrow bounds of the foreign settlements.

The small group of islands known as Japan is inhabited by a people of unknown origin. We are content to speak of them as Japanese, and for our present purpose it is not required to know more concerning them. But scattered along the coasts from the north as far as to the extreme southern end of Kiushiu, there are found traces of a different people, who must have occupied the country in prehistoric times.

Recent explorations have led to the conclusion that these aborigines are representatives of a race known as Ainos, who are now confined to the island of Yezo, in the north of Japan.

Figure 3.4 Romeyn Hitchcock 1890. Courtesy: Smithsonian. William W. Fitzhugh and Chisato O. Dubreuil, *Ainu: Spirit of a Northern People.*

The church later became known as the Moto-Urakawa Church (Former-Urakawa Church) when the town center for Urakawa was moved several kilometers up the coast.

Western Contact with the Ainu

Meanwhile, the condition of the Ainu natives was rapidly worsening. In 1890, Romeyn Hitchcock, a collector for the Smithsonian Institute, visited the northern island of Japan and wrote a series of articles for American newspapers as well as reports to the Smithsonian. One of them read:

> We have here a remarkable instance of the close association of two distinct races, one superior and powerful, the other degraded and weak, working together day by day, living in contiguous villages, intermarrying more or less, and yet, after a century of such intimacy, as distinct in their characters, habits of life, superstitions and beliefs, as though they had never come together. The Aino [*sic*] has not so much learned to make a reputable bow and arrow, although in the past he has had to meet the Japanese who are famous archers, in many battles. It is a most remarkable example of the persistance [*sic*] of distinct types together, when the conditions are apparently favorable for the absorption of one by the other. The Ainos, being unable to affiliate more closely with the Japanese, remain distinct and apart, and are therefore doomed to extinction from the face of the earth. (cited in Shinichirō and Harrison 1999)

The "degraded and weak" condition of the Ainu was of course a result of the colonization practices of the Meiji government. They could no longer practice their traditional fishing and hunting culture. Like many other native peoples in the world, the Ainu population is particularly susceptible to alcohol addiction. The wretched social conditions drove many to drink.

The Ainu people were stripped of their ancestral lands, and all of Hokkaido was considered *terra nullius*—empty and ownerless—and thus the property of the Japanese emperor. The Japanese government passed the Hokkaido Former Aborigines Protection Act in 1899 and the Regulation for the Education of Former Aborigines' Children in 1901. These and other laws made it impossible for the Ainu to engage in fishing and hunting, forcing them to become agriculturalists—but they were given the worst land to till. If they did not engage in farming, they were assumed to have abandoned their land for public seizure. The Ainu were

Figure 3.5 Ainu people in 1888. Courtesy of the National Anthropological Archives, Smithsonian Institution.

forbidden to use their native languages in public or engage in any public ritual performance. Men could not wear earrings, and women could not be given their traditional tattoos. Native children were taken away from their homes and put into boarding schools where the Ainu languages were forbidden. Many in the Japanese government hoped that the Ainu would intermarry with the mainlanders and over many generations, the "problem" would cease to exist whatsoever. It became fashionable to call the Ainu *horobiyuku minzoku*—"the dying race" (Howell 2004, 13).

In 1925, Kyosuke Kindaichi, a linguist at Tokyo Imperial University, proclaimed: "It is common knowledge that the Ainu population will completely disappear from the earth within the next two generations."

Imu Shamanic Practices among the Ainu

At this point we take a slight detour from the historical narrative to talk about some of the ritual practices of the Ainu, who had a condition called *imu* that was associated with shamanism. *Imu* in its severest form manifested as a loss of self-control (especially in speech) and disassociation from reality. Anthropologist Emiko Ohnuki-Tierney wrote about this condition in her classic 1981 volume *Illness and Healing among the Sakhalin Ainu:*

> The first category [of *imu*] is a mild state in which an individual becomes surprised, but not necessarily frightened, and mumbles nonsensical phrases. The second category is a more severe state in which the individual loses touch with reality and has no self control . . . other symptoms include echolalia, echo praxia, . . . and coprolalia and copropraxia—the involuntary utterance of obscenities and performance of obscene behaviors.
>
> The Ainu do not classify *imu* as an illness or a sign that the individual may be sick. They simply regard the behaviour during an *imu* seizure as amusing. If a respected shaman or a political leader happens to be a victim of *imu,* it in no way affects the respect he commands; the others laugh at him only during the seizure. . . .[8]
>
> Chiri and K. Wada convincingly argue that in the past the Ainu saw a close association between *imu* and shamanism. . . . When I checked a list of individuals who were victims of *imu,* more than half of them were also shamans. (Ohnuki-Tierney 1981, 175–176)

Ohnuki-Tierney analyzes *imu* as a culturally sanctioned way for people—especially women; all of the Hokkaido shamans were women—to express discontent:

> There is at least partial evidence that *imu* among Hokkaido Ainu women is linked to their marginal status vis-à-vis Ainu men, who form the dominant group in Ainu society, and also vis-à-vis the Japanese, who constitute the dominant group in a larger universe of the Ainu, who have become a minority group in Japanese society. . . .
>
> During a possession trance, individuals are not held responsible for their behavior. Thus, they can assume the identity of that which has possessed them—a demon, a god, a general, a deceased patriarch, and so on. Possession therefore serves as a culturally sanctioned mechanism that has a definite therapeutic function for the individuals who, either because of their personality or role constraints, cannot otherwise express themselves in a manner that is possible during a possession trance. (Ohnuki-Tierney 1981, 175–176)

It would be tempting to look at this historical description of the Ainu and imagine a past where people with *imu* attacks were not only not marginalized as mentally ill but also held respected positions within their communities as shamans and leaders. But this is problematic on several levels. First, having *imu* wasn't a sufficient or even a necessary condition for being considered a shaman. Rather, Ohnuki-Tierney's work and the work of other anthropologists make it clear that shaman status relies on a complex interaction of social status and internal politics.

In her 1990 *American Ethnologist* article "The Woman Who Didn't Become a Shaman," cultural anthropologist Margery Wolf relates an incident that happened during her fieldwork in a very small village in rural Taiwan in the 1960s. A young woman suddenly engaged in very aberrant behavior. Her family, the village, and the resident anthropologist were then enmeshed for the next few weeks in a struggle to determine what was wrong with her. Was she possessed by the spirits and thus a shaman, a *tang-ki*? Or was she simply sick in the head and in need of medicine (traditional and western) to be cured? In the end, it was determined that she was not a shaman, which was a disappointment to her family, as that would have provided a source of income. Wolf's analysis was that as newcomers to the village, her family did not have the social status and appropriate relationships—what anthropologists call social capital—to enable her to become accepted as *tang-ki*.

Secondly and more importantly, we should not fail to situate *imu* within the horrendous conditions of colonization of the Ainu by the Japanese and the social dislocation and psychological damage that this caused. In a pivotal essay on the future of transcultural psychiatry, Lawrence Kirmayer and Harry Minas write of the dangers of isolating "native" psychological or cultural phenomena from the colonial contexts in which they emerge:

> This is made strikingly clear by the example of *pibloktoq*, or arctic hysteria, among the Inuit. Most comprehensive psychiatric texts mention *pibloktoq* as a culture-bound syndrome characterized by sudden wild and erratic behaviour. Recently, the historian Lyle Dick collected all the published accounts of *pibloktoq*, of which there are only about 25. It seems that psychiatric case description transformed a situation of sexual exploitation of Inuit women by explorers into a discrete disorder worthy of a new diagnostic label. With hindsight, we can see how insensitivity to the impact of exploration on other peoples distorted the picture when vital information on social context was not included. The legacy of these colonialist blinkers is still with us. . . . [9]

Unfortunately so. Let us now return to the general historical narrative of Hokkaido in the early twentieth century.

Christian Missionaries in Hokkaido

In the early 1900s, a British Christian missionary by the name of John Batchelor began proselytizing and educating Ainu youth in the prefectural capital of Sapporo. At his mission and elsewhere, young educated

Ainu men started to talk about the plight of their people. By the 1920s, these men (and some women) had become the core of the Christian Ainu movement, but their early goals, far from being radical, were assimilationist. Eager to incorporate themselves in Japanese society, they focused their efforts on the abolition of schools for native children, the eradication of alcoholism, the repeal of discriminatory laws that treated Ainu differently from Japanese, and an improvement in the general social and economic situation.

Through their efforts, they fostered a great amount of intellectual and artistic expression that ironically helped sponsor a newfound sense of Ainu pride. One of the more radical members of the emerging next generation was Iboshi Hokuto, who wrote a series of powerful poems criticizing colonialism and its aftereffects. This one is from 1930:

> Adjusting my necktie, I glance at my face
> The mirror tells me
> You are Ainu after all (cited in Siddle 1996, 130).

Christianity and Christian beliefs became one way that these young Ainu men and women could resist mainland influence and improve themselves. Western discourse itself became a countercolonial technique (cf. Fanon 1968). In the early decades of the twentieth century, Christianity had established a niche in the peripheries. In western Japan, Hiroshima and Nagasaki had rekindled their strong Christian communities. There were Christian outposts in northern Japan, including the tip of Honshu (Aomori) as well as Hokkaido.

The Church at Urakawa

The Moto-Urakawa Church that had been built in 1886 by the Sekishinsha colonists attracted parishioners from the entire region. But travel was difficult, especially in the middle of winter. Furthermore, the church was located in Ogifushi, a small hamlet in comparison to the town of Urakawa, which was rapidly growing as a result of the booming fishery trade.

In 1956, several parishioners took it upon themselves to build a small prayer house in Urakawa. The church was nowhere near as nice as the one at Moto-Urakawa, being a simple wooden structure with a tiny meeting space that could barely accommodate more than a dozen worshippers. And despite the hopes of those that prayed there, the church was

Figure 3.6 Bethel Member Shoko Katohgi being baptized by Rev. Yamamoto at the Urakawa Church, December 23, 2007. Minoru Sasaki is holding the baptismal chalice. Mr. and Mrs. Mukaiyachi are standing to her left. Photo by the author.

never given a permanent resident minister by their parent organization, the United Church of Christ in Japan. While the church at Ogifushi had a full-time minister, the Urakawa church relied on a minister who came once a month, if that, on a traveling circuit that took him through the small towns of the region.

This small church at Urakawa eventually became the backdrop for the founding of Bethel.

CHAPTER FOUR

The Founding of Bethel

On a brisk spring day in 1978, a young man got off the train at Urakawa Station and despaired for his future. The boulevards in front of the train stations in Japan are usually quite lively. But when Ikuyoshi Mukaiyachi stepped off the train, all he could see were abandoned storefronts and dilapidated houses. He felt that he had come to a godforsaken land. In a way, though, he was pleased, as he was there to do God's work.

Mr. Mukaiyachi was a devout Christian. He wasn't originally from Hokkaido but from northern Honshu, the main island of Japan. When he was in middle school, his mother had converted to Christianity, and he soon followed suit. He was, by his own admission, quite passionate about his beliefs and an idealist at heart.

Mukaiyachi-san had majored in social work at Hokusei Gakuen University in Sapporo. His family was quite poor, so he had to make ends meet by working the night shift at a nursing home for the elderly. He remembers feeling quite alienated from the other college students, who were enjoying a much more free and secular college experience. When he graduated, he looked far and wide for social work positions but couldn't find anyone to hire him. He had almost abandoned hope when he found the opening at the Red Cross Hospital in Urakawa.

The Japanese Red Cross Hospital in Urakawa was then, as now, the only general hospital in the region (for more on the hospital and its psychiatric ward, see chapter 5). Mukaiyachi was hired to be the facility's social worker, charged with bringing the hospital out into the community. This was a radical concept at the time, as most hospitals thought that health care was something that they provided only inside their walls. Mukaiyachi-san's job was to reach out to the families in the area, to help educate people about healthier living, and to work with improving the social condition of an area that had severe problems with alcoholism and domestic violence.

The Acorn Society

When he moved to Urakawa in 1978, Mukaiyachi-san was literally penniless. He had to borrow money from his parents to buy a suit for his job interview, and he had pawned his English dictionary to pay for the train ticket.

When he got to Urakawa, he looked for the local Christian church. He was delighted to find a tiny church nestled on the hill near the station but became despondent upon learning that the church had no resident minister. Instead, a traveling minister would come once every few weeks. The rest of the time, the parishioners would hold the services themselves. Ikuyoshi discovered that this turned out to be quite to his liking, as the simplicity and honesty of individuals coming together to celebrate Christ and study the Bible was a refreshing break from ponderous sermons.

The church itself was a simple wooden building that had been erected in 1956. It had no insulation, and the only protection against the elements was a thin metal roof and a single layer of siding. It was so cold in the building that if you left a kettle with water on the stove, it would be frozen solid by morning (Sasaki 1992, 46). The church originally had some rooms for a resident minister, but they had been empty for several years. As he couldn't afford anything else in town, Ikuyoshi asked the regional Church of Christ in Japan office if he could move in. Because no one else was using it, and because it would be helpful to have someone there during the week to keep an eye on things, he was granted permission.

One of the first things that Mukaiyachi-san did was start a support group for discharged psychiatric patients, a category that also included people who were alcoholic. As we saw in chapter 2, the usual model for psychiatric care in Japan in the postwar period was extended stays. This was profitable for the hospital and amenable to many families—but often not in the interests of the patients themselves.

The group that Mukaiyachi-san founded his first summer in Urakawa was nicknamed the "Acorn Society" (*Donguri no Kai*), and they met at his place in the church once a month (Mukaiyachi 1992, 13). Early members

Figure 4.1 Bethel House in 2007. Photo by the author.

remember this time with fondness, as the meetings were loud and raucous but full of sharing, mutual support, and trust.

A New Minister Moves In

In 1980, one of the parishioners in the town donated enough money to erect a new church.[1] The need was quite dire, as the old church where Mr. Mukaiyachi was living was tiny, cramped, and literally falling apart. The new church, built right next to the old one, was a new and gleaming white ferroconcrete modern structure with a tall spire that reached up toward the heavens. The first floor was designed to house a minister and his family, while the second floor provided a chapel and a meeting space.

After it was built, the new church was granted a resident minister. In August of the same year, Reverend Miyajima and his wife and three children moved in. They came from Wakayama in central Japan. The minister's wife, Michiko, remembers those early days. Mr. Mukaiyachi would spend Sunday afternoons picking up children in the neighboring houses and housing projects in his minivan and bring them to the church for Sunday school. Michiko would make them a hearty lunch, as many of the children weren't getting full meals at home. Many of these kids were from Ainu families or families with histories of mental illness or alcoholism. At the time, Mr. Mukaiyachi was working aggressively in the community to address issues of alcoholism and domestic violence, so he knew many of these families quite well.[2]

With the minister living in the new church next door, the old church building could now accept more occupants. The first resident was a man who had spent time in and out of the psychiatric ward of the hospital because of his alcoholism.

The second resident was Minoru Sasaki, a young man who was born in the area. Like many young men of his generation, Sasaki-san had gone to Tokyo after high school to make his fortune. But in Tokyo, he experienced symptoms of schizophrenia and returned to Urakawa for hospitalization. According to Michiko, even after he was discharged from the hospital and was working again at an auto repair garage, he encountered a lot of discrimination from his coworkers when they found out he was an ex-patient (Miyajima 1992, 38). Sasaki-san had already encountered Christianity in his childhood—he remembers going to Sunday school and Christmas parties when he was a child.

Sasaki-san had become the head of the Acorn Society when he decided to move into one of the rooms of the old church. The church quickly became a sort of clubhouse for other former patients, and their monthly dinners attracted up to twenty people (Miyajima 1992, 40). Other people asked the Miyajimas if they could also live in the church building. By that time, Mr. Mukaiyachi had married Etsuko, one of the nurses at the Red Cross Hospital, and had moved out of the old church building.

About a year later, Sasaki-san's housemate moved out, and Kiyoshi Hayasaka moved in (as detailed in Kiyoshi's story earlier in this book). The year was 1983.

Bethel House

In April of 1984, a group of volunteers got together to try to make the old church building more habitable by putting in some insulation in the bare walls and renovating and expanding the living facilities (Mukaiyachi 1992, 12). Reverend Miyajima used this opportunity to officially christen the old church building Bethel House (*Beteru no Ie*). The name, which appears in the Old Testament and means "house of God," was also a reference to the

Bethel Institution, a psychiatric hospital in Germany that in 1940 courageously resisted orders given by Adolph Hitler to euthanize their patients in a prelude to his Final Solution for the "Jewish question" (Miyajima 1992, 43).

Around the same time, Mr. Mukaiyachi got into a dispute with the chief of psychiatry at the Red Cross Hospital over his handling of psychiatric patients. Apparently Mr. Mukaiyachi thought that the doctor was an arrogant bully (Mukaiyachi 2006, 32). Mr. Mukaiyachi remembers that for five years, he was forbidden to enter the psychiatric ward, although of course he was doing a lot on the outside with the discharged patients and area families.

The first year or two of Bethel House were rather hectic. Michiko Miyajima remembers the police often coming to the church with one of its drunken residents in tow or of parents telling their children to avoid the area (Miyajima 1992, 38). But there was a bigger task of trying to find jobs for the residents—what good was leaving the hospital if you couldn't live independently?

For instance, Mr. Mukaiyachi and Mrs. Miyajima struggled to find Kiyoshi a job. Although he had worked several years as a projectionist at a movie theater in a town near Sapporo, his mental state had deteriorated since his return to Urakawa. Every time he would get a new job in town, he would feel too much pressure, seize up, and get hospitalized. This happened several times before they realized that this just wouldn't work. They'd have to find something that he could do in-house.

One of the side jobs that many housewives in the area did was packaging *kombu*, a type of seaweed used in making soup stocks and as a garnish. The coast of southeast Hokkaido is famous for its seaweed. Urakawa and the surrounding areas used to provide 90 percent of the *kombu* seaweed for Japanese consumers.[3] In fact, if you go to any convenience store in Japan, you can buy *onigiri* rice balls that proudly proclaim that they use Hidaka seaweed.

All that seaweed needed to be dried and packaged. There were no large seaweed processing plants in the Hidaka area, as it was all done as by people in their homes as piecework, which meant that it could be done at your own schedule at home. Perfect for housewives—and, thought the minister and his wife, maybe something that Kiyoshi and the others could do.

Not many people would have predicted in 1988 that packaging and selling *kombu* would be one of the things that Bethel would become famous for.

Bethel's Principles

With increasing sales from their seaweed packaging, Bethel was able to expand. In July of 1989, they started up the Welfare Shop Bethel, which would sell paper diapers and other rehabilitation products to the elderly in the community and the patients at the hospital. In 1990, Bethel House was renovated yet again, this time so that it could accommodate up to six residents. At that point, Bethel was engaged in three main activities: (1) caring for residents in the old church building at the Group Home Bethel House; (2) packaging seaweed and doing other jobs at the Bethel Sheltered Workshop; and (3) running a diaper delivery service at the Welfare Shop Bethel.

As the president of the Acorn Society and a former patient himself, Sasaki Minoru had strong feelings about what Bethel House could provide:

> There are many people in the hospital who want to get discharged but have no place to go. If there were halfway houses to help them, they could take that first step toward independence. I can't help but pray for more of these halfway houses to be developed. We need to put pressure on the government toward making people with psychiatric disabilities more independent. Meanwhile, we need to understand that we too are members of society and actively engage in activities oriented toward improving our independence. We disabled people cannot be only be on the receiving end of assistance from society. On our end, I believe we all have roles that contribute to society. As people in recovery, we need to realize that we have social value and can find meaning in our existence. (Sasaki 1992, 46)

As it expanded, Bethel was trying to avoid becoming yet another welfare organization with bureaucratic rules and regulations. As Mr. Mukaiyachi noted,

> I was once asked, "What do you think the main feature of Bethel is?" I responded by saying, "It's a place where management is just impossible." If I think about it, Bethel House doesn't have any of the rulebooks or management manuals that other organizations do. There was a time when we had come across the rules and regulations that other group homes or workshops used, and while we were impressed by the totality of the rules, we thought, "We don't need this at Bethel." . . .
>
> If we did have those types of rules and regulations, then we felt that everything could get answered by "looking it up in the regulations." Every individual act of generosity or thought might become end up becoming squelched. (Mukaiyachi 1992, 16–17)

Although Bethel was in fact running a sheltered workshop, Mr. Mukaiyachi hated the idea of them. He felt that sheltered workshops and other work-rehabilitation facilities for people with disabilities reeked of the paternalism that had marred the social welfare landscape. People with disabilities in these workshops would do menial tasks at very little pay (often much below minimum wage)—and were supposed to be grateful to their benefactors to boot! In addition, they had very little say over their own working conditions. He wanted something different for Bethel.

To counter that, Bethel was set up to operate under the principle of "management by every member of the staff" (*zen'in keiei*), one of the trendy management buzzwords flitting around Japan at the time. But in their case, it was close to the truth. They thought that it was important that everyone decide how they wanted to participate. If that morning, you felt ill or too sick to come in to work, you didn't have to. You only had to go to Bethel if you felt up to it. They developed a set of core principles that laid out their philosophy for the new company. Many of the principles were derived from their Christian faith or from Alcoholics Anonymous teachings:

- Meeting is more important than eating.
- We want a workplace where you can goof off without fear.
- Move your lips, not your hands.
- We welcome prejudice and discrimination.
- From "auditory hallucinations" to "Mr. Voices."
- Trust in the power of the group.[4]
- Weakness binds us together.
- Bethel's colors [diversity] make sales go up!
- We welcome the mixing of public and private.
- When you come to Bethel, your illness comes out.
- Let's value our lack of profits.
- Don't try too hard.
- Don't try to fix your illness by yourself.
- Just letting it be is good enough.
- Go from a "life of ascent" to a "life of descent."
- Reclaim your problems.
- You're right on schedule.

Meeting before Eating

Perhaps the most important of Bethel's core principles is "meeting before eating." Meetings go on constantly during the day at Bethel. They always start the same way, with each of the participants giving their name and how they feel today, both physically and psychologically. Morning meetings go over all of the activities of the previous day—how the sales team did in terms of selling things, or how many packets of *kombu* the packaging team did, and so on. The goal of these constant meetings is so that everyone has the feeling that they know what is going on—both in terms of Bethel the company and in terms of each other.

Because everyone talks about how they are feeling psychologically and physically, you know whether someone might be grumpy and best left alone. Or that another person might really need a hug and someone to talk to. Or that someone might be feeling sleepy or nauseous and that it might be best to not ask them to take on too much that day.

Going over the previous day's logs also helps in another way. At Japanese companies, many workers feel great pressure to show up each day, because if they don't they will let down the entire team, which might be counting on them for a crucial element. This causes a huge amount of workplace stress. By making everyone aware of what is going on, Bethel tries to reduce the pressure on any one person feeling that they need to show up, either to complete a job or to let the next shift know what needs to get done. Psychologists call this the development of transactive memory. The end-of-day meetings are debriefing sessions, so that everything that happened that day can get noted in the records. This provides the day-to-day continuity a company needs, despite the individual weaknesses of its members.

At the end of the week is the Friday afternoon meeting, where people talk about the struggles they had during the week. In *Bethel*, one Friday meeting resulted in a great deal of tension when one of the members said that they were struggling with another member's strong body odor. Still, these meetings are an important place for these feelings to come out, so that no one feels as though people are hiding things from each other. It's notable that the entire meeting was run by Bethel members; despite the strong emotions expressed, there was no staff intervention at any time. This was typical of Bethel meetings.

Bethel Is Full of Problems

Bethel prides itself on being full of problems, another one of its core principles. Mr. Mukaiyachi felt that the "ability to worry" (*nayamu chikara*) was a critical skill that was denied from people with psychiatric disabilities.

Hospital environments are designed to take away all of your problems: you didn't have to worry about your job, your relationships, or even what you were going to have for breakfast or wear that day. You assume the sick role, the hospital manages everything else.

In contrast, Mr. Mukaiyachi felt that people should be given back their problems and worries. The ability to worry represented a step toward real social rehabilitation and social participation. Problems should be welcomed, not feared. You should reclaim your problems. The fight scene mentioned above is yet another example of a problem that should be welcomed. Similarly, the philosophy of Bethel prefers that all prejudices and discrimination to be aired because if they aren't expressed, then nothing can be done to work around them.

Dr. Kawamura, the chief psychiatrist at the Red Cross Hospital, also welcomes people's problems, but from a different angle. He believes that there is something fundamentally wrong with most of Japanese psychiatry. He says that in any other hospital, if a patient goes to the psychiatrist and says that they are still hearing voices, the attending doctor will increase their levels of antipsychotics. Eventually, the patient is either taking so many pills that they don't feel anything and can't do anything, or they learn not to tell the psychiatrist anything at all. The doctors in this scenario aren't bad people or pawns of the pharmaceutical industry; they are just trying to fix their patients using the only tools that they know.

Dr. Kawamura feels that the best thing that he can do is the opposite. He reduces the levels of antipsychotics that his patients take until they are able to function socially again. They might still hear some voices, but as long as the voices aren't too bothersome, he would rather have his patients learn how to deal with them than dampen them pharmaceutically. Allowing his patients to become full social beings again—to reclaim the problems that everyday life gives people—is his stated goal.

When asked in an interview in 1992 what he thought was the defining characteristic of the Bethel members, the doctor responded:

> It's overwhelming the richness of their self-expression. They're very loud! [he laughs] I think it's very important that they are able to express anger and get into fights with their peers. When you're angry at someone, in reality you want their love. So being able to express your anger is extremely healthy. If you aren't able to express anger, what happens is that the anger turns into malice. In contrast to anger, malice is the desire to destroy the other party and is pathological. (Kawamura 1992, 164)

From a "Life of Ascent" to a "Life of Descent"

It may sound surprising, but the purpose of Bethel is not to get better. Many psychiatric pilgrims come to Bethel expecting miracles—that the doctor will be able to cure them or cure their children—of their mental illnesses and restore them back to society. Ultimately, they leave disappointed.

Dr. Kawamura calls himself a "doctor that can't cure, a doctor that won't cure." The psychotropic medications he gives can alleviate some symptoms, but they cannot *cure* the underlying illness, whether it be schizophrenia, depression, or bipolar disorder. This is just the reality of modern psychiatry. At best, the medication can temporarily quieten the voices, calm the feelings of anxiety, or make the pain of living a bit more bearable.

But even before that, both Dr. Kawamura and Mr. Mukaiyachi don't believe that the mental illness is the true problem. Many people think that *if only* they are cured of their mental illness, then everything will be OK. The real problem that people with mental illness have is that their lives get interrupted by the illness and the subsequent treatment.[5] After they become ill, all of their energy (and all of their parents' energies) gets directed toward treating the illness. Their lives effectively stop. They leave school or their jobs, fall out of social interactions with others; in many ways they become non-people. They may be living, but they die social deaths.

This is where some of the alcohol treatment background to Mr. Mukaiyachi and Dr. Kawamura comes in. Neither believes that they can fix a

Figure 4.2 Mr. Mukaiyachi working with Kiyoshi in a self-directed research session at the hospital. Photo by the author.

person with mental illness; rather, they believe that people need to learn how to *live in recovery* from mental illness. Just as an alcoholic will always be an alcoholic and needs to learn to live with their disease, someone who is schizophrenic also needs to learn to live with that condition. In Urakawa itself, the philosophy manifests itself in some of the other core principles: You're right on schedule; don't try too hard; we are linked by our weakness.

Mr. Mukaiyachi wants to counter the notion of getting "better." He feels that much of the problem is that people try too hard to be better than what they are. In a series of lectures that he gave while I was at Bethel, he talked about the notion of a "life of descent," which he later turned into a book by the name of *Anshinshite Zetsubō Dekiru Jinsei* (How to live a worry-free life without hope, 2006); he also appeared in a 2009 film called *Oriteiku Ikikata* (How to live in descent).

This philosophy, which one might call a pragmatic or realistic pessimism, is that life isn't going to get better. We all reach our peak fairly early in our twenties, and we need to live with the fact that our bodies and minds will forever after be in decline. By accepting the fact that we live "in descent," one can live a better life with fewer unrealistic expectations.

This philosophy of descent is particularly well suited to post-bubble Japan. The Japan of the 1960s through the 1980s was consumed by economic growth and prosperity. When that bubble burst in the early 1990s, the future became very murky. Japan has no natural resources. The birth rate has been steadily declining; in 2008 it was 1.4 children per woman, well below the self-sustaining rate for a country. This means that the one resource Japan has—human resources—is not being replenished. Politicians and the media constantly tell us that Japan is headed for a demographic nightmare—too many old people and not enough young people. In a sense, the Japanese have become their own *horobiyuku minzoku*—a dying race, just like the Ainu people that they tried to destroy a century ago.

With the global recession further dampening any hope of a recovery, a philosophy that says that life is not about ascending but about descending—this has resonance not only in Urakawa but in broader Japan as well.

The Heart and Mind of Bethel

It should be clear by now that Mr. Mukaiyachi is both the heart and mind of Bethel. Without him, the first meetings at the church would have never taken place, and Bethel House would never have been founded. Dr. Kawamura might never have been inspired to stay in Urakawa permanently. Mr. Mukaiyachi has written over a half dozen books on Bethel and edited many more. He writes regularly for a number of magazines in Japan, on topics ranging from psychiatric social work to Christian philosophy. He's a voracious reader, and his books are filled with citations from a broad range of scholars in Japanese and Western philosophy, psychiatry, neurology, and spirituality. Now that he's a college professor and no longer employed by the hospital, Mr. Mukaiyachi travels all across Japan lecturing on the Bethel system, recruiting new members at psychiatric facilities and institutions.

I was once driving with Rika as we followed Mr. Mukaiyachi's car to Health Sciences University of Hokkaido in Sapporo, where he works. Rika and another member were going to give a self-directed research presentation to his class. The road to Sapporo City hugs the coast. I noticed that Mr. Mukaiyachi's car would drift to the left and the right of the small, two-lane highway. I was surprised and asked Rika what she thought was going on—was Mr. Mukaiyachi dozing off? Oh no, she responded, he's most likely reading something. He does that all the time. When we stopped off at a convenience store for a break and asked him about his driving, Mr. Mukaiyachi chuckled and said he was reading an especially interesting article in an academic journal.

Mr. Mukaiyachi has a unique charisma, especially within the Bethel community. His monthly lecture series in Urakawa, even when they are on rather dry German social philosophy, is always packed. His mobile phone is constantly ringing with phone calls or text messages from members. He has dedicated his life to Bethel and its members, and they in turn have entrusted their lives to him.

The Urakawa church has a Christmas party every year. After the service, there is a shared dinner with a Christmas cake. The two years that I was in Urakawa, Mr. Mukaiyachi also gave a demonstration of his psychic powers. With the room packed with Bethel members, he would choose a small object like a coin. He would briefly leave the room, with instructions that one of the members should hold onto the object without telling him who it was. There would be a flurry of activity. Some people would be scared of the coin; others would be eager to have it. After a few minutes, someone would decide to hold it, stuffing it into a pocket or a purse. Mr. Mukaiyachi would come back into the room.

He would scan the room, looking at the crowd of people, some with Cheshire grins on their faces, others furtively avoiding his gaze. He would approach one of us, peer into our eyes, and ask, "Do you know where the coin is?" That person would deny it, and he'd move on. Invariably within just a few minutes, he would declare who had the coin, to the astonishment of everyone. It was an awe-inspiring demonstration. While Mr. Mukaiyachi was most likely not psychic, he could still easily read the minds of the Bethel members.

The other significant figure in Urakawa is Dr. Kawamura, the chief psychiatrist at the Urakawa Red Cross Hospital. In many ways, Bethel was able to flourish because of the unique partnership between Dr. Kawamura and Mr. Mukaiyachi. I've talked about the doctor several times now in the context of Bethel but neglected to introduce him formally. Perhaps it's best to talk about the doctor and the hospital in the chapter after our next life story.

UFOs and Other Mass Delusions: Kohei's Story

When I first came to the town of Urakawa to make *Bethel*, I was interested in the stories that circulated in the community—what anthropologists might call central myths.[1] Humans love to tell tales, but we don't choose stories at random. Myths often reveal important structural or symbolic belief systems that underlie society.

Talking to people in the Bethel community, one such narrative that emerged was the story of Kohei Yamane's UFO hallucination and delusion. This story won him the Grand Prize at the Hallucinations and Delusions Grand Prix at the 2002 Bethel Festival. In the version that appeared in *Bethel*, I chose not to do a dramatic recreation because I felt that it would appear artificial, choosing instead to focus on how Yamane-san and his friends told the story. I intercut the narrative of two of his friends and colleagues at Bethel, Rika Shimizu and Shio Hayasaka.

The segment in the film begins with Kohei trying to remember the events that led up to the UFO incident. He was staying at Bethel House when suddenly he heard the voice of a woman who had worked at his former company. She told him that he needed to go to Erimo Park in order to catch a UFO and save the world. He packed his bags and was trying to figure out how to get to Erimo Park (about fifty kilometers, or an hour's drive, from Urakawa) when he bumped into a Bethel member who (being schizophrenic himself) immediately realized that Yamane-san was hallucinating and delusional. This member convinced Kohei to go to one of the group homes to talk with the other members about going to catch the UFO. He said that there is a woman there who is in regular contact with UFOs, so maybe she can give him some advice.

Various Bethel members and a couple of staff gathered at Rika House to talk with Yamane-san. He explained the situation, and the members asked him questions. It's the middle of winter; Erimo Park will be absolutely freezing—is he sure the UFO will land? How many people can ride in the UFO? Does he have a UFO license?

He responds to their questions with ease, but this final question stumps him. He didn't realize that he needed a UFO license to ride a UFO in Urakawa. The members all agree that he does—after all, the last person who tried to ride a UFO without a license fell off a roof and broke his leg. Kohei needed to go talk to Dr. Kawamura at the UFO Research Center to get his license. Agreeing, he went with them to see Dr. Kawamura at his house, whereupon the good doctor convinced him that he should check into the psychiatric ward to rest for a couple of days before leaving on his UFO expedition.

It's important to note that at the time, Yamane-san wasn't a Bethel member, which means that he wasn't considered to have a psychiatric disability by the others around him. In fact, before coming to Urakawa, he hadn't seen a psychiatrist and hadn't been diagnosed with any mental illness. This contrasts with almost all of the other members, many of whom had spent years in and out of psychiatric facilities and had come to Urakawa with diagnoses and heavily dosed on medications.

What doesn't appear in the film is the backstory to Yamane-san's experience. There is also no exploration of what this story reveals about life at Bethel—and why it won the 2002 Hallucinations and Delusions Grand Prix. The short narrative style that I used in the film is useful for dramatic events but is not as well suited for the slower unfolding of people's lives or for intellectual commentary. In these areas, written text allows for a more careful pacing and interweaving of exposition and narrative. Here, I textually interweave extended portions of an interview that I had with Yamane-san with background material and analysis.

Kohei's UFOs and the 2002 Grand Prize at the Hallucinations and Delusions Contest

As a child, Kohei had always wanted to be an automobile designer. Like most Japanese children who had grown up in the economic boom of the late 1980s, Kohei had studied hard to get into a good elementary school, studied hard to get into a middle school, then high school, and then finally into a good college—one of the best private universities in Japan. Kohei followed the mantra of postwar Japan: study hard and work hard and you will be rewarded with material success and stability. "Salarymen" at top-tier companies had lifetime employment and great benefits. By getting into a top university, Kohei was well on his way to achieving the Japanese Dream.

Unfortunately, the year that he graduated from college, 1996, was the beginning of the longest and bleakest recession that Japan has ever faced. The economy had stalled, and the stock market and real estate prices had crashed. To make matters worse, the previous year a massive earthquake devastated the port city of Kobe, and a doomsday cult named Aum Shinrikyo had orchestrated a terrorist attack using poison gas in the subways of central Tokyo. Dark times, indeed.

So Kohei was thrilled when Mitsubishi Motors chose to hire him. It wasn't his first choice; he would've been much happier if the much more successful Honda or Toyota Motors had picked him up, but any job was better than nothing. Many of his friends had ended up with no jobs, something that would have been inconceivable just a few years earlier. Mitsubishi was still a top-tier company, who could complain?

Mitsubishi was founded in 1870 as a shipping company and grew rapidly as Japan opened up in the wake of the Meiji Restoration. It played a central role in the industrialization and then militarization of Japan. During World War II, Mitsubishi was famous for making the Zero airplane. In the postwar period, it reorganized itself and now consists of rather diverse interests such as Mitsubishi Bank, Mitsubishi Petrochemicals, Mitsubishi Atomic Industries, Mitsubishi Heavy Industries, Mitsubishi Fuso Truck and Bus, and Mitsubishi Motors, among others.

A member of the Mitsubishi conglomerate, Mitsubishi Motors is the fifth-largest automobile manufacturer in Japan, well behind Toyota, Nissan, and Honda. They do, however, have a solid line of utility trucks and some sporty sedans. So it was not the end of the world for Kohei when they hired him. Or so he thought.

When he entered Mitsubishi, he asked the Human Resources department to place him in the design and engineering department, since that was his major in college. HR instead placed him in data analysis. This wasn't unusual. HR divisions in large companies in Japan will often place people in unfamiliar areas in order to develop new skills in them, rather than areas in which they already have training.

Kohei didn't particularly like computers or data analysis, but he decided that if he was going to be in that division, then he was going to do the best job that he could. Maybe then, HR would see that he was a talented and hard-working employee and move him to automobile design and engineering.

He was assigned to analyze defect data that was coming in from consumers and the dealerships. These were problems that appeared after the vehicles were on the road. Car manufacturers in Japan would normally pore over defect data in order to make improvements to the line or engineering changes to future designs. This was part of the philosophy of *kaizen*, or "continual improvement." Kohei was puzzled then when his boss told him to ignore the reports of problems and accidents that were happening to Mitsubishi cars and light trucks due to defects in design and manufacturing.

Kohei thought that surely Mitsubishi wanted to make the safest cars on the road. His boss must have been mistaken (or possibly he had misheard him) when he told Yamane-san to suppress the defect data. So Kohei tried to network with others in his company who might be interested in the defect data. He started up an internal newsletter to share information. He thought he was doing the best he could to make Mitsubishi the safest car manufacturer in the world.

He got the exact opposite reaction from management and his coworkers that he expected. Suddenly he was removed from all of his group projects and was given meaningless idle work. His coworkers started to ignore him. In my interview with him in 2005, he spoke of the bullying that started to occur:

> I was isolated from all of my other coworkers.
>
> If I went to one of them with a question, they would stand up and walk out the room. If I tried to go talk with someone, they would all disappear. I was totally blocked from communicating with other people, and in the end I was totally isolated. They even put up cardboard boxes between my desk and other desks so that I was totally boxed in.
>
> I was told things like, "If you try anything, we'll kill you," "Don't say idiotic things about making safe cars," "Stop defaming our company." Things like that.

The psychological bullying wasn't only from his coworkers. It came from management as well.

> There was a retreat where all of the staff had to go. And there I was forced to write reflection essays (*hanseibun*) describing what a worthless person I was. I would be forced to write about my own death—they said that I had to write for five minutes on that topic, and I wasn't allowed to stop writing

> or set down my pencil during that time. I'd have to write on how worthless I was. I was also forced to write four last wills and testaments—addressed to my parents, my friends, my girlfriend, and someone else. They had to say that my life up to that point was entirely misdirected and that I was a bad person.
>
> And so I started to think that maybe I had actually died. . . .

Although this might sound fantastical, this sort of thing actually happened in Japanese companies, although it wasn't widely known at the time when Kohei was going through it. In the investigations following the horrendous JR Fukuchiyama Line train accident in 2005, the Japan Railways Corporation was discovered to have widely engaged in "reeducation training" as punishment for even such minor infractions as a slightly delayed train.[2] The driver of the Fukuchiyama train was so afraid of being reeducated again that he went over the speed limit on a sharp corner in order to make up time, derailing the train and causing the death of 107 people, including himself.

In Kohei's case, his tormentors offered him a way out:

> And then they said that they would teach me how to live a new life: "So you understand that how you've been living your life up to now was wrong, right? So we'll tell you how to live your life. You need to think how each conversation you have, each step you take, each glass of water you drink, every movement that you make contributes to the betterment of the company. Think about that and put it into action. If you do that, your life will turn around."
>
> I thought about it and wrote a contract to them. I promised that each movement I made, each thought I had, every single little thing I did would be for the company.
>
> And I thought it was wrong for me to criticize the cover-ups that the company was engaged in and how I should have helped my coworkers with the cover-up. It wasn't fair that I didn't participate in the cover-up exercises.

Cover-up exercises?

> People from the Ministry of Transportation would occasionally come for site inspections. We had two sets of books going at the time. One set was the real documentation, and the second would be the fake or cover-up documents. [In our cover-up exercises,] we'd have to hide the real documents within ten minutes of the warning siren. We didn't have any push-carts to hold all the documents, so we'd put some of the documents on our office chairs that had casters and push the office chairs with the documents on them. We'd all run down the hallway with this stuff. Behind the computer room was a hidden room, and we'd all rush to put the documents in that room.

> There would then be a bucket relay to put all the boxes away. The section chief had a stopwatch and was yelling at us, "You got to get it to under ten minutes, hurry up!"
>
> If it took twelve minutes, for example, he'd yell, "That's no good!" And we'd have to put all the documents back on the chairs and carts, take them back to their original location, and then run the cover-up exercise again and try to get everything hidden within ten minutes. If we'd succeed, we'd all clap our hands in happiness and tell each other that we did a great job.

Kohei hated the training exercises and would try to avoid them:

> I worked in the computer room, and so I'd look behind me, and there would be a bucket relay of boxes piling into the hidden room, stopwatches going and whatnot. I used to look at that whole scene and think, what a stupid thing they were doing.
>
> We even had double sets of books on computer as well. I used to think that instead of going to all this trouble, why not just make safer cars, but when I said that, that was when I was forced to write more reflection essays and such.
>
> I took all the reflection essays back home with me and put them up on the walls of my room, looked at them every day, and mumbled to myself that I would strive to do my best to help with the cover-up. I promised that I'd do anything for this company.

It was at this point that Kohei started hearing the voices of his coworkers berating him, even when he was in the privacy of his own home. He tried working even harder. Kohei's mother started to worry about him. She thought that if he continued in this vein, the company would kill him. This wasn't an idle fear. Enough salarymen literally work themselves to death that the Japanese have a word for it: *karōshi*.[3] Kohei took a medical leave of absence.

Kohei's mom confided her fears to one of her neighbors, another housewife. As Kohei relates:

> One of our next-door neighbors just happened to be the mother of a television producer for TBS [Tokyo Broadcasting System] Television named Michio Saito. My mom and his mom were good friends. My neighbor told my mother that her son was going to Hokkaido to do a piece on a place called "Bethel" and wondered if I might be interested in going with him.
>
> But at that time I was thinking only about the company and that I had a lot to do at work. But my mom insisted that I had to go. And so I went as sort of a production assistant, carrying the bags of the cameraman and so forth.

After about of week of filming, Saito-san said he had to go back to Tokyo and said goodbye to me.[4]

And somehow I ended up staying at Bethel House.

The TBS television crew didn't have any money to rent a hotel room for him, so Kohei was lodging in the original Bethel House, the old Urakawa church building. I asked him why he stayed behind when the rest of the crew went back to Tokyo.

Well, if I kept living in Tokyo, all I was doing was yelling out loud to myself things like, "For the company, for the company." My mom thought that if I kept going to work that my mental state would deteriorate even further.

The director, Saito-san, thought the same thing and said that rather than going back to work, I should stay here [in Bethel] for a while.

I asked him if Kohei was aware of his mental condition at the time.

I didn't have any awareness that anything about me was wrong. And so when I came here, I'd say things to the other members like, "Well, if it's for Bethel, you should do everything you can, including committing a crime."

Why?

Well, you know I had initially skipped going to the cover-up exercises but came around to believe that I needed to do everything for the company. And so I thought that people in Bethel also should give their entire life to Bethel. I thought that they should . . . that they should commit any crime for Bethel's sake. They should cover up mistakes, falsify information, and do anything needed in order to increase sales. I had heard that they [Bethel] were a company whose sales were booming, so I thought that they had to be doing all sorts of evil things, cover-ups and whatnot in order to do that.

So I would go around saying things like, "We need to work to death here." And the people here would yell at me, "Are you an idiot??? Shut up!" No one understood where I was coming from.

Instead they would say, "You're in such a pitiful state, you're really in a bad state, huh? You must have suffered a lot, huh. If you're tired, you need to take it easy, get some rest, OK? If you don't like yourself, then you got your priorities wrong: it's not company first, yourself second."

Everyone said things like that. And when I get angry and tell them that they were liars and that wasn't the case, they'd all look at me with sad eyes and tell me that I must have really suffered a lot. I had no idea what to say back to them.

Every time I'd say things like, "For the company, for the company," they'd ask me, "Are you ok? You must be really tired. Take a rest, take a rest."

Was everything I had believed in and done up to then wrong? Was doing everything and anything for my company wrong?

I was so confused and didn't know what to believe. And so I felt like I couldn't trust anyone.

Kohei's fears that people were out to get him followed him to Urakawa and to his group home at old Bethel:

In any case I had to eat, so I went out and bought groceries, some meat and things, and put them in the refrigerator downstairs. I went back down after a while, and someone had eaten everything!

And I thought: even here, someone is out to get me!

Later on, when I was better, I asked and found out that the refrigerator downstairs was the common refrigerator for the house and anything left there was considered fair game for everyone. I was told that it was my fault for putting such tasty meat in it. If I had wanted to eat something tasty by myself, I was supposed to have taken responsibility myself and put it in my room for safekeeping.

So I gradually realized that people here weren't out to get me.

When I was at my worst, there was a period when I didn't trust anything anyone said to me. I'd say stuff like: "We need to try harder! We need to do anything we can to make better sales!"

My next-door neighbor at Bethel House at the time was Kiyoshi Hayasaka. And I noticed that all these people who were in really bad shape would go visit him, and they'd leave his room later on with smiles on their faces. And I thought he must be the central figure, the "key man," in this group. Maybe if I copy what he does, I'll get better too. So I started copying everything he did.

Like what?

One of the things that Kiyoshi still kids me about is. . . . Kiyoshi-san eats five or six meals a day, about twice what I eat [*author's note: Kiyoshi weighs about twice what Kohei does*]. So I thought that maybe if I ate more, I'd get better. So I tried eating as much as he did, but ended up gaining 6 or 7 kilos (15 pounds) and was so full that I threw up at night. But I felt I had to keep eating, so I'd eat more after that. That didn't seem to work, so I gave up trying to eat as much as he did.

Another thing was that Kiyoshi . . . well, he grew up in this area, so he's used to the cold . . . in the winter he'd be sitting in his underwear right by the stove, with an *uchiwa* fan in his hand, fanning himself and saying, "It's so hot, it's so hot."

So I thought sitting around in your underwear must be a good thing in the winter, but I caught a cold and was bedridden for a few days.

> So I tried to do everything he did, but after a while slowly figured out that some things worked for me, other things didn't.
>
> I didn't tell Kiyoshi at first, but after about a year, I finally told him that I had tried to copy everything he did. Some things worked, but wearing just my underwear in the cold and stuffing myself full of food didn't. After I told him that, he said that, "You really are a true idiot, huh. . . . Well, you're still young, so you'll most probably take another 20 years to settle down, but until then don't make too much of a fuss."

I asked Kohei if he went to see Dr. Kawamura, the chief psychiatrist, at all.

> I first went in . . . at the end of November of 2001. At the time, I couldn't admit to Dr. Kawamura that I was hearing voices: the voice of my superior, for example.
>
> When I looked at Dr. Kawamura. . . . I couldn't tell him that the faces of my old boss and my coworkers would appear and tell me, "If you say anything, we'll kill you" or "If you talk about safe cars, we'll kill you" and things like that.
>
> At the time, I couldn't talk at all, and if I tried to say anything, all of the memories of fear would well up in my stomach, my head would get pulled into pain, like a *hachimaki* headband was being tied tight around my head and if I tried to talk, the words would get stuck in my mouth, and all I could say would be, "Ahh . . . yes . . . oh . . . OK. . . ."
>
> Dr. Kawamura would nod his head and tell me that it seemed like I was having a hard time and tell me to make friends, to try to work on communicating with the other people here. Being able to express my feelings was the most important thing. He'd say that being in Urakawa was like being in a foreign country, so it's OK if you express your feelings here.
>
> At the time, I didn't understand what he was trying to say, but after attending the meetings, I saw that people were expressing how they felt. And I realized that this was how I should proceed too.

As we talked, the caretaker of the Bethel facility walked into the room and, after realizing that an interview is going on, walked back out.

> The person who just stepped in right now, Ms. Akao, is intimately related to this [story] as well.
>
> When I started living in Bethel house. . . . It was filthy. I couldn't believe the conditions that I was living in. My meat was being eaten by other people, and I didn't understand why, but in order to figure that out, I began communicating with the other residents here. And I started to feel like I should do something here too.
>
> The kitchen seemed like it was a mess and that no one was washing any of their dishes, so I started working on cleaning it up. I also made some

rice. And while I was washing the dishes, people would come up and plop their dirty dishes right next to me and walk away without saying anything. Nobody said, "Thank you" or "You're doing a good job." I was pissed off but kept on washing the dishes.

I said to someone that I was disappointed that I was diligently washing the dishes and making rice, yet no one said anything to me. He told me that if I had problems, I should tell them at the meetings. Kvetching by myself wouldn't result in anything; I had to talk about it at a meeting.

But I said that if I complained, it would lead to a fight. He said, "You idiot! That's your misunderstanding. Don't worry about it, spit it out." So at the house meeting, I said, "I wash the dishes and make the rice, how come none of you are encouraging me?"

That's when [the caretaker] Ms. Akao said . . . well, it's kind of gross, but she said, "A person like you who can't even wipe his own ass shouldn't even think of wiping other people's asses. You're a hundred years too young for that."

GAAAAN! [The sound of a metaphorical frypan hitting my head, waking me up.] That was a huge shock for me! I retorted, "That's not what I was thinking, I was thinking of helping you guys. . . . Am I supposed to just wash my own plate?" And they all said, "Yes, yes, just wash your own plate. When you get well enough to wash your own plate, then you can think of washing other people's. Don't go parading around here with such a big face."

And although I was pissed off, I said that I understood. And starting the next day, I only washed my own plate.

And gradually I realized that other people were washing the plates too. Sasaki-san, who lives next door, wakes up at 1 a.m. or 2 a.m. and washes all the plates and puts them away. And then Takashio-san, who doesn't really say much, also washes the plates and puts them away at lunchtime.

I was out during the day, so I hadn't noticed but people were washing the plates at midnight and noon. I was just noticing things were piling up in the morning and evening. I gradually understood how things worked. And I realized that not saying anything but getting all worked up inside wasn't helping me make any connections with my peers.

People will voice any complaints they have at the meetings, so ill feelings don't have a chance to build up. And you're able to address problem areas directly. Even if you can't resolve the complaints, at least voicing them helps you feel better.

For example, one of the things that often comes up in meetings and never gets resolved is trash. One of the members is really bad at throwing away his trash. For example, he leaves the trash can cover open, and there will be used tissue paper scattered around.

And we all know that Taki-san (that's his name) is bad at trash and that he won't ever get better at it. But still, we bring it up each week at meeting and talk about it. Because we talk about it in the open with everyone there,

> it doesn't become bad gossip. And because we can all see that everyone else also understands that Taki-san is bad at throwing away his trash but we're all trying to support him anyway, that makes each of us better. Fundamentally, it doesn't resolve anything, but at least we all feel that everyone else is aware of the situation as well. So it makes us feel better.
>
> So even though it appears at first glance that people here don't really have any communication skills, it turns out that they do know how to communicate with each other, and if you can get used to that, it's actually a relaxing place to live.

And it was a totally different environment from the business world that you were in?

> Yes, the business world that I was in was all about taking individual responsibility for getting things done, to take any steps necessary to get things done.
>
> At first I didn't understand when I started living here, but everyone has their strong points and their weak points. And we each support each other with our strong areas. The fellow Yoshi-san who washes dishes in the afternoon? He can't speak, and he doesn't know how to calculate his money. So when he goes shopping, he doesn't know how to give or get the right amount of change. So when he goes out, one of us tries to go along with him. On the other hand, he's really good at cooking, so he cooks for us. So we all support each other.
>
> This [Bethel House] is the oldest group home. Because it's so old, we're very good at knowing each other's [strong and weak] points and being able to support each other. And it's an unspoken rule: I'll help you here, if you can help me in another way.

And so now that you understand how Bethel works, do you have any plans on returning back home?

> Not really. Going back home would mean that I would have to help support the cover-up again. There's no way that I want to do that. Even remembering those days makes me feel ill again.
>
> I don't think there is anyone here who feels that by going back and denouncing or suing the people [that caused our problems], that we'd feel better afterwards. By finding the one or two people who we can tell our problems to and by having them understand, we can find balance again. So I don't think there's anyone who thinks that we could get balance by suing someone or by trying to forget what happened.

I asked Kohei about the UFO incident, cautious that he might not want to be reminded of that difficult period. He said it was okay to continue.

The first time [I was hospitalized], it's hard to explain. . . . I was out grocery shopping, and when I came back to the house, the voices were waiting for me and ambushed me. I heard a voice saying, "Save the world and the company!"

And I thought, that's right! I'm the only one who can create the perfect defect cover-up system for the company. I needed to go home, so I went up to my room and packed up all my bags so I could go back home to Tokyo.

And then the voice that was saying, "Save the world and the company!" told me that I had to catch a UFO to do that. And so I told everyone that I had to go to Erimo Misaki National Park to get on the UFO, go back to Tokyo, and save the world and the company.

And the people that heard this nodded their heads as they listened, and they said, "It'd be good if you told everyone else this." An emergency meeting was called. The Rika House [group home] weekly meeting was that day, and it was changed at the last moment to be about me.

And everyone took me there and they said, "Yamane-kun wants to go catch a UFO and save the world and his company, let's listen to what he has to say." So people asked me what the voices sounded like and what they were saying. And told them that I had to leave to do [my mission].

It was January at the time, and people said to me that it was −10 degrees Celsius at Erimo Misaki this time of year. There's nothing there, there are no trees, and there's strong winds, it must be tough to land a UFO there. And people said things like that. But the voices in my ear said, "It's OK, the UFO can land in those conditions." And so I told them that the UFO was most probably OK in the cold and wind.

And then one of the members said that in order to ride a UFO in Urakawa, you needed a license—did you know that? And I said, no, no, I didn't know that. I've never even heard anything like that.

And so someone decided to hold a vote on whether this was true or not. Anyone who thinks that you need a license to ride a UFO in Urakawa, raise your hand. All of the members—except me—raised their hands. I was taken aback! I thought that this might really be the case here, since everyone raised their hands so quickly and all at the same time. And so I ended up believing this.

And so I asked them to take me to the place where the licenses were issued. And we all got into the cars. And I asked them before getting into the car what the name of the place was that issued the licenses. And they said that there was a place called the Kawamura Space Center, and I nodded my head.

And we got into the cars and went off. When we arrived, it was the Urakawa Red Cross Hospital. And Dr. Kawamura was there in the consulting room waiting for me. And I talked about the voice that said to save the world and my company, that I was to go to Erimo National Park and catch a UFO there. And so I'd like to go there.

Dr. Kawamura pushed his chin deep into his chest and said, "I can understand your feelings, Yamane-kun, but there was someone three years ago who wanted to go ride a UFO, but he fell out of his second-floor window. It was Christmas Eve, the 24th of December, and he fell out. He shattered his leg in a compound fracture, but there was no one around, so he had to drag himself on his elbows to the hospital. If I let you go to Erimo Misaki in your current condition, you'd pretty much end up in the same state as him. So I can't issue you a license just right now. Why don't you take a rest here for a while?"

And so I ended up staying at the hospital for a week.

The day after I checked in, everyone came to the hospital and told me that the previous night a huge blizzard had struck Erimo Park and that they hadn't heard any news of a UFO landing there that night.

After thinking about it deeply, I thought that the whole thing did sound pretty implausible. And so I was able to check out of the hospital [a few days later] without any worries.

And that's the story that won the Hallucinations Contest?

Yup, the 2002 Hallucinations and Delusions Grand Prix.

Dr. Kawamura said that the reason that it won the grand prix wasn't because I talked about a UFO coming to take me away. He said, you won because after you talked about the UFO, everyone came to your aid, it's important to recognize and value that. I don't want you to forget that everyone came to your help.

I thought about it and agreed. If I had been by myself, I most probably would have tried to go ride the UFO.

What was hospital life like?

I realized that other people weren't really interested in an analysis of what happened but just told me, "You sure went through a lot . . . but everyone is also going through a lot, so you're OK."

I slowly realized that I didn't need to analyze my problems. So I did a couple of overnights [outside of the hospital, at Bethel House] for the next two weeks and was able to talk about things more. And so I was able to have a conference. . . . At the Red Cross Hospital, we have three support conferences: one when you check in, one in the middle, and one when you check out. In addition to the doctor, there are members of Bethel there as well as the person who is in the hospital. And we talk about how they are doing, whether they are ready to be discharged, and if there is agreement, then they can be discharged from the hospital.

And at the discharge conference, they said that I was struggling right on schedule. Someone said that they also had a couple of problems when they checked out, so you'll most probably also have those same problems. But it's still OK. Just talk about it with us. And so I was able to check out without any worries on my mind.

Was that the last time you were hospitalized?

Actually I was hospitalized a third time. The third time was in 2003. . . .

About a year had passed, and I was in better shape and could talk, could express my emotions. But the one thing I couldn't do was remember.

I was at my worst when I first showed up in Bethel. I couldn't even remember what had happened ten minutes before. If I tried to remember anything, the thought that "if you say anything, we'll kill you" would jump up at me. Even if I tried to remember something that had just happened, these terrifying and terrible memories would come out instead, making me shrivel up in fear.

I lived during those days by writing memos to myself. At such and such a time (x hours and y minutes), I did this; and such and such a time, I did that. I made it through the day by looking at these memos. Trying to remember anything at all was just too painful, so I just wrote a lot of memos to myself.

After about a year of that, I was able to write just an occasional memo to myself. One day I was driving to a presentation. I thought to myself, I think I'll be able to remember this time. I was driving in Dr. Kawamura's car, and another car approached us in the opposite lane. I thought to myself, that car's tire is going to come off . . . huh . . . oh no, that car's engine is going to catch on fire, that car's steering wheel is going to come off, that car's axle is going to fall off, oh no. . . . We erased the data for defects in over one million cars. . . . There are a lot of dangerous cars on the road. . . .

This was before the news of the cover-ups had hit the airwaves. And I thought, if I talk publicly about the cover-up, they'll just put me back into the hospital. . . . But if I don't say anything, maybe someone will die in an accident. . . . What should I do? And I was thinking all these thoughts while trying to drive.

And finally, when we got to our destination, there was a really beautiful lake; something broke inside of me, and I turned around and asked Dr. Kawamura, "Dr. Kawamura, Dr. Kawamura, why do people have desire? Is it OK to do anything in order to satisfy our desires?"

I stared at the doctor but he answered my questions with: "Humans are complex beings. People live their lives carrying many problems." He answered my questions straightforwardly.

I was shaking. All these voices were talking about conspiracies and cover-ups in my ear. I was remembering all these things and freezing up. I was part of the conspiracy. I did this, I did that.

On the way back, Dr. Kawamura said, "You know Yamane-san, you're in pretty bad shape. Why don't you check straight into the hospital?" I was there for around a month.

It wasn't as bad as before. I wasn't as frozen up like before. I did several overnight stays outside. I was able to express myself. I practiced expressing how I felt when my memories came up. I was terrified. . . . Many of my coworkers had been terrorized into leaving the company, and I was worried that many some of the perpetrators would come to Urakawa. It was hard to go back to the group home, but I thought that the hospital would be a safe place to be. I was so scared it was hard for me to check out of the hospital.

After about a month of being in the hospital and doing a couple of outside overnight stays, I felt like Bethel house might be safe as well. My housemates said, "We're right here, leave it to us [to make sure it's safe]."

Just around that time, Kiyoshi-san said to me, "If you're hearing voices, you need to come right out and tell us. We're professionals when it comes to voices. Don't try to struggle with it by yourself and burn yourself out. If you hear voices, we'll decide what to do, so tell us what they're saying. There's nothing as bad as trying to do it by yourself."

And that led me to think that the group home might be a safe place for me. And I was able to successfully check out.

That was the third hospitalization.

And the third time was just around the time that the news of the cover-up was just appearing in the newspapers?

I think it was around six months after my third hospitalization. The Kanagawa Prefectural Police began their first investigation around then. But they ended up without enough evidence and had to drop the case.

It was the next year, 2004, that things became clearer in the mass media.

Were you able to watch or read any of the news about it?

No.

I wasn't able to watch any of that coverage.

I hadn't noticed . . . but there was coverage of when the president [of Mitsubishi-Fuso Truck and Bus Corporation] was arrested on the television. And my eyes had become "cat's eyes."

Kiyoshi says that when people at Bethel start to feel bad, their eyes become like cat's eyes. Their pupils dilate in fear, and so it looks like their eyes become entirely black and look like cat's eyes. [At Bethel] we try to find people in that state and make sure they get proper care, confer with the doctor, check them into the hospital, and so forth.

Even if someone is pissed off and fuming or depressed and withdrawn, you can still talk with them about it. But if they're all frozen up in fear, then you don't know what they might do because they feel like they're trapped in a corner, so it's really important for all of us to work together to help them.

And so when I saw the president of the company being arrested on the news, my eyes had become cat's eyes, and I was frozen up. Kiyoshi told me, "You can't watch the news by yourself. If you are going to watch any news about Mitsubishi Motors, you need to watch anything about Mitsubishi when all of us are here."

> And so for the next six months or so, anytime there was some news coverage of Mitsubishi, I'd go running around the house to see if there was anyone home so that they could watch it with me. And they'd watch it with me and nod their heads and say, "Huh. . . . Huh. . . . You must have had a really rough time, I see, I see. . . . We'll listen to anything you want to say, so relax."
>
> And so gradually, I was able to relax.
>
> And people also began to see what I was talking about.
>
> "When you were talking about tires coming off of running cars or engines catching on fire, you were telling the truth! We understand now."
>
> And so I was able to relax.

Apparently up to then, people at Bethel thought that Kohei's talk of defective cars and a company-wide conspiracy to cover up the facts was just one of his delusions, so they were surprised when it made national television and proved to be true!

Folie à Deux, Trois, Quatre, Plusieurs and Other Mass Delusions

One of the significant aspects of Kohei's UFO story is that everyone at Bethel joined in when he talked about the UFO coming to pick him up.

Figure 4.3 Senior executives of the Mitsubishi-Fuso company apologizing at a press conference at the Ministry of Transportation in 2004. Copyright © The Yomiuri Foundation. Used with permission.

They took him to another woman who was also in communication with space aliens. In the meeting at Rika House, they asked him how many people could ride in the UFO (it was only a two-seater, so he couldn't take everyone). They inquired where it was landing and whether he was sure that it wouldn't be called off on account of the cold weather. And finally, they told him that in Urakawa, you needed a UFO license in order to ride a UFO and took him to see Dr. Kawamura of the Kawamura Space Research Center, who was moonlighting from his regular job as the chief psychiatrist of the hospital.

One could read this a couple of ways. First, some audiences that I've screened the film with have commented that the other Bethel members must have been lying to Kohei in order to get him to go to the hospital with them. Others criticized the way that the members were interacting with his delusional beliefs, saying that it wasn't appropriate and that it could be dangerous. Certainly, the handbook for psychiatric nurses in Japan apparently cautions nurses to not respond to any delusions or hallucinations of the patients.[5]

I believe that what was instead happening was a tempered version of what French psychiatrists call *folie à deux*, or shared delusion.[6] The other members, who we must recall also have their own psychiatric history, knew that Kohei was having a psychotic episode and that he genuinely believed that there was a UFO landing. Not surprisingly, UFOs attempt to land quite regularly in Urakawa. Bethel members recognize that the most dangerous thing is when a member tries to go out to meet the UFO by himself or herself.

Just a few years before Kohei's incident, one of the Bethel members heard from his voices that a UFO was about to land. On Christmas Eve, he climbed up onto the roof of his group home to catch the UFO but slipped on the slippery, snow-covered shingles onto the ground below and broke his leg. Because it was the holidays, there was no one else around, so he had to drag himself on his elbows to the hospital. After that incident, it was clear that going to meet a UFO by yourself was dangerous.

Bethel members wanted to make sure that UFO-catchers were physically and psychologically ready for the event. The best way to make sure someone was ready to catch a UFO was to make sure they had a UFO license. And the best authority on whether someone was ready was Dr. Kawamura, who had plenty of experience talking to people with UFO experiences.

Kohei won the 2002 Hallucinations and Delusions Grand Prix precisely because he successfully created a *folie à plusieurs*, a type of mass delusion, although in this case the other members were quite aware that the existence of UFOs was a reality only in Kohei's head. There is always safety in numbers; the most dangerous thing is a delusion or voices that you keep to yourself.

But in addition to creating a shared delusion, Kohei also created a shared memory at Bethel. His story became a legend, shared property of the community. It was raised as an example of everyone doing the right thing to save one of their peers.

In 2007, when I was in town for the Bethel Festival, the winner of that year's Delusions and Hallucinations Grand Prix was the entire Kireiso House. The various members were convinced that there was an invisible man in the house who was playing tricks on them. The pranks the invisible man played were usually related to whatever neurosis the resident had, whether it was a thing that they misplaced or doors that were being slammed too hard. The various members started talking about the things that the invisible man was doing to them. In this case, the *folie à quatre* helped the four residents to talk to each other and to find out what each was worried about, which was why it was awarded the prize that year.

Where Is Yamane-San?

Kohei's story has a happy ending, but I'll make you wait until the end of the book to read it. He's one of the few Bethel members who has graduated from Bethel, a problem that will become more apparent as you read on.

CHAPTER FIVE

The Doctor and the Hospital

Toshiaki Kawamura was born in 1949 in the small town of Mori, on the southwest tail of the island of Hokkaido. He was fortunate enough to have been born in the middle of Japan's postwar baby boom. By the time he was in his teens, Japan had managed to rebuild itself out of the rubble of the war and was enjoying unprecedented economic prosperity.

The young Toshiaki wanted to please his parents, so he became an aquatic and fishery sciences major at Hokkaido University. He stuck with it for three years before dropping out, not sure what he wanted to do with his life. Deciding that he wanted to become a physician, two years later he applied to and was accepted at Sapporo Medical University.

In medical school, Toshiaki wasn't sure which specialty he wanted to enter. Unlike some of the major medical schools on the mainland, Sapporo Medical University was relatively free of the radical communist student movements of the time, so Toshiaki wasn't influenced by the antipsychiatry critiques they offered at that time.[1] One of his internships was at a psychiatric unit, and he was surprised by what he saw. He was observing a clinical interview, and the psychiatrist was just quietly nodding while a patient laughed and cried as she talked to him. At the very end, the doctor nodded his head and said, "Great, I'll see you in two weeks." The patient thanked the doctor and left. Toshiaki thought that there surely had to be something profound going on there. How could you heal someone just by nodding your head?!

After graduating from medical school and spending a year in residency at a university hospital's psychiatric ward, Dr. Kawamura's first placement was to the psychiatric ward at the Urakawa Red Cross Hospital. He was there for only two years, from 1981 to 1983, but during that time, he met Kiyoshi Hayasaka and helped him get discharged into what would become Bethel House.

But like many doctors in Japan who aren't in private practice, Dr. Kawamura wasn't in control of his own career. He found himself rotated out of Urakawa and then transferred to the Alcohol Dependence Ward of the Sapporo Asahiyama Hospital. The four years at Asahiyama proved to be a pivotal experience for him. Much of his later philosophy about the treatment of serious mental illnesses such as schizophrenia came from his observations of the recovery process for alcoholic patients. Quite simply, he believed that patients needed to be in control of their own recovery; there was very little that he could do as a doctor if the patient didn't want to get better.

Dr. Kawamura realized that a fundamental problem was that most doctors were psychologically dependent on their patients—they lived in fear of being abandoned by them. They so badly wanted to be seen as a "good doctor" and as a "good person" that they tried too hard to *cure* people, by piling on treatments or drugs. They didn't realize that they needed to step back and take themselves out of the focus. He felt that the patient needs to be the main actor, and the doctor needs to do what it takes for the patient to regain his or her autonomy. That's the only way that patients can build the courage to work toward recovery.[2]

> As a medical professional, I think it's important to realize just what we are not able to do and what our limits are. This has to be a fundamental starting point. Even if new drug therapies are discovered or new clinical therapies are created, all they do is increase the availability of different approaches; they don't represent the only or even the major solution. In that sense, until we understand what our limitations are and can distinguish what our proper role in society is, I think psychiatrists and psychiatry are destined to go down the wrong path. (Kawamura 2005, 264)

In 1988, Dr. Kawamura returned to Urakawa. His brief taste of Urakawa had whetted his appetite for more. While he missed some of the formative years of Bethel, he ended up changing Bethel every bit as much as Bethel changed him. And his main contribution was the way he revolutionized psychiatric care at Urakawa Red Cross Hospital.

Figure 5.1 Dr. Kawamura at his home on New Year's Day 2008. Every year he invites Bethel members to his house to pound mochi ricecakes. Photo by the author.

The Urakawa Red Cross Hospital

The Urakawa Red Cross Hospital is run by the Japanese Red Cross Society. Despite the name, the JRC has nothing to do with Christianity. Created in 1887 after Japan joined the Geneva Convention, it is an independent, nonprofit, nongovernmental organization, and a member of the International Red Cross. In addition to disaster relief and blood drives, the Japanese Red Cross also runs a number of hospitals and clinics in Japan.[3]

The history of the Urakawa Hospital itself begins in 1904, when it was built and run as a public hospital by the town of Urakawa. In 1939, when the town asked the Red Cross take over its operations, the hospital had forty-two beds, two doctors, two nurses, and five departments: internal medicine, surgery, pediatrics, OB-GYN, and otolaryngology (ear, nose, and throat).[4] This was enough to treat the needs of the local residents, most of whom were farmers and ranchers or worked at the fisheries.

In 1954, a large earthquake struck the region, and the Urakawa Red Cross hospital suffered a considerable amount of damage. It was decided that rather than patch up the old building, it would be better to build a larger and more modern facility. When it was completed a few years later, the new hospital was an imposing five-story, ferroconcrete building designed as a large square with an open center. With everything from pediatrics to ophthalmology, the new hospital was granted recognition to operate as a general hospital, the only one in the region.

By the late 1950s, the hospital board decided to add a psychiatric ward with inpatient facilities. They discovered that there was great unmet demand. According to the medical anthropologist Sachiyo Ukigaya, a study done at the time showed that there were approximately six hundred people with mental illness in the Hidaka area. Many were Ainu residents, who were at risk for alcoholism and mental illness due to social discrimination. Others were mainlanders who had come to Hokkaido to seek their fortune in the coalmining business but were being laid off as the mines closed down. As there were no other psychiatric facilities in the area, these people were receiving "care" at home.

The new ward opened in 1959 as an annex to the hospital with a total of fifty beds—twenty for women on the first floor and thirty for men on the second floor. The hospital advertised the availability of free psychiatric care in the local newspaper (Ukigaya 2009, 54).

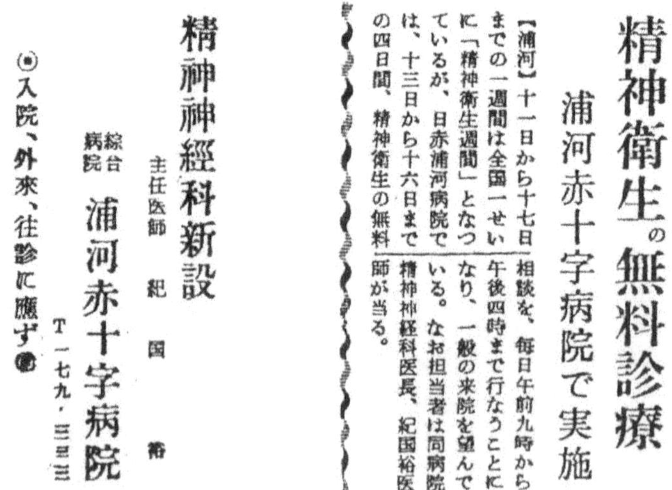

精神衛生の無料診療

浦河赤十字病院で実施

【浦河】十一日から十七日までの一週間は全国一せいに「精神衛生週間」となつているが、日赤浦河病院では、十三日から十六日までの四日間、精神衛生の無料相談を、毎日午前九時から午後四時まで行なうことになり、一般の来院を望んでいる。なお担当者は同病院精神神経科医長、紀国裕医師が当る。

精神神經科新設

主任医師 紀国 裕

綜合病院 浦河赤十字病院

T 一七九・三三三

◉入院、外來、往診に應ず

精神神経科新設を告知した新聞広告と
無料診療開設の記事（いずれも日高日報）

Figure 5.2 Advertisements for free psychiatric care at the Urakawa Red Cross Hospital in 1959.

In 1960, Urakawa Red Cross Hospital became a nationally-designated psychiatric hospital, which allowed it to receive additional government funding. This led to it accepting more patients, so by 1962 the psych ward was running over its maximum capacity. Attracting patients from the entire region, the ward had people with schizophrenia, alcoholism dependency, dementia, and other psychological and neurological issues.

The Red Cross Hospital Today

Today, the Urakawa Red Cross Hospital still remains the largest and only general hospital in the surrounding area. The main hospital building remains much as it was originally built, although on September 26, 2003, there was another earthquake, and the aging structure did not fare well. The entire east wing of the building was condemned, so the hospital is now shaped as a squared-off U.

According to the hospital's 2007 annual report, the Urakawa Red Cross Hospital has 278 beds: 210 beds in the general ward; 4 in the tuberculosis ward; 4 in the infectious diseases ward; and 60 beds in the psychiatric ward. On an average day, the hospital has 248 inpatients and sees 668 outpatients.

Officially, the hospital has nineteen doctors in its nine wards: five in internal medicine, two in pediatrics, four in surgery, one in ophthalmology, two in neurology and psychiatry, two in orthopedic surgery, two in anesthesiology, and one in vascular surgery. Like many hospitals in remote outposts, Urakawa Red Cross has great difficulty getting doctors to come there—and to stay permanently once they arrive. As a result, the hospital is chronically understaffed.

For example, the hospital does not have any intensivists (emergency room doctors), so the entire physician staff has to take turns on rotation in the after-hour emergency clinic. Even Dr. Kawamura, the chief of psychiatry, has to take a couple of the overnight shifts each month. At one staff meeting I attended, he mused about a diabetes patient he had seen the previous night in the emergency clinic and the similarities between diabetes and psychiatric patients in making sure that they take their medications and are attuned to their own condition. The psychiatric nurses and social workers also have to take turns helping the night shift in the emergency clinic, which further exacerbates the turnover in this small community.

The Department of Psychiatry and Neurology

The Department of Psychiatry and Neurology at the Urakawa Red Cross Hospital is staffed by two doctors, with Dr. Kawamura as the department head. The other position seems to be a rotating slot; every time I have visited Urakawa, it is a young doctor fresh out of medical school who is there for a two- or three-year stint. They usually leave at the first opportunity. The social workers mused that even if a new doctor himself were to find Urakawa amenable, the wife or the family of the doctor would rebel at the prospect of spending the rest of their lives in such a backwater town. Having spent the past thirty years in Urakawa raising six children (four biological and two adopted), Dr. Kawamura is certainly exceptional among the staff at the hospital.

The name of the hospital's department of psychology and neurology (*seishin-shinkeika*) is an anachronism, harking back to the 1930s when psychiatry (*seishinka*) and neurology (*shinkeika*) were considered the same discipline in Japan (Kitanaka 2012). But it also serves a useful purpose. In an ethnographic study of a Japanese psychiatric hospital in the 1980s, John Russell noted that one of his informants was hesitant to go to a hospital department labeled psychiatry[5] rather than one labeled neurology "since the former designation is associated with disorders of the mind, while the latter connotes physiological, and hence more socially acceptable, disorders" (Russell 1998, 29).

In other words, the department's old-fashioned name gives its patients plausible deniability if one of their neighbors sees them: I'm not mentally ill, I just suffer from a weakness of my autonomous nervous system.

Like most hospital physicians in Japan, Dr. Kawamura does not take appointments. If you want to see him, you have to show up early in the morning and put your name on the waiting list for the day. Psychiatric outpatients are seen at the outpatient ward on the first floor of the building. Starting at around 7:30 in the morning, people start to line up, as they are seen on a first-come, first-served basis. By mid-morning, all of his appointments for the day are usually taken, although his nurses can slip someone in if there is an emergency.

Most hospitals in Japan operate this way, as it allows for more flexibility; some patients can be seen for only a few minutes, while the doctor is free to take much more time on others. No one needs an appointment, and you can usually be seen the same day. But it does mean that seeing the psychiatrist (or any other doctor or specialist[6]) can take up much of the day. The nurses take the medical cards of patients and tell them their number in the queue.

Almost all of the patients are regulars, so they know about when they need to come back to the waiting room. Some stay around and wait in the hallway. Some wander over to psychiatric day care, where they smoke in the smoking room, read the newspaper, browse the internet, or simply lay down on the couch or tatami mats for a nap. If they had not been there first thing in the morning, it can be quite a wait until they are called. Other patients go off to the nearby convenience store or to the hospital cafeteria.

Dr. Kawamura's office in the outpatient psychiatric ward is narrow and sparsely decorated. The only personal touch is a row of potted plants by the window. The doctor sits at his plain metal desk listening and taking notes, and the patients sit in chairs while they talk to him.[7]

Dr. Kawamura's consultations are usually short. If you are a regular patient, you might be finished in five minutes—especially if you are one of his patients who likes to see him every day. People whom he hasn't seen in a while or new clients might take up more time, thirty minutes or longer. Because he isn't on an appointment system, consultations can take as much time or as little as needed.

Dr. Kawamura tries to deprecate himself in front of his patients. Although hospital regulations require that he wear a white doctor's lab coat, the plaid shirt and jeans he wears underneath often poke through, and work boots convey a similar message. He often talks about his family and the various amusing situations he gets himself into. He cracks jokes and makes the worst puns imaginable. He likes to claim that he is a doctor who won't heal, a doctor who can't heal (*naosanai, naosenai isha*) (Kawamura 2005, 265). He deemphasizes his own role in the recovery process. He thinks that the role of the psychiatrist and medications was important, but only as the first step to recovery. It is much more important that the clients be able to move out into the real world and begin to have a life—with all of the problems that life entails. Encountering and overcoming these problems is where the real recovery begins.

One of his common phrases is, "You've been having a really tough time, huh?" This simple acknowledgment is often enough to send his patients into tears.[8] Dr. Kawamura writes notes in their charts with a fountain pen in German, the way he learned to do it in medical school many years ago. I've never seen him rush a patient out; the conversation often reaches a natural end, and then the patient thanks the doctor. Dr. Kawamura writes a new prescription if necessary; the patient leaves, and the next patient shuffles in.

Where the old psychiatric inpatient ward used to be is a dialysis unit. After the earthquake in 2003, the hospital moved the psychiatric ward to the west wing of the old building and constructed new facilities for the dialysis unit and the psychiatric day care unit, which now had its own two-story building with a private back entrance, something that has positively affected the climate there.

Psychiatric day care runs a number of programs that are open to both patients in the ward as well as those living in the community. For example, it runs social skills training (SST) workshops, various forms of group therapy, and sports therapy. There is a music practice room and a large kitchen on the first floor. Two parent-child groups meet regularly in the kitchen—one for parents of children with psychiatric issues and the other for parents who have psychiatric issues. Day care is well staffed, with two psychiatric social workers and two full-time nurses.

The psychiatric inpatient ward is on the third floor of the west wing. Technically it is a closed psychiatric ward, which means that in order to enter or leave, you have to be buzzed in by one of the nurses on staff. According to the Urakawa hospital's data, psychiatry inpatients stayed an average of 99.5 days, well below the national average of 317 days (see chapter 2).[9] Using the average length of stay is unreliable, as the spread is usually quite wide, with a great many people staying only a few days, while a handful of patients are there for several years. It has been Dr. Kawamura's long-term goal to discharge as many of these long-term residents as he can, but the process is not as easy as just releasing from the hospital into the community.

Reducing the Psychiatric Ward from 130 to 60 Beds

Dr. Kawamura first served at the Red Cross Hospital from 1981 to 1983 and then returned in 1988, this time for good. In 1989, the Red Cross Hospital in Urakawa had just completed a major expansion of the psychiatric ward to accommodate 130 inpatients (Ukigaya 2009, 54–55). This was certainly not the work of Dr. Kawamura, as he had only arrived the preceding year. Rather, it might have reflected the optimism of the hospital that their new psychiatrist would be able to bring in more patients. With extended hospital stays that didn't require much in the way of advanced equipment or extensive nursing care and hefty profits for the hospital pharmacy, a large psychiatric ward represented financial stability for hospital administrators.

At the time, the psychiatric ward at Urakawa was being run as what sociologist Erving Goffman would call a "total institution." Every aspect of the patients' lives was controlled by the nursing staff: what time the patients woke up, the breakfast they ate, the morning's activities, lunch, the afternoon's activities, dinner, to lights out. This was all sustained by the bureaucratic regime of the nursing staff.

As Dr. Kawamura recalled, if a patient wanted to go to the supermarket next to the hospital to buy a snack, that patient would have to apply in writing three days ahead of time with the exact time he wanted to go, the name of the product that he wanted to buy, and how much it cost (Kawamura 1992, 161–162). Dr. Kawamura says that this was done under the mantra of "social rehabilitation," but it made no sense to him. He joked that anyone who knew in advance what they would want to have for a snack three days later would be, by definition, quite sick in the head.[10]

Dr. Kawamura said that such rules were really for the benefit of the staff rather than the benefit of the patients; he also felt that such regulations led to social isolation and dependency on the part of the patients. Soon after he arrived, he did away with this rule and others like it. Now the ward operates much more like an open ward, with patients who have leave privileges able to come and go as they please and visitors also able to come in to visit without prior notice.

When I visited the psychiatric ward on a warm July day in 2007, a board by the nurse station listed all 63 patients in residence. Of those, seventeen were written in red, which meant they were not permitted to leave. Six were coded blue, which meant that they were restricted to the hospital premises. The remaining forty were able to come and go as long as they had an escort. Almost anyone could serve as an escort—a family member, a Bethel member, or even myself. When I went out with a nonrestricted patient to the day care room or to the nearby supermarket, there was no elaborate signout procedure; we just told one of the nurses that we were heading out right before we left.

The psychiatric ward had three isolation rooms. That particular day, only one of them was being used, and I recognized the occupant as a

Figure 5.3 Main lobby and smoking room of Ward 7 of the Urakawa Red Cross Hospital. Photo by the author.

Bethel member who had been having a lot of difficulties recently and had been hospitalized. According to the head nurse, the patient himself had asked for the isolation room, as he was afraid of human contact at the moment. From the closed-circuit video monitor, I could see him pacing back and forth in the small room. The only other thing in the room was his futon mattress and blanket.

When Japanese anthropologist Sachiyo Ukigaya visited the inpatient ward in 2006 for his field research on psychiatric nursing care, he made a detailed record of the number of patients, their lengths of stay, and their diagnoses. He noted that around 70 percent of both male and female patients had schizophrenia. There were four alcoholic men in the ward, but no women who were alcoholic. On the other hand, seven women were diagnosed with mood disorders (depression, bipolar disorder, or adjustment disorder) but no men. Two men had been in the ward for over thirty years (one was undoubtedly Yuzuru Yokoyama, who appears later in this chapter), and one man was 95 years old. This demographic data gives us a glimpse into the gendered nature of psychiatric care in Japan.

Table 5.1 Number of patients by age, length of stay, and diagnosis

		Male	*Female*
Number of patients		33	27
Ages		26–95	27–76
Length of stay	< 2 years	16	17
	2–9 years	9	8
	10–19 years	3	2
	20–29	3	
	30+ years	2	
Diagnosis	Schizophrenia	23 (70%)	18 (67%)
	Alcoholism	4 (12%)	0
	Depression/ Bipolar	0	6 (22%)
	Adjustment disorder	0	1 (4%)
	Intellectual disabilities	2 (6%)	
	Dementia	2 (6%)	
	Other	2 (6%)	2 (7%)

Source: Ukigaya 2009: 110.

Forced Medication/Forced Restraint

Although I visited the inpatient ward over a dozen times during my stay in Urakawa, I never saw the use of restraints, forced medication, or other forms of physical force on the patients. I'm not the only one to have noticed this. In an interview in 2005, Dr. Kawamura responded:

> Many people think that the best way to prevent patients from becoming violent is to make sure they give them a lot of drugs ahead of time. There was an era when that was believed here too. But what we've learned here is that that isn't effective at all. All we are doing is choosing the most effective method for our situation.
>
> It's strangely rare to find the stereotypical image of the violent psychiatric patient here at Bethel. When someone is acting out, it means that at the core they have something that they vehemently need to express. When they are acting out, they are really saying, "Argh. . . . I have all these problems, can't you see, can't you see?" There are only a few times a year when we have to involuntarily hospitalize someone. It's not because their symptoms are mild, but because the members have learned how to signal an SOS for help before blowing up. (Kawamura 2005, 266)

While the hospital building itself was old, the ward itself was clean and bright. Most of the patients were in shared rooms with six western-style hospital beds. There were also two tatami shared rooms for people who preferred to sleep on futons. Patients were allowed to have their own possessions, with personal lockers for valuables. In the lobby was a dedicated smoking room partitioned off (and, thankfully, externally ventilated) from the rest of the lobby by glass windows.

Downsizing the Ward

In 2000, Dr. Kawamura held a number of meetings with hospital staff and Mr. Mukaiyachi about downsizing the psychiatric ward. Looking at the roster of 109 inpatients, Dr. Kawamura and Mr. Mukaiyachi noted that 37 might be able to be moved to nursing homes for the elderly, another 23 into psychiatric group homes, 6 into facilities for the physically disabled, and another 10 back to their own family homes. As a result, in just over a year of hard work, the staff of the hospital was able to reduce the inpatient unit from 130 beds to 60 beds. This radical downsizing was almost unprecedented in the realm of psychiatric care in Japan (Ukigaya 2009, 63).

Other hospitals were beginning to feel government pressure to shorten psychiatric stays, given growing international attention and criticism. But most hospitals had simply exchanged their long-term patients with other hospitals, driving down each of their average lengths of stay by playing an elaborate shell game with people's lives. In Urakawa's case, the nearest psychiatric hospital was in Tomakomai, almost two hours away. This would mean that transferred patients would be cut off from their families, which Dr. Kawamura thought was unacceptable. The doctor insisted that each discharge be entirely voluntary and under conditions that were amenable to the patient. He thought that forced deinstitutionalization was just as bad as forced institutionalization. In order to convince people to discharge themselves, they would both have to want to leave as well as have a place to go.

Bethel's Expansion

This is where Bethel comes in. The reduction in the size of the hospital's psychiatric unit was made possible by an expansion in the number of Bethel's group homes. Bethel started out in 1984 with just the old church building, which had only a few spare rooms that could be used as bedrooms. In 1990, they expanded the back of the church so that six people could live there; by 1992, it was at capacity at seven people. If Bethel was going to help more people get discharged from the hospital, it would have to find more room for them.

Starting in the 1990s, Bethel started buying and leasing properties in Urakawa. One of the first of these was Rika House, named after one of its residents, Rika Shimizu. This was a large modern home that had originally been built to accommodate a family with an elderly grandparent, which meant that it was entirely accessible by wheelchair. Furthermore, it was next door to Mr. and Mrs. Mukaiyachi's new house, on top of a large hill that overlooked the town of Urakawa. Rika House could accommodate five residents.

Urakawa's declining economy and shrinking population helped Bethel in its expansion, as they were able to buy up several properties for a pittance. Landlords that might not previously wanted a group of former psychiatric patients as residents were now much more willing to negotiate. Bethel was practically the only aspect of the Urakawa economy that was actually growing.

Furthermore, the law changed in 2005 so that psychiatric group homes could receive government support if they provided certain services, such as meal preparation and supervision. This caused Bethel to differentiate between its group homes (which had meal and other support services) and its shared living facilities, which were not subsidized by the government. The people who needed more assistance went to the group homes, while those that were stable and could take care of themselves went into the shared living facilities or into private apartments in the community.

By 2008, Bethel owned three group homes and three shared living facilities, while several other private properties were leased by Bethel:

Group Homes:

"Original" Bethel (the church)

Flower Heights

Shiomi Heights

Pia House

Shared Living Facilities:

Rika House

Rainbow House (women only)

Hikari

Mikan

Private Apartments and Houses

Kireiso

Hot Hime

Shiosaiso

Takeda House

Tanoshiso

While I was at Bethel in 2007 and 2008, the group had just bought a large dormitory conveniently located behind the Urakawa Central Police Station, which could house another twenty residents. Mr. Mukaiyachi had also built a new house and was leasing his old house to Bethel as another group home. In 2011, Bethel completed their purchase of an apartment complex that they would use to help house the families of Bethel members.

There was some resistance from area residents when Bethel started expanding and buying up properties. Mr. Mukaiyachi explained that in an area where most people were struggling to get by, the anti-Bethel sentiment came from a small minority of people who were envious of Bethel's prosperity. As a result, a number of Bethel's purchases were made by third-party Bethel supporters in their own name and then deeded over to Bethel. This was done in order to obscure who was really buying the property until the sale was over. It occurred to me that this would not help the image of Bethel as cultish and secretive in the eyes of their detractors.

The Town's Response to the Expansion of Bethel

I tried to ask people in the town what they thought of Bethel, but most were much too polite to say anything negative on the record. And Bethel certainly had many supporters, including the hotels and merchants on main road that had seen increased tourist traffic because of the many visitors to Bethel.

The local Urakawa police unquestionably thought that the Bethel members were a pain in the neck. They were tired of being called to deal with problems caused by the members or attributed to the members—or being called by the members themselves. One thing that particularly irked the local police was that the emergency telephone number 110 (the same as 911 in the USA and 999 in the U.K.) didn't go to a local dispatch office but to the main emergency dispatch center in Sapporo, which would then relay the message back down to the local level. Many Bethel members would often call emergency services whenever their feelings of persecution flared up. The local police must have felt embarrassed that their division received so many emergency calls, which counted against them in their regional statistical rankings.

It must have also bothered the police that Bethel's latest real estate purchase was literally in the backyard of the Urakawa police station. The windows of the facility looked directly into the police office windows, and after the Bethel members moved in, the police started closing their blinds more often, cutting themselves off from a gorgeous view of the ocean.

There was even talk of the police asking that Bethel build a large wall between the two facilities so that the Bethel members wouldn't be able to look at them. And, Mr. Mukaiyachi said that the police had requested that the gates of the Bethel facility be locked so that the residents couldn't wander over to the police headquarters to ask for an air pump for their bicycle tires. One of the members had done just that, repeatedly, which apparently the officers felt lowered them to the status of service station attendants. Managing the tender egos of the local police constabulary was just another task that Bethel found itself constantly engaged in.

Much of the negative sentiment also seemed unfair. One day while I was at the New Bethel office, I heard fire sirens and ran outside to see what was going on. One of the old wooden buildings in the neighborhood was in flames. As the firefighters doused the flames, I could hear one elderly woman in the crowd mutter to her friend that it must have been a Bethel member who had caused this. I later found out that there indeed was a Bethel member who was living in a room on the second floor of that building, but she was fortunately not home when the fire broke out. The fire department later reported that the noodle restaurant on the first floor of the building had been the cause of the blaze.[11]

Bethel House would also get phone calls from local stores asking them to come pick up someone who had shown up on their premises drunk. When they'd send a member to go pick this person up, it would

Figure 5.4 Firefighters rush to put out a blaze at an apartment and restaurant complex near New Bethel. Photo by the author.

often turn out to be someone entirely unrelated to Bethel. In the minds of some of the townspeople, all the drunks and crazies emanated from Bethel.

One of Bethel House's residents, Okamoto-san, liked to take naps outside in the summer. The problem was that he liked to take his naps by the side of the road or in the corner of parking lots. It didn't help that he was usually dressed in dirty clothes and often smelled awful. Worried passersby often called the Urakawa police to report a "dead person." In response, Bethel honored Okamoto-san at the annual Hallucinations and Delusions Contest in 2009, awarding him with the "Best Exemplar of a Slow Life." They gave him a small lawn sign that he could stick in the ground when he took a nap that read, "Taking a Nap."

Aside from the examples above, there were numerous other reasons why some residents of the town might not like Bethel. For example, they were embarrassed to be known all across Japan as living in a town famous for having "crazy" people. Some people were afraid of what unstable Bethel members might do. And truth be told, some Bethel members did on occasion cause public disturbances. Some townspeople were jealous that Bethel members were living off social welfare checks while they were working hard for a living. In the same vein, others were jealous that Bethel was apparently doing very well financially and was able to buy real estate at steep discounts, all while the town as a whole was dying. To ameliorate the feelings of jealousy, one of the goals of the Bethel Festival each summer was to convince the town and the area merchants that Bethel was a good thing for the community because it brought in tourist dollars.

From Hospital to Group Home to Apartment to Hospital

The mixture of different types of housing stock in Bethel's arsenal had an intended consequence. Because Bethel owned or had long-term leases on the properties as a group, they had a great deal of flexibility. They could accommodate someone who was being discharged from the hospital and might still have serious special needs with a group home where they could receive meal services and be observed regularly by a visiting nurse, Bethel staff, and other members. Once this person had gotten used to life outside the hospital and was more independent, he or she could then move into a shared living facility or a private apartment.

Dr. Kawamura and the Bethel staff worked to make it easy for members to check out of the hospital into the group homes and shared homes, but the opposite was true as well. Checking into the hospital was not seen as a failure. Rather, it was seen a natural part of the rhythm of mental illness. People would become hospitalized, feel better, check out of the hospital, resume life. At some point they might taper off their medications or something would trigger a flareup of their symptoms, and then they would check back into the hospital. The doctor and the social workers tried to get people to understand the cycle of their mental illness so that they could predict when they might need hospitalization again. What were the circumstances in which they stopped taking their medications? What triggered these flareups? Of course, it would be ideal if the members could then figure out ways that they could disrupt this cycle so that they wouldn't need hospitalization, but hospitalization in and of itself was not seen as a negative thing.

Kiyoshi regularly checked back into the hospital when he started to feel his body freeze up again. Other members would have flareups of their psychotic symptoms and would check into the hospital, sometimes for weeks, before returning back. This fluidity meant a lot of work for Bethel, but it gave members great peace of mind, because they knew that they could check into the hospital easily as well as check back out when they got better, without having to worry about what would happen to their housing or jobs.

Hospital—Bethel—Town—School Relationships

The hospital and Bethel's efforts at resettling people into the community were aided by excellent relations among the hospital, Bethel, and the town government units. In September of 2007, I went to a meeting at the public health clinic. A support meeting (*ōen mītingu*) had been called for Akiko Kimura, a Bethel member with two young children, one in grade school and one in day care. Akiko needed help.

At the meeting, Akiko sat at the head of the conference table. To her left sat Eriko, the hospital's social worker[12]; to her right sat Oya-san, one of the staffers at the public health center. Dr. Kawamura was also there, along with one of the nurses who ran the mother-child group at the psychiatric day care unit. There were two people from the local school board as well as the head teacher at the local elementary school and a teacher from the day care center. One of Akiko's friends was there too. There were also a few people from the town hall's Child Consultation Center, a social welfare office that helped parents with raising their children. In all, there were fourteen people in the conference room (and one anthropologist), all there to work with Akiko.

Eriko, the social worker at the hospital, started the meeting. The main issue was that Akiko's kids were being teased at school. The two kids (whom I often met at the psychiatric day care when the mother-child group was in session) were bright and intelligent, but apparently the other kids would often taunt them by saying "You smell," "Don't come here," or "You're dirty."

Eriko continued. She said that you could tell how stressed out Akiko was by the amount of garbage in her house. It was her "stress barometer." Unfortunately, Akiko felt a strong desire to keep up appearances, so she had a great deal of difficulty asking for help. She was also deeply embarrassed by her domestic situation and was afraid that if she called attention to it, people would look down on her even more. Sometimes she would take her frustrations out on her kids. Parents in Japan tend to use more physical punishment with their children than in the United States, but there seemed to be more than was being openly said on this issue.

The head teacher at the elementary school chimed in. He had been worried about this issue. The older daughter had been acting up even in first grade, and he thought that there might be something going on at home. Now that she was in the third grade, she seemed to be doing much better. The day care center worker noted that she hadn't been aware of the situation. She had noticed that when Akiko would come pick up her younger daughter, sometimes she would be in a bad mood, and the staff at the day care center didn't quite know how to handle her. Now she had a better idea of what had been going on and was glad that she knew.

By this time, Dr. Kawamura had closed his eyes, and his head was starting to slowly bob back and forth. Some glances were passed around the conference table, and someone giggled (it might have been me). Dr. Kawamura had a habit of napping in meetings, but we were never sure if the doctor was really asleep or not, as he had a habit of suddenly opening his eyes and jumping back into the conversation, as if he had been awake the entire time. It may have been that he was genuinely narcoleptic, or he could have been trying to make sure that he wasn't seen as the authority figure in the room. Or both.

Ignoring the doctor, one of the Bethel members mentioned that they would be happy to help Akiko clean up her house again. The last time that Bethel had come to clean up her house, one of the members joked: "Is this all? This isn't even that much garbage!" (That very summer, one member's apartment had so much raw, stinking garbage in it that it started to produce methane gas. One of the neighbors called the fire company thinking there was a gas main leak—nope, just two feet of rotting garbage.) In Akiko's case, the Bethel members were happy to come again to help her out. The psychiatric day care nurse said that she'd also ask the other parents in the mother-child group at the hospital if they would assist her.

With the meeting almost over, Akiko herself spoke up. She said that one of her main problems was that the public housing unit that she was in didn't have a bath. She had to take her kids to the public bath, but the distance to the bathhouse made it expensive and difficult. She wanted to find a new apartment that had a bath, but she was on public assistance, and the amount she could spend on rent was limited. The various social workers around the table took notes. The meeting was called to an end. Akiko left happy, feeling that she had been heard. The doctor woke up with a start, and headed back to the hospital.[13]

This scene was unimaginable to me from an American perspective. First, it would be extremely unlikely for staff from an American hospital to be working closely with the social workers from the town, members of the school board, schoolteachers, day care workers, and a nonprofit community-based mental health program to solve the problems of just one individual.[14] And what's more important, it was clear throughout the hour-long meeting that Akiko was in charge, that she could refuse anything if she didn't want it or ask for additional help if she needed it. She wasn't being accused of wantonly mistreating her children. These meetings kept the communication lines open so that the schoolteachers knew what types of difficulties the children were facing, while the hospital staff were working on her self-confidence and mental health issues, and Bethel was helping out with her garbage problem.

Smaller versions of these support meetings happened regularly at Bethel or at the hospital. The Bethel members and staff, as well as the hospital social workers, would try to help people figure out what they needed and help them to achieve it. Sometimes these meetings were staged as interventions, called by someone who was worried about how a friend was doing. Usually the meetings didn't end with firm resolutions, as that wasn't the Bethel style. Just knowing that help was available and that people cared was the most important message being imparted anyway.

Several months later, Akiko invited me to her home for Christmas. We saw each other regularly at the psychiatric day care when she came for the parent-child group. I drove up to her apartment, which was in a squat concrete public housing unit on the top of the bluffs overlooking the town. With small gifts for her kids in hand, I rang her doorbell with some trepidation, given my memories of the meeting earlier that fall. I was surprised when she opened it. Her tiny apartment, while certainly packed to the gills, wasn't dirty or messy at all. She was delighted that I had come and went to make tea while her kids buzzed around me. After we had tea and snacks, she showed me her place; the grand tour took around two minutes. As she had said in the support meeting, her place didn't have a bathtub or a shower, so she had to go into town to use the public bathhouse. I also didn't see a washing machine. In such an environment, I could easily see a busy single mother of two children falling behind on laundry and bathing her children, even without having to deal with her own mental health issues. Since the support meeting in September, Akiko had gotten some more help in dealing with her problems, and her children seemed to be doing better.

The Invisible Doctor

Watching some of the videos made by Bethel in the 1990s, I'm aware of how much of a presence in Bethel the doctor once was. He used to help with their activities regularly, even helping mop the floors of a supermarket when one of the members froze up and wasn't able to finish. While he still has members come over to his house often for dinner or just to hang out, and while he still hosts Christmas parties and the summer *tanabata* festivals at his house, I rarely saw him at Bethel events anymore.

Dr. Kawamura also didn't seem to engage in Bethel's self-promotion efforts. While Mr. Mukaiyachi has written more than half a dozen books about Bethel and edited another half-dozen, Dr. Kawamura's name is only on one coauthored volume (with Mr. Mukaiyachi) about Bethel's clinical practices.

I went to dinner one summer night at the Kawamuras. I told him that the previous day I had done a sociogram with Kiyoshi. A sociogram is a tool that anthropologists (and some sociologists and therapists) use where you ask a person to draw the social relationships in their lives. People who are closer to you in real life are closer in the diagram.

I told that doctor that after Kiyoshi drew his sociogram, I noticed that Dr. Kawamura seemed to be missing. "Oh yeah!" said Kiyoshi and drew him in. I told the doctor that I was surprised that he seemed to be an afterthought.

Dr. Kawamura said that he thought that this was for the best. He said that he always asked patients who were leaving the psychiatric ward what had helped them the most in getting better. They often said that it was the friendships in the ward, the nurses, or the social workers. In these cases, the doctor thought their prognosis was good. If they said that it was the doctors or the medication that helped them the most, then he thought that they would probably soon return to the ward. This was a constant refrain for the doctor. I remember another conversation we had where he was talking about his experiences at the alcohol treatment clinic where he had worked after medical school. He said that it was the patients who had the hardest time that were successful in the end. It was the patients who seemed to be able to give up alcohol without trying, the "star patients," who always seemed to relapse.

Dr. Kawamura remembers when he was jealous of the social workers at the hospital, because they seemed to get to see much more of the patients' lives than he did. As he says in *Bethel,* the doctor's office is the loneliest place to be. But in a sense, he has decided that his proper place was in the doctor's office and that trying to put himself into too many aspects of his patients' lives would actually be counterproductive.

This was part of his desire for his patients to be able to struggle. He didn't want their lives to be easy. They needed to work through difficult social relationships, money problems, and family issues. Recovering their lives also meant recovering their struggles (*kurō*). A life without struggle is not one worth living. It's the same as living in a total institution. You never have to think or worry. Real life is all about worrying and trying to decide which direction to go. That was the life that the doctor wanted for his patients.

The Sick Role, Disability, Recovery, and a Life in Descent

There are multiple competing frames that structure the lives of people who live in Bethel. Many members undoubtedly come in believing in the biomedical sick role that constitutes the mentally ill as *ill* and thus in need of treatment. While you are sick, they think, you should be a patient patient, waiting for your doctors to cure you and release you back to the world. The notion of the sick role is quickly discouraged within Bethel. Passivity is not a virtue.

The second frame is that of recovery (*kaifuku*), which draws on Alcoholics Anonymous–style step programs as well some similar theories in disability activism. Here, mental illness is framed as a chronic illness or disability. One will never be cured of mental illness, just as one is never an ex-alcoholic or an ex–blind person. Rather than waiting patiently for a cure, people need to work on recovering their interrupted lives. Medical professionals will always be needed, but they are not enough in themselves. Social accommodation is also needed, but it is not enough in itself. Responsibility for one's own life is the remaining critical factor. Related to this is a notion of a life in descent. Rather than expecting things to get better, they will almost certainly get worse. What we choose to do with this harsh reality is up to us as individuals. We can't pine for the days when we were young, beautiful, or mentally whole; we have to accept that not everything is possible and that we need the help of others. Bethel is designed around the philosophy that everyone needs the help of other people in their lives.

Recreating Bethel

In July, a group of doctors from Hannan Hospital on the mainland came to Urakawa for a seminar retreat. They stayed at the local hot springs hotel and visited Bethel and the hospital. This sort of visit was quite common in Urakawa. My name for these people was "psychotourists." Often, they wanted to know how they could recreate a bit of Bethel back in their hometowns.

One evening, Dr. Kawamura and several members went up to the hotel to give a seminar on the philosophy underlying the Urakawa system, what Dr. Kawamura calls the "Philosophy of Non-Support" (*Hienjo Ron*), which he contrasted to the medical model that dominated psychiatric care in Japan.

In his PowerPoint presentation, Dr. Kawamura noted that in the medical model, the focus of attention was to determine the root cause of the disease and to eradicate it. In the Urakawa-Bethel non-support model, he felt that the goal was to determine the possibilities created by the "problem" and to work on the possibility of negotiation rather than eradication. In order to do this, you needed to shift the attention away from the pathology or the symptoms toward the particular needs that people are having. In this perspective, the "caregivers" are also seen as people with needs.

In the nonsupport model, the goal is not to cure or even to "help"—a position that too often is unilateral. In the non-support model the "expert" takes a position of powerlessness. Their goal is to help heal and recover, to encourage, and to help people get a better understanding of themselves through self-directed research (see chapter 6). People are encouraged to talk with other people in similar and different situations and make their own connections.

It is important that doctors not take the usual position of authority, domination, and objectification that they normally would in the medical model. Rather, Dr. Kawamura encouraged his peers to think about respect for subjectivity, to try to encourage mutual growth of both doctor and patient, and to build trust on both sides.

Dr. Kawamura's final slide noted the following bullet points:

Points about a Philosophy of Non-Support

- To recover the "self-help" potential of the person as position and attitude of encouragement
- A position and attitude of: affirming, believing, and trusting
- To be able to discern "what I won't do" as more important than "what I can do"
- To be able to discern that there is potential even in the most difficult of times
- To have discretion and modesty in not making your role (as a doctor) the core of your self-image or reason for being
- To be able to laugh even in the darkest times (the ultimate courage)

As to the many people who come to Bethel seeking the solution to all of Japan's problems, Dr. Kawamura was more critical:

> Just as I think patients who only thank the psychiatrist when they get discharged from the hospital are not going to do well, I think the trend of people saying, "At Bethel, they do this, at Bethel, they do that. . . ." is also not a good thing. Bethel is not a holy land. If we do something different, it's because that's the appropriate thing to do given someone's personal experiences. Based on our interactions with the various people here, we've created various types of actions and activities. What people who visit here need to do is to take the core of those experiences back with them and figure out how to make them work their own way. (Kawamura 2005, 274)

Just as patients had to struggle in order to make their lives meaningful and there was no easy solution for life, other places would also have to come up with their own ways to integrate people with psychiatric disabilities into the community. The Urakawa-Bethel way was appropriate for Urakawa and Bethel, but it was not the only way. In the next chapter, I will look at some of the therapies that were being used in Urakawa.

Thirty-Seven Years of Institutionalization: Why Did Yuzuru Never Want to Leave the Hospital?

Most weekday mornings, I'd take the short walk from my home to the psychiatric day care ward. I'd enter through the back entrance and walk past the kitchen and the library/music room up to the second floor, where the conference room, staff room, and main room of the psychiatric day care were. The day care ward used to be located inside the hospital, but it was moved after the earthquake in 2003 that severely damaged an entire wing of the hospital. Psychiatric day care was moved to a newly constructed building on the hospital grounds.

The morning would start off with a short staff meeting attended by the hospital's three psychiatric social workers,[1] a nurse, and a nurse's aide. Dr. Kawamura would also come in on the days that he was seeing patients. After the staff meeting, the morning's events would start. At that point, I would decide whether to stay in day care or to drive over to New Bethel to observe the activities there. One morning in early October, after the staff meeting, I headed for a peer support meeting in Ward 7, located on the third floor of the west wing of the hospital proper. The meeting had been called for Yuzuru Yokoyama.

Yuzuru had been hospitalized in Ward 7 since 1970, the very year that I was born. When he was finally released in 2007, he had been hospitalized for thirty-seven years, the longest of any resident in the ward. For quite a while, Mr. Mukaiyachi had said, "The goal of Bethel House is to create a society where someone like Yokoyama-san can discharge himself and live in the community without worry" (Mukaiyachi 2008, 137). And so for the past two decades, the hospital social workers and Bethel members had been trying, on some level, to convince him to leave the hospital and also make the appropriate social changes to enable this.

Yuzuru's story is helpful in understanding why Japan has some of the longest institutionalization figures for people with mental illness in the industrialized world.

Early Years

When Yuzuru Yokoyama was a teenager in the 1960s, he attended Urakawa High School, which was located directly across the street from the hospital. From the school grounds, students could see the patients in Ward 7 looking at them through the bars of their windows.[2] The schoolchildren would often taunt each other by saying, "You're heading to Ward 7!"

Yuzuru graduated in the aquatic and fishery sciences division of the high school (i.e., the non-college, vocational track) and worked for a while as an automobile mechanic and then in Japan's Self-Defense Forces before the symptoms of schizophrenia caught up with him and he had to be hospitalized. Looking at the school from the other side of the bars, Yuzuru felt deeply embarrassed and ashamed at how his life had turned out. As he put it, "In the town of Urakawa, the most miserable thing that could happen to someone would be to come down with a mental illness and to be hospitalized in Ward 7, the psychiatric ward of Urakawa Red Cross Hospital."[3]

In the 1980s, Yokoyama-san had been one of the early members of the Acorn Society, the patient support group that was the predecessor to Bethel. He was more social back then, playing baseball with the other Acorn members or going on camping trips with them. But as more and more of his friends left the hospital to join Bethel, Yuzuru found himself more and more isolated in the hospital. But he didn't want to leave. He had been discharged once, very early on, and, finding life on the outside incredibly difficult, went back to the hospital almost immediately. As more and more of his peers left to Bethel, Yokoyama-san started to isolate himself more and more.

Yuzuru was comfortable in the hospital. He didn't have to worry about anything. There was no financial reason for him to leave. The national health care system paid for his long-term hospitalization, and he received a small pension for his smokes. While he didn't talk to anyone, at least he was never lonely in the hospital. People didn't look at him oddly. Life was good on the inside.

According to Mr. Mukaiyachi, Yuzuru pleaded with his doctor not to discharge him, and since it was Dr. Kawamura's philosophy never to discharge someone into circumstances that they didn't want, he agreed to keep Yuzuru in the hospital (Mukaiyachi 2008, 137). In fact, whenever talk of discharge came up, Yuzuru would become so upset that for many years the staff couldn't even raise the topic with him. He had started to shut down, closing in more and more into himself. He wrote magical numbers and words on his body and the wall of his room, protecting himself from the terrors of the outside.

Peer Support Program

New guidelines issued by the Ministry of Health, Labor, and Welfare in 2006 encouraged the creation of registered peer supporters who would help people with disabilities live independently. The vast majority of these peer supporters were people with physical disabilities, showing other people with similar disabilities how to live outside of institutional life. The blind were leading the blind—literally—and people in wheelchairs showing people in wheelchairs how to live independent lives outside of institutional care. Unfortunately, not many people volunteered to become psychiatric peer supporters.

When news of this initiative circulated around Bethel, the first person to sign up for the peer support program was Noboru Sakai,[4] one of the older Bethel members. He was soon joined by a young fellow named Gen'ichi Nakayama. Suffering from psychosis and other psychiatric symptoms, Gen had also spent a number of years in Ward 7 but was now living in one of the Bethel shared homes.

Gen and Sakai-san worked to help Yuzuru and others leave the hospital. The problem was that Yuzuru had been in the hospital so long that he was inured to hospital life. He didn't want to leave, as he saw nothing in the outside world that appealed to him. All of his relatives were dead or wanted nothing to do with him—nobody really knew. When he left the hospital for the first time in decades, he found that he couldn't even recognize the streets of Urakawa—they had changed so much in the intervening times. He said he felt like Urashima Taro—a fisherman in a fairy tale who rescues a turtle and is taken to a palace under the sea. There he is bewitched by the Dragon God and when he returns to the surface, he finds that several centuries have passed in his absence.

Gen started by visiting Yuzuru every day in the hospital. Every single day, at 7 a.m. sharp, he would show up at the hospital. At first it was just short visits, just to say hello. More and more, Yuzuru warmed up to the amicable and good-natured Gen. He started opening up. Eventually, Gen started taking Yuzuru out on a regular basis. At first they'd go out for a smoke, then for a bowl of ramen soup, then to the supermarket to buy cigarettes.

Eventually they did longer day trips together—to Erimo National Park to see the southeastern edge of the island or to a local factory. Finally, Yuzuru spent a night in one of the group homes, just to see what it was like. After much hard work over a period of two years by Gen, Sakai-san, and other Bethel members and the psychiatric social workers and staff, Yuzuru decided that he was ready to leave the hospital. On a final meeting at the doctor's house on June 29, 2007, Yuzuru Yokoyama's discharge date was fixed: It would be October 17 of that year. Gen wasn't present at that June meeting, as he was in the hospital, in Ward 7, for exhaustion after his activities organizing the Bethel Festival. Nonetheless, it was the culmination of everything he had been working toward for several years.

There was a final peer support meeting in early October to help Yuzuru through the discharge process and to help make sure that everyone in the community was ready. Kiyoshi from Bethel House was present as well as Sakai-san, Yuzuru's other peer supporter. The nurses and social workers

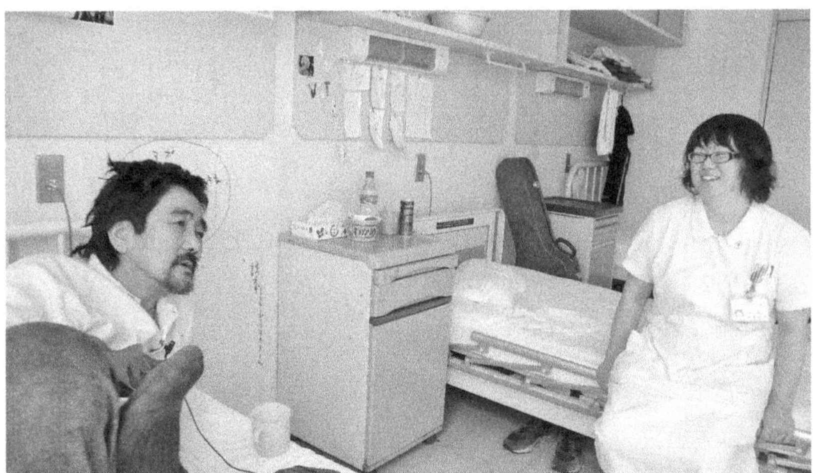

Figure 5.5 Yuzuru Yokoyama talks to a nurse in his hospital room on the last day of his thirty-seven-year stay. Photo by the author.

from the hospital, Bethel staff, and a woman from the public health center also attended. I was there as well. We were all crammed into a small conference room in the hospital.

There were some lingering issues that Yuzuru was worried about. He had always had a problem with money. In the psych ward, if he wanted to buy cigarettes, he could always ask the nurse on duty for some money out of his account so that he never had to manage it himself. On the outside, he was worried that people might ask him to lend them money and then not return it. Or that he might get money on a Monday and run out by Friday and then have no money for food on the weekend.

One of the members mentioned that Yuzuru should sign up for the Civil Rights Protection service (see chapter 1) for help with financial management. Kiyoshi was already using it, as were several other Bethel members who had made the transition from long-time ward residency to independent living. He'd still have control over his money, but the financial assistant could help him stay within his budget and avoid mishaps.

Yuzuru was placed in the original Bethel House group home. It had a caretaker who made all of the meals, and it was also on the circuit for the visiting nurse, who checked in with everyone to make sure they were healthy, taking their medications, and had no other issues that they wanted to talk about. More importantly for Yuzuru, Bethel House had become a community for him. Through the many dinners that Gen had initiated,

Figure 5.6 Dr. Kawamura sees Yuzuru as an outpatient for the first time after his discharge. Kiyoshi Hayasaka accompanies him. Photo by the author.

Yuzuru was close friends with Kiyoshi, Minoru Sasaki, and the other residents. It would feel like coming home, which it would be.

Coming Home

On October 17, 2007, Yuzuru Yokoyama discharged himself from the psychiatric ward of Urakawa Red Cross Hospital after thirty-seven years. The entire nursing staff lined up to say good-bye to him. His worldly possessions fit into three large shopping bags. One of the first things he did was to go down to the psychiatric outpatient ward to talk with Dr. Kawamura for his first session as an outpatient. Then Yuzuru got into one of Bethel's vans and went to Bethel House, his new home.

Yuzuru was given a room on the second floor, right next to Kiyoshi Hayasaka. He watched silently as the social workers helped bring his stuff up to the room and pull out the futon mattress and blankets that he could use. Kiyoshi was there to make his new housemate feel welcome.

One of the psychiatric nurses had also come from the hospital with Yuzuru to help him move in. In a strange way, they were two birds of a feather. The nurse, Yu Itoh, was retiring after four decades on the psychiatric ward. He was just as used to institutional life as Yuzuru was. They

Figure 5.7 From left to right, Yuzuru, Kiyoshi, and nurse Yu Itoh talk about old times on Yuzuru's first day in his new room at Bethel House. Photo by the author.

both were coming to a slow realization that an old chapter had closed, and a new chapter of their lives was just beginning.

Coming Home (Again)

Three months later, Yuzuru checked backed into the hospital. Dr. Kawamura joked that he was "right on schedule" (Kawamura and Mukaiyachi 2008, 65). Life on the outside was difficult. While the hospital rooms were kept at the same pleasant temperature throughout the day, the rooms in the old Bethel House were drafty and cold. Furthermore, he felt lonely during the day when most of the members were out doing various activities. He yearned for the physical and social warmth and comfort of the hospital. But Yuzuru doesn't rule out leaving the hospital again. According to Mr. Mukaiyachi, he says that he might try leaving again in the spring, when the cherry blossoms bloom.[5]

CHAPTER SIX

Bethel Therapies

During my eight months of intense fieldwork in Urakawa from June of 2007 until February of the following year, I tried to approximate the rhythm of life of a Bethel member.[1] During the day, I went to as many meetings as I could, at Bethel or at the hospital. Most of my evenings were spent at the homes of Bethel members or at Bethel events. I'd go to the house of my friend, Yanagi-san, to talk about rock music or to listen to Tsutomu play music on his guitar. I'd sing karaoke with my friends at the local karaoke box or go to Rainbow House to eat pizza for dinner.

Dr. Kawamura had arranged housing for me on the hospital grounds. The hospital maintained a number of small houses for doctors and nurses. My neighbor across the gravel road was the head nurse of the hospital, while my next-door neighbor was a doctor who had just moved to the area. The staff houses were located behind the hospital, squeezed along the side of the parking lots and on the side of a hill. They were very simple affairs, all the same shape and size—free-standing, wood-frame, one-story homes. The basic design was what Japanese like to call "2LDK," which stands for 2 bedrooms and a combined living room/dining room/kitchen.

The only heat for the house was a single forced air heater in the living room fueled by a large kerosene tank outside the house. It ran fairly well, but it could really warm the living room only, so the rest of the house would get quite cold in the winter. Rika-san loaned me her portable kerosene stove for my bedroom, but I was terrified of carbon monoxide poisoning, so I didn't run it at night. Some winter mornings, it was very difficult for me to get up, as I had piled futon mattresses on myself, and it was nice and warm under them—and freezing in the rest of the house that awaited me. I had little privacy, as my house faced the hospital parking lot—perhaps the reason that that particular unit was vacant in the first place. If I sat on my back porch, I could wave hello to the nurses and doctors as they came in for the day or left for the night. Alternately, the social workers could see me struggling with my laundry in the late mornings or running out to take it down during the sudden afternoon rainstorms.

Despite the humble amenities, living in the staff housing was very pleasant. The supermarket was just down the street, right next to the hospital. It was a cooperative supermarket, which always had fresh vegetables, fish, and meat. I particularly enjoyed the fresh fish, direct from the wharfs. Hokkaido milk was also exceptional—Hokkaido is the dairy capital of Japan. Japanese milk has a much higher buttermilk content than in the United States—in fact, until very recently, the high fat content of the milk was something that was advertised as a positive.

My home in Urakawa was also perfect because it was located very close to the psychiatric day care unit, which I tried to visit almost every day. When Dr. Kawamura saw me bicycling around Urakawa with my camera equipment (and wondered what I would do in the winter), he loaned me the use of his beloved Porsche. Of course, this particular Porsche could barely make the legal speed limit on freeways. Still, that Porsche pick-up truck was my legs in Urakawa, and for that I am eternally grateful to the doctor, as New Bethel was located on the opposite side of town from the hospital, and life in Urakawa, especially in the winter, would have been almost unimaginable.

Having a car was one area where I differed from most of the Bethel members. If you are on public assistance in Japan, as most of the Bethel members are, it is very difficult to get permission from the social welfare office to own a car. In addition, people with severe symptoms of schizophrenia, such as hallucinations, can also be legally denied driver's licenses.[2] As a result, there were very few Bethel members who had cars or driver's licenses. Rika Shimizu and Tsutomu Shimono were the two main exceptions, and the other members constantly asked them if they would drive them to the grocery store or other errands. I tried as much as possible to drive people around town as well. Because I had a car, I was much more mobile than most other Bethel members, who tended to stay in one location for most of the day.

Daily Life in Urakawa

My usual routine was to wake up around 8 a.m.—usually to the sound of car tires crunching gravel in the staff parking lot behind my house. I'd make myself breakfast—usually a slice of processed cheese on toast with some "pizza sauce" topping in between, toasted in my small oven toaster. I'd drink down some instant coffee or make some tea.

In summer, I'd air out the house in the morning, maybe hang the futon mattresses and blankets outside along with the laundry. Japanese houses don't commonly have clothes dryers, so you have to hang your laundry either outside or, in inclement weather, inside. It was the sign of a good housewife to have your brightly washed laundry out early on sunny days and back in well before dusk. I was a very bad housewife.

After breakfast, I would decide whether to go to the psychiatric day care unit or to New Bethel. Much of this depended on what day of the week it was. I found most of the morning meetings at New Bethel to be stultifying, as most of the time was spent going over production reports and orders from the previous days. The one exception was the Friday meeting, during which people talked about their week and there was an opportunity for people to get things off their chests if they had any complaints. This was the occasion of the fight in the last scene in *Bethel*.

Psychiatric Day Care

If I decided to go to the psychiatric day care unit, I would make my way down the gravel road to the hospital. It was only around five hundred feet from my house to the back entrance of the day care ward. I would go in through the back, up the stairs, and drop my bags off at the staff office before making my way to the main activity room. There would be only a few people there in the early morning. Some were waiting for the day care activities to begin, some were waiting for their morning hospital work shift in the laundry room to begin, some were waiting for a consultation with the outpatient psychiatrist, and some were there just because they had nowhere better to go in town.

The psychiatric day care building was a prefabricated two-story annex to the main hospital building. The original psych day care ward was created in 2001 when the hospital downsized the psychiatric inpatient unit from 130 beds to 60, freeing up space for outpatient day care. The unit used to be housed inside the hospital itself, but in the massive Urakawa earthquake of 2003, an entire wing of the hospital was damaged and a new annex was built to house the psych day services.

In many ways this was ideal because the annex felt separate from the hospital. It didn't smell like ammonia, and its rooms were bright and sunny. There were no bars on the windows, and the doors leading to the hospital or outside were always unlocked during business hours. It had a bright and open feeling, entirely unlike being in a hospital ward. The psychiatric social workers and nurses in the psych day care aided in this impression by wearing regular clothes and not uniforms (unlike the white and pink garb the nurses in the psychiatric inpatient ward wore). The only visible difference between the patients at the day care and the psychiatric social workers was that the latter wore hospital ID cards around their necks.

The main room on the second floor of the day care was a large 6 x 20 meter (20′ x 65′) space. In one corner was a large comfortable sofa. There was a television that could be coaxed to yield a very fuzzy image—or could be used to watch VHS tapes. Along the side wall was an old Windows 2000 computer that had access to the internet and a printer. People used it to log into the Bethel SNS-Net social networking site account and update their blogs. No one used it to check their e-mail as almost everyone used their mobile phones for that.

On the far side of the room was a small *koagari* of tatami mats, with a small coffee table, beanbags, and *zabuton* cushions. Often I'd walk in to find someone deep in sleep there. Next to the *koagari* was the smoking corner. This was a glass-partitioned area with a large ashtray in the middle. It had its own door so that smoke couldn't seep out—but this also meant that inside the smoking corner was a toxic zone of cigarette smoke. There was an air filter, but it had long ago succumbed to the accumulated layers of tar and no longer worked.

On sunny days, the smokers would open the window in the smoking corner; apparently they were able to obtain some oxygen that way. There were times when I had to enter the smoking corner in order to follow a conversation. I dreaded when this would happen, because I knew I'd spend the next few days with a hacking cough, and no amount of Febreze deodorizer would be able to get the smell out of my clothes.

Except for some of the women of Sunshine House, almost everyone I knew at Bethel smoked. Kiyoshi smoked up a storm, and taking a cigarette seemed to be the only way he knew to allow himself a break. Rika-san didn't smoke; her personal vice was alcohol, and she took it in liberal amounts to compensate. I think that part of attraction of tobacco is that there is not much to do when you are mentally ill. The medications or the illness can blur your vision and your mind, so reading is not an option. Television and the radio can be confusing when you have voices swirling around your head. Smoking is one way at grasping at reality, a socially sanctioned way of whiling away the time, of standing around and not looking stupid, of looking like an adult man or an adult woman, of seeming normal.

For those at Bethel, normalcy seemed a major goal. This is a component of what Dr. Kawamura would call the right to "struggle" (*kurō*) in life. People wanted the trappings of normalcy: a home, a relationship, work. Bethel provided that framework. The hospital, on the other hand, was the antithesis of that. It was anti-normal. You had no responsibilities in the hospital, no roles but the sick role. No requirements except to get better. Nothing to do but sleep until sleeping itself became painful. It is often said by medical professionals that what people with schizophrenia need most is structure, but hospitals are anti-structure. There is an attempt to fill that with various rehabilitation activities, but many of them are transparently useless. Patients will never make a living selling clay figurines, so what is the purpose of making them all day long? Patients know the futility of this more than anyone.

While in the hospital, I was not issued an hospital ID card, nor did I display my Yale ID. I wore casual clothes but not the sportswear that the psychiatric nursing staff wore. I noted that all of the interns and visiting guests were issued ID cards, but I never was. A stranger walking into the psychiatric day care unit might easily have mistaken me for another patient, since all I did was lounge around and scribble incomprehensible things in my notebook.[3]

After spending the morning at day care or at New Bethel, I would look at my schedule to try to figure out what to do for the rest of the afternoon. Bethel members were usually engaged in their various jobs, such as seaweed packaging, fish drying and salting, noodle making in the sheltered workshops, or helping staff the two stores that Bethel operated. Those who weren't working or were in the hospital had a wide variety of various group meetings to go to. My own weekly schedule of events, which is (of course) just a partial snapshot of everything that was going on in Urakawa, looked like this:

Table 6.1 Weekly Schedule of Activities at Bethel and Urakawa Red Cross Hospital.

	Monday	*Tuesday*	*Wednesday*	*Thursday*	*Friday*	*Saturday*	*Sunday*
AM	New Bethel – Morning Meeting	New Bethel – Morning Meeting	Day Care – Staff Meeting	Day Care – Morning Meeting	Day Care – Staff Meeting		Sunday Mass
	New Bethel – Self Study Research	New Bethel – Event Meeting	Day Care – Peer Meeting	Day Care – Occupational Therapy	Ward 7 – Bethel Meeting		
			New Bethel – Shinsengumi Factory Meeting	New Bethel – Social Skills Training			
PM	Day Care – Staff Meeting	Day Care – Member Meeting	New Bethel – Social Skills Training	Day Care – Gencho Meting	Day-Care Parent-Child Cooking Class		WA Meet-ing at Sunshine House
	Day Care – Self-Study Research	Yonbura – Member Meeting			Day Care – Friday Special Event		
		Day Care – Uwatsura Meeting			Yonbura – SST		
EVE	Shiomi Heights House Meeting	House Meetings – Flower Heights, Takeda Heights, Rika House	Bible Study at Church	House meetings – Rainbow House, Sunshine House, Old Bethal House			
		SA Meeting at Hospital					

Individual Therapies

Although I spent most of my time visiting the various weekly group meetings, I should note that people went to a variety of individual treatment sources on an ad hoc basis:

- Psychiatric treatment: There were two psychiatrists on staff at the Red Cross Hospital. Dr. Kawamura was by far the more popular, but patients often saw the other doctor at the hospital for various reasons. There was also a private mental health clinic in town, which also saw a number of Bethel members and their families as well as townspeople.[4]
- Social workers: The Urakawa Red Cross Hospital had three social workers on staff, one dedicated to the psychiatric day care unit and the other two to community-based care. There was a counseling office for one-on-one sessions in the hospital that was deliberately designed not to look like a doctor's office. It was built like a traditional tea room, with tatami mats and *shōji* windows. And plenty of stuffed animals for role-playing.
- Mr. Mukaiyachi: Although he was no longer working for the Red Cross Hospital as their social worker (nor for Bethel, in any formal capacity), Mr. Mukaiyachi was the counselor of choice for many Bethel members, who had his mobile phone number on speed dial. Often when I was driving with Mr. Mukaiyachi, he'd pull over to take a call from a member and we'd spend up to a half-hour there on the side of the road.

Bethel's Group Therapies

Outside of the doctor's office, the majority of psychiatric care happened in various types of group therapy. The main ones were Schizophrenics Anonymous (SA) and Women's Anonymous (WA), social skills training (SST), and self-directed research. The hospital also ran a number of interventions such as gardening a small plot of land, playing sports, or occupational and art-based therapy. I'm also leaving out the therapeutic value associated with the work done at the Bethel seaweed packaging and noodle-making sheltered workshops.

For the rest of this chapter, I focus on social skills training and the self-directed research groups as they were practiced at Bethel. Both of these group therapies are based on the principles of cognitive-behavioral therapy (CBT), which is a treatment modality that tries to get people with mental illness to understand the underlying cognitive and behavioral processes that underlie their symptoms or their reactions to or behaviors caused by their symptoms. By better understanding these processes, people with mental illness can find ways to break a behavior cycle or change their psychological reactions to events. First used in the treatment of depression, CBT has now been extended to the treatment of anxiety disorders, mood disorders, schizophrenia, and other severe mental illnesses.

Social Skills Training (SST)

Social skills training (SST) was developed by Dr. Robert Liberman at UCLA in the 1970s to help people with severe psychiatric disabilities recover a degree of social skills through role-playing, modeling, interactive feedback, and coaching (Liberman et al. 1989). SST workshops were introduced to Japan by Kei Maeda, a Japanese social worker who received her Masters of Social Work from Columbia University in New York. Maeda started practicing and promoting SST for the treatment of psychiatric disorders in the 1990s from her position at Japan Lutheran College, and her treatment methods became known to Mr. Mukaiyachi, who then introduced them to Urakawa (Itoh and Mukaiyachi 2007, 167).

SST workshops were held several times a week in the hospital's psychiatric day care, New Bethel, and Bethel's Yonbura Store. The SSTs at day care were usually run by the psychiatric social workers while Mrs. Mukaiyachi or her staff ran the SSTs at New Bethel and Yonbura. As such, they catered to different audiences. The hospital's SSTs were not generally open to the public, and the people presenting there tended to be in the early stages of social participation. Bethel's SSTs were open to the general public, and the people presenting tended to be those who were already participating socially in the community. Regardless of where they were run, SST meetings were always well attended by members, staff, and visitors. There was usually an audience of fifteen to thirty people each time, which greatly facilitated interaction.

There are two SST presentations in *Bethel*, both filmed at Bethel's Yonbura Store. The audience is composed of Bethel members as well as a few out-of-town visitors from another psychiatric support community, which is why the faces of the audience aren't shown in the clip.

The purpose of social skills training is to help people overcome various social difficulties that they might be having. If Bethel members have problems, it's common for the social workers to suggest that they bring these issues to SST where the community can talk about. For example, in *Bethel,* Takei wants to ask his friend Kaku if he will help with the end-of-year cleanup, but doesn't know how to ask. The facilitator, Mrs. Mukaiyachi, has Takei role-play the scenario in front of the audience with one of the other members playing his friend's role.

After the role-playing is done, Mrs. Mukaiyachi asks the audience for feedback. What went well, what could have been improved? The audience members are asked what went well with the presentation and what could be improved. A couple of suggestions are made and the facilitator, Mrs. Mukaiyachi, writes them on the whiteboard. She also seeds a few ideas into the process. Takei is asked to do the role-play again, this time incorporating the suggestions. The role-playing and the modeling help Takei overcome his internal hesitation and shyness about asking someone a question, even someone who is a close friend.

There are many benefits to the SST. Takei directly benefits by getting feedback on his problem with his friend. In addition, the audience gives him (and also gets) insight into what might be going on in Kaku's life that is preventing him from attending events (his bad back, his girlfriend, and so on). As with other rituals at Bethel, information is also being brought out into the open—Takei's own concerns as well as what is going on with Kaku's dating life. By making members present again with a report on how things went—their homework assignments—SST encourages them to act on the advice given and to resolve the situation.

The second SST deals with internal psychological issues. One of Rainbow House's residents, Nozomi, is having difficulty articulating what is going on when she telephones Mr. Mukaiyachi for help. Her bad voices are constantly berating and belittling her. She had come to SST the last time, and group members had given her some feedback on how she could combat them by recruiting good voices such as the prime minister or policemen. Her "homework" presentation this week had been designed to let them know whether their advice had been useful.

After the SST workshop, I interviewed some of the Bethel members, who credited the workshops with helping them get out of their social withdrawal. Overwhelmingly, members viewed the SST sessions as very useful, and there was often a waiting list to present. Even if you weren't presenting, though, many of the situations raised commonalties to everyone: how to ask someone for a favor, how to ask someone for his or her opinion, what to do in a particular type of situation, and so on.

Self-Directed Research

By the early 2000s, self-directed research projects (*tōjisha kenkyū*) were rapidly becoming an acclaimed aspect of treatment at Bethel. The self-directed project reports were a hallmark of Bethel presentations all across the country, and in 2005, Mr. Mukaiyachi published a collection of reports under the title *Bethel House's Self-Directed Research*. Two more books titled *Let's Do Self-Directed Research, Vol. 1* and *Vol. 2* followed in 2009 and 2011.

Self-directed research follows certain premises. Many types of mental illness such as schizophrenia are characterized by a lack of awareness by the individual that their mental processes are unstable or deluded or that they are engaging in unusual behavior. The individual believes that they are fine, they are healthy—and that it is the world that is not right.

This lack of awareness is one of the most difficult aspects of mental illness for families, loved ones, therapists, and other caregivers. How do you help a person who doesn't believe that he or she needs any help? Some professionals advise against engaging with the hallucinations or delusions that someone with schizophrenia might have. By asking someone about the UFO that he says is going to pick them up before the end of the world comes, are you validating the existence of a UFO and abetting his denial of reality—that there are in fact no UFOs that are coming to land tomorrow? How do you make people understand that they are in a delusional state? Yelling at them "There are no UFOs!!!" is usually not efficacious, as it just leads them to think that no one believes them, so they need to act on their beliefs by themselves.

This is why self-directed research became one of the most important of the innovations within Bethel. It not only gave members insight into their illnesses, it also gave them a socially sanctioned and ritually defined narrative structure in which to talk about their experiences and feelings. Medical anthropologist Lawrence Kirmayer has talked about the importance of the "narrativizing function" in the creation of psychological mindedness, the first step to building insight and self-awareness in people with schizophrenia. In the Japanese context, Junko Kitanaka has also noted that psychiatrists at one hospital she studied tried to encourage their patients to achieve "narrative integration" (*katari no tōgō*) in talking about their symptoms at case conferences (Kirmayer 2007, 235; Kitanaka 2012, 100; see also Tranulis, Corin, and Kirmayer 2008).

The phrase *tōjisha kenkyū* is composed of two words. *Tōjisha* is a legal term in Japanese that means the interested parties in a suit. In Japanese social movements, the term has become a useful gloss to mean all people who have encountered discrimination or members of a discriminated class. But it is also used as a polite way within discriminated communities to indicate membership: Are you a *tōjisha?* Yes, I am a *tōjisha.*[5]

Kenkyū means research. The grammatical ordering of the phrase makes it clear that it's research done *by* the affected parties, not research done *on* the affected parties. The use of formal term *research* in this context is designed to help the patient separate themselves from their symptoms as well as emphasize that the positive aspects of understanding one's own condition.

Thus the combination of the two words, *tōjisha* + *kenkyū,* means research on yourself-as-part-of-an-affected-class. I've chosen, though, to translate it as *self-directed research,* well aware that it unfortunately negates the some of the political aspects of the term *tōjisha.*[6]

In the introduction to his 2005 volume, Mr. Mukaiyachi recalls that the first self-directed research project was created in February of 2002 when he was working with a member named Hiroshi Kawasaki who had been hospitalized with schizophrenia:

> Even though he was hospitalized, [Hiroshi] would ask his parents to order sushi to be delivered to the ward or to buy him video games. One time, his parents refused his request, and he got so angry that he broke the payphone in the psychiatric ward. He was feeling dejected about it afterwards when I [Mr. Mukaiyachi] went up to him and asked him, "How would you feel about doing research together on how to get along with Hiroshi Kawasaki, as well as on the topic of 'blowing up'?" I'll never forget the sparkle that came to his eyes as he immediately responded, "I'll do it!" Something about the word *research* managed to overcome the feelings of hopelessness that he had been mired in and encouraged him to do research on himself up to present moment. Another member responded to the same invitation by saying, "In contrast to phrases such as 'look intently at myself' or 'to reflect on my past,' the phrase 'to do research' somehow makes me tremble with expectation. My spirit of adventure gets tickled!" (Mukaiyachi 2005, 3)

Mukaiyachi continued to detail the various steps necessary to conduct self-research:

1) **Differentiate between the "problem" and the "person":** Change how you think about yourself from, "I'm Hiroshi who keeps blowing up" to "I'm Hiroshi who is struggling with the issue of how to stop blowing up even when I don't want to." This is very important not only for you-as-*tōjisha* but also for the people around you.
2) **Create a self-diagnosis:** Don't just use the medical diagnosis but create your own self-diagnosis that encapsulates the meanings and circumstances of what you are struggling with. For example, "Schizophrenia: Runs-out-of-money-by-the-end-of-the-week type." This helps your peers (i.e., other people who might have experienced similar situations) understand what you are struggling with and helps them talk about it. It's an important part of you feeling ownership over your problems.
3) **Figure out the patterns and processes of your problems:** There must be some rules that regulate how your symptoms occur, actions that lead to them occurring, or things that lead to problems such as "running out of money."
4) **Try to think of concrete ways that you can help yourself or protect yourself and scenarios where you can practice them.**
5) **Verify your results.** (Mukaiyachi 2005: 4–5)

Self-directed research was designed to be done "individually within a group," with people working out the broad contours of their own analysis and then reporting back to a group with other members and Mr. Mukaiyachi or one of the social workers serving as research advisors.

To that end, Bethel printed up a series of self-directed research workbooks so that members could fill out each step of the process, bring it to the group, come up with new hypotheses about what was troubling them, test their hypotheses, and then report back to the group again. Various interventions and coping strategies that came from self-directed research were also tested and put into action through social skills training workshops, and the two were seen as part of the overall system of Bethel's cognitive-behavioral therapy (cf. Itoh and Mukaiyachi 2007).

One of the Bethel members, Gen'ichi Nakayama described the benefits of the self-directed research process:

> Through research, I was able to get a much better understanding of myself. It's funny to think about it, but when I engaged in research sessions with my peers, they were able to understand things about me that I couldn't,

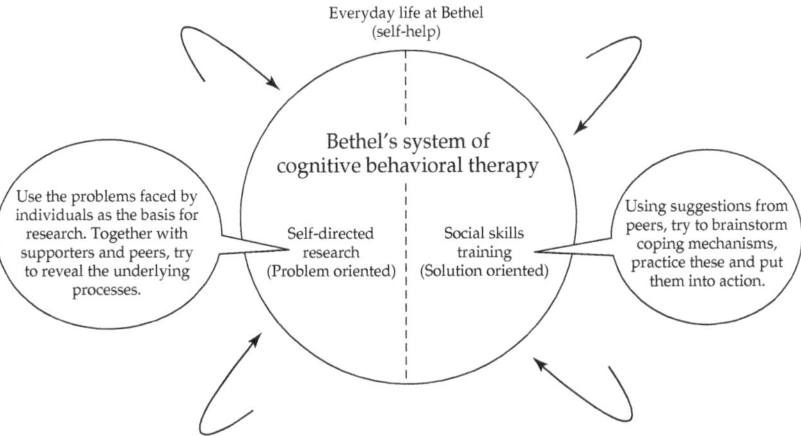

Figure 6.1 Bethel's system of cognitive behavioral therapy
Source: Derived from Itoh Emi and Mukaiyachi Ikuyoshi (2007)

> and in turn I could often perceive things about them that they couldn't. Through the process, I was able to learn the value of other people's opinions and experiences. (Mukaiyachi 2006, 222)

One of the goals of self-directed research was formal research presentation at various private and public venues. For example, while I was in Urakawa, I saw presentations at Bethel, the hospital, and the local middle school as well as one for local nursing students. There were also presentations for visiting pharmaceutical representatives, at regional conferences for independent livings centers, and also a formal presentation in Tokyo for a group of psychiatrists.[7] Finally, there were presentations at the annual Bethel Festival and of course the many books by Bethel on the subject.

A Self-Directed Research Presentation

One November morning in 2007, I went to New Bethel for their weekly self-directed research meeting. One of the Bethel *tōjisha* staff, Noriyuki Itoh, was serving as the facilitator.[8] Mr. Mukaiyachi was sitting near him but not otherwise playing an active role in the proceedings. About thirty people had gathered for the meeting. Noriyuki opened the proceedings by asking for a volunteer in the audience to introduce the self-directed research process to the rest of the members and to the several visitors that had come that day. A young woman raised her hand and came to the front of the room:

> My name is Mai Suzuki.
>
> Self-directed research is where we talk about our illnesses or our symptoms in front of everyone and we all try to think through what is going on . . . and we don't try to solve the problem [there and then], but by presenting the struggles [that that person is going through] . . . something usually comes out of this space. . . .

Mai struggled a bit with her words. Noriyuki asked her to talk about her own research project:

> I am going through schizophrenia right now[9] . . . my self-diagnosis is "Schizophrenia: Codependence on my Gencho-san [auditory hallucination] type."
>
> By codependence I mean . . . that when my Gencho-san is around, I find him to be really irritating, but if he isn't around, I feel lonely.
>
> The name of my Gencho is Michiaki. When Micchi is around, it's very difficult, but when he's gone, I'm lonely. I'm trying to learn how to live with my Gencho-san.

Noriyuki thanked Mai for her introduction and told us that Mai had just arrived in Urakawa and was actively working on her self-directed research project. We all clapped, and Mai sat down. After one more introduction, Noriyuki then asked if anyone else had brought his or her research presentation for the group.

Katsuko Miyanishi raised her hand and walked to the front of the room. Katsuko was a young woman in her early twenties. Like Mai, she had just arrived in Urakawa a few weeks earlier. She had been languishing in a psychiatric hospital in the neighboring town of Tomakomai but wasn't feeling that she was making any progress there toward recovery. After reading one of his books, she wrote a letter to Mr. Mukaiyachi, who invited her up to Bethel to "study abroad" in Urakawa for a while.

Katsuko was dressed quite nicely in a cardigan with a white blouse. But for the fact that she never made eye contact with anyone, you'd have thought she was just another preppy college student. This was her first public presentation before many of the Bethel members.

> My name is Katsuko Miyanishi.
>
> My diagnosis is "Schizophrenia with Self-Destructive Tendencies."

As she talked, Noriyuki wrote this on the whiteboard behind her.

> My research project involves feelings of guilt.

She paused, unsure how to continue. . . . Noriyuki asked her if by "feelings of guilt" she meant that she thought that bad things happening in the world were her fault?

> I read the *Hokkaido Shimbun* newspaper. . . . All my crimes are always being exposed by the *Hokkaido Shimbun,* so I have to read it every day.

The audience giggled. Noriyuki asked her why she feels so compelled to read the paper:

> I get very anxious, so I have to read the newspaper.

After writing the basics on the whiteboard, Noriyuki took the microphone and said that now that we know the basics of Katsuko's issues, did anyone in the audience have any questions for her?

Mr. Mukaiyachi asked her if the revelations of her crimes were written in newspapers other than the *Hokkaido Shimbun,* such as the national newspapers: the *Mainichi Shimbun* or the *Asahi Shimbun.*

> Only the *Hokkaido Shimbun.* All of my crimes are local to Hokkaido, so they aren't covered in the national papers.

Mr. Mukaiyachi asked her if she doesn't plan to make a break to the nationals?

> The nationals just aren't interested in me, so it's hard for me to get listed in them. I want to debut in them, but there's just no offer from the nationals.

I raised my hand and asked whether she gets listed in the prefectural edition of *Hokkaido Shimbun* or in the local editions. And just what were the crimes that she gets reported for?

> When I lived in the Iburi region, I read the Iburi local edition [of the *Hokkaido Shimbun*]. Now that I've moved to Urakawa, I think that the Urakawa local edition will cover my crimes. . . . My crimes involve things like embezzlement of public funds, public lewdness, assault, murder, violation of public election laws. . . .

You must be very busy, I added.

> I'm very busy.

Mr. Mukaiyachi asked if these are crimes she really committed, or is she being framed for them?

> I did some research together with the day care worker at my last hospital and realized that I was being falsely accused of these crimes. The real criminal is someone named Waruo,[10] who is the head of a gang. He's the one who is committing the crimes and trying to blame me for them. One of Waruo's henchmen is named "Agent"—he's also one of my voices [Gencho-sans].

Noriyuki asked Katsuko to draw a picture of Waruo.

> Waruo is also secretly controlling the security police. He's also very good at manipulating information and is able to deceive the people into thinking that I'm a very evil person. He is brainwashing the public. He also managed to convince me that I was responsible so that I would confess to these crimes.

One of the Bethel members, Masako Yoshino, asked her why she thinks that she is responsible for the crimes, is this a kind of delusion by association (*kanren mōsō*)?

> When I read the paper, my Gencho-san voice tells me, "You did it. You must have done it." He whispers these things in my ear, and that's how I come to believe it.

Figure 6.2 Katsuko Miyanishi talks with Mr. Mukaiyachi about Waruo, the secret agent who plots against her. Photo by the author.

Masako asked Katsuko, so that's why you think that you did it, even though someone else did it?

> Even though the article in the *Hokkaido Shimbun* might say that someone else with a different name or even a different nationality did the crime, I know that there are certain codes embedded in the newspaper that go beyond mere chance. That's how I know that I did it after all.

Masako continued: so you force yourself to believe that it's your fault? Katsuko paused, not sure how to respond. Mr. Mukaiyachi, who had been sitting down, took the opportunity to stand up and says that he's found a copy of the *Hokkaido Shimbun* (Urakawa edition). Maybe you can show us what is going on? Mr. Mukaiyachi asked for some volunteers to play the role of Katsuko's voices. They role-played her reading the newspaper while the voices behind her were telling her that she's responsible for the crimes listed in the articles:

Mr. Mukaiyachi asked if we all understand what Katsuko was going through. We all nodded our heads. He asked Katsuko what she would like to achieve from her self-directed research:

> I want to be cleared of the crimes that I was falsely accused of. I want the public, who is agitated about the . . . assassinations . . . and expelling me from society. . . . There's an assassination squad out there, and

Figure 6.3 Katsuko Miyanishi, Noriyuki Itoh, Kōichi Yoshii, and Mr. Mukaiyachi role-play the critical voices inside Katsuko's head as she reads the newspaper. Photo by the author.

> before the assassination squad comes around, I want to be cleared of my crimes. . . .

Mr. Mukaiyachi said that she had told us that she feels accused of various crimes. What does that feeling feel like? He asked all of us to point our fingers at Katsuko. Is that what it feels like? Katsuko saw all of us pointing at her. Her eyes dilated, and she breathed in sharply.

> That's exactly it.

So what do you do?

> I run away.

And what happens when you run away? Do you feel better?

> Temporarily. But the feeling that the public is after me continues. The police don't have enough goods on me to arrest me, so they are just following me for now. I don't know who they might be. They might be in disguise.

Mr. Mukaiyachi went through another role-playing exercise with some members playing the agents that are trailing her. He then asked us if we can understand what she is going through. He concluded that her goal is to be able to relax, to get away from the fears of persecution. Her research topic, he said, is, "How I can relax." He invited the group to do research with her on this topic. Mr. Mukaiyachi handed the microphone back to Noriyuki, who then asked us if we have any ideas on how Katsuko can relax. Mai asked her if she is cleared of her crimes and found innocent, what will she do?

> I can't even think about that. . . . That's a terrifying thought.

Mr. Mukaiyachi stepped in and asked her, but I thought you were innocent of these crimes?

> Maybe. . . . I'm not sure.

Then Mr. Mukaiyachi said, "Japan has just introduced a jury system for their criminal courts. So guilt or innocence isn't being judged by judges but by people like you'd see on the street, by regular people. So let's ask everyone to serve as the jury here. You've heard about Katsuko's many crimes from rape, to murder, to shoplifting, to election fraud. It's a wonder that she's still alive; she ought to have been found guilty and condemned to death long ago. But let's ask everyone here to be jurors and decide whether she is innocent or guilty. You're all jurors. Who thinks Katsuko is guilty? Raise your hands. Hmmm. . . . no one. Who thinks that she is innocent? Raise your hands."

Noriyuki looked at the crowd of hands and said, "Hmmm. . . . it seems that by a unanimous verdict of the Bethel jury, you've been found innocent."

> I'm very puzzled. . . . I don't think that you people have enough information to make that decision. . . .

Mr. Mukaiyachi said that this is very puzzling to him: "Most people would be very happy to be found innocent, but Katsuko is very worried by this."

Several members raised their hands and talked about their own experiences with feelings of guilt and persecution and how they dealt with their feelings that they were responsible for various crimes that were going on in Japan.

Mr. Mukaiyachi then led Katsuko on another role-playing exercise in which he showed the rest of the audience how Katsuko wants to make connections with other people, but the voices are constantly preventing her from getting close to other people. They constantly put up a barrier, causing her to retreat. At times, she feels compelled to punish herself by hitting herself on the head or smashing her head against the wall, to the point of causing serious head wounds.

After several more suggestions from various Bethel members about how they have dealt with their own feelings of persecution, Katsuko sat down. This was Katsuko's first self-directed research presentation.

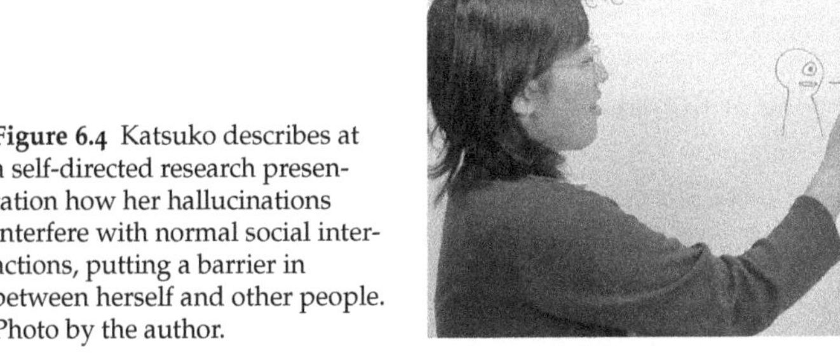

Figure 6.4 Katsuko describes at a self-directed research presentation how her hallucinations interfere with normal social interactions, putting a barrier in between herself and other people. Photo by the author.

It served a dual purpose of introducing her to the Bethel community as well as letting them know what issues they might encounter as they interact with her. It also served as the first step in her self-directed research process. Over the next several weeks, both by herself and with other members, Katsuko used the worksheets in the *Bethel Self-Directed Research Workbook* to think about her condition.

In a conversation with Mr. Mukaiyachi and Bethel members about self-directed research, Dr. Kawamura described his thoughts about the process:

> It's now been several years since we started doing self-directed research. It's my impression that the people who are engaged in self-directed research—how would you say it—no longer seem to be trying to be cured [*naosō to shinakunattekita*]. They seem to be engaged in something much more important. "Losing the desire to be cured" [*naosu ki ga nakunatta*] in this case doesn't have bad connotations. It doesn't mean that they want to be left alone. Rather, it means that the people with the illness themselves become really involved in the research process. In addition, there's something about what you might call the gaze of your peers [i.e. people who have experienced the same things you have].
>
> Up to then, the goal of those people might have been to try to become like a healthy person. They were concerned with what their doctor thought about them, or they were judging themselves by the standards of people without their illness and striving to meet those standards. In these types of circumstances, their doctor feels compelled to help by reducing as much as possible any symptoms of their illness. I feel that clinical treatment up to now has been based on this type of relationship. This has become even more evident after we started doing self-directed research.
>
> This comes through not only in how they talk about their symptoms. Because they are engaged in the research together with their peers, they are able to relate clearly and appropriately the larger context of their symptoms, as well as details about their worries and their struggles, in ways that other people can understand. Another way of thinking about it is my thought that because self-directed research has progressed so well that I think to myself, "What's a psychiatrist supposed to do now?" (Mukaiyachi 2006, 231–232)

Studying Abroad at Bethel

In 2010, Mr. Mukaiyachi published the second volume of *The People of Bethel*, which was also his twelfth book on the community. One of the chapters was titled, "The Proliferation of Self-Directed Research—Encouraging Studying Abroad." The chapter begins with a description of Bethel's activities within Urakawa as well as their efforts to promulgate their philosophy through their public lectures throughout Japan. Then he raises a third way that people can experience Bethel, which is their "study abroad" (ryūgaku) program. He talks about two recent study abroad students and their experiences with the self-directed research program. One of the examples is Katsuko Miyanishi. As before, she gives her self-diagnosis as: "schizophrenia with self-destructive tendencies."

Katsuko herself presents her self-directed research in *Let's Do Self-Directed Research, Vol. 1* (2009). With her permission, I include a slightly abridged excerpt from one of her self-directed research reports:

RESEARCH ON MY FEELINGS OF GUILT

by Katsuko Miyanishi

Research Purpose

The purpose of this research is to understand how I can exist without always hitting my own self-destruct button. Up to now, I've brought myself to my own criminal court, found myself guilty, handed down convictions, and punished myself. But I'd like to stop doing that and think of new ways to free myself from this kind of suffering.

In order to do this, I need to figure out why I always feel this sense of guilt, that I did some sort of crime. I need to do research on the mechanisms that underlie such feelings of guilt. I want to figure out how to stop myself from unfairly judging myself and to be able to hold a fair and equitable trial and judgment of my actions. Finally, I want to be able to understand other ways of releasing the pent-up magma of my difficulties without exploding.

Research Methodology

By talking with the social workers and other members of the self-directed research groups about my problems, I want to explicate the patterns behind my self-destructive actions, and in order to improve the mechanisms that I can use to help myself, I want to continue advancing my research through SST and self-directed research meetings.

Explicating My Self-Destructive Patterns

The general pattern of my problems begins with my Gencho-sans telling me, "You've committed a crime." Then I begin to be put under surveillance. If I can see even the smallest crack in my front door, I get worried and can't even go outside for work. Furthermore, my crimes are reported in the local edition of the newspaper. They don't use my name but instead use special codes and symbols. My Gencho-sans tell me repeatedly and in accusatory tones, "You must be the one that's being talked about in the papers." It's just like I'm being put through a police interrogation, even though I don't think I did it, I'm under such emotional pressure that I begin to think that I might have done it. Finally, I confess to having done it.

Up to now, it's like I've been putting myself on trial, finding myself guilty, and punishing myself. I've been my own judge, jury, and executioner. My punishment has always been to hit myself with my fist on my head, or to hit my head against the wall, or to slap myself. Once I complete my punishment, the Gencho-san quiets down, and I am able to relax.

New Ways of Helping Myself

New Mechanism #1—Putting Criminals on the Most Wanted List

Through self-directed research, I was able to come up with the hypothesis that because I didn't do the crimes, it must be the Gencho-san who were trying to convince me that I was a criminal. . . . Right now, I've put the real master criminal who is behind all of this on the "most wanted list."

New Mechanism #2—Responding to the Accusations of the Gencho-san

2a—Bring in Legal Counsel

The first thing that I came up with was to bring in legal counsel. The staff said that they would serve as my lawyers, so when the various Gencho-sans come in with their accusations, I will tell them to go talk to my lawyer and to leave me alone.

2b—Being Open about My Problems

I now participate in Schizophrenics Anonymous. I find that my feelings of persecution become stronger when I'm keeping secrets, so being open about things with my peers makes life easier for me.

2c—Checking In with Myself

At Bethel we have a self-checklist with the mnemonic "Natsu Hisao." The letters in Japanese stand for Worrying-Tiredness-Boredom-Loneliness and Lack of Money-Hunger-or-Medicine. . . . I'm trying to look at myself and my Gencho-sans in as objective a fashion as possible, so I will ask people around me for their opinions so that I don't act on my own judgments by myself.

2d—Talking about My Problems. . . .[11]

2e—Recruiting a Good Gencho-san to Help. . . .

2f—Coming Up with a Hypothetical Guilt Filter. . . .

2g—Understanding My Self-Destructive Cycle. . . .

2h—Freeing Myself from a Dependence on Injections

When I was in the hospital, I was dependent on injections [of sedatives] to help me sleep. On the positive side, I was happy when the nurses would take my pulse and blood pressure. I felt taken care of and valued. And I could go to sleep without facing any of my problems. The negatives were that none of my problems ever went away and just repeated themselves. When I would wake up, I would feel unloved by the nurses. I think my low self-esteem was at the root of this. When I was dependent on the injections and caught up in my feelings of guilt, I never had to do the hard work of looking at myself. Since coming to Urakawa, I've been able to distribute and defocus my feelings of dependence onto several other people and other things; in doing so my burden has become lighter and easier. And now I no longer need the injections that I was so dependent on.

Conclusions from Self-Directed Research

Before I started doing self-directed research, I felt very caught up in my illness and surrounded on all sides by it. But now I am able to put the illness front and center while at the same time being able to gain some distance and objectively evaluate it. Even when I'm going through difficult times, I'm able to think to myself, "This might be good research material!"

I want to say to other people who also suffer from the same feelings of guilt and persecution: "You're suffering under false charges." Because they are facing false charges, I want them to keep on trying until they are able to proclaim their innocence to the world.

(Miyanishi 2009: 70–79)

Katsuko Miyanishi has become one of the new superstars at Bethel. When I visited in early 2012, she was out of town giving a talk at one of Bethel's lecture series. She's also hosted the annual Bethel Festival and is well on her way to becoming one of the new core members. Not all of the new people that come to Bethel work out so well. A good many are turned away at the door, as both Bethel and the hospital are at full capacity and can choose which members to accept. Of those that stay, some leave disappointed that there are no quick fixes. Others have adopted quieter lives in slow recovery. There are few "failures," as Bethel has accepted failure as a fundamental part of what they do ("failure is an opportunity" is an oft-heard mantra), but there are also more downs to ups to the lives of many of the people there.

The Repeatability of the Bethel Experiment

An alternative to moving to Bethel is to try to bring a bit of Bethel back to where you live. There are Bethel study groups scattered all across Japan, where people read Bethel books, watch Bethel's videos, and invite Bethel members to come down from Hokkaido to talk. They engage in SST workshops or create self-directed research teams. These study groups are composed of family members of people with mental illness, those with the illnesses themselves, social workers, and medical professionals. When I talk with the some of the study group participants who visit Bethel and ask them what is different from their hometowns, they almost always answer that the "people at Bethel are really lively [*genki*]." When I ask them if it would be possible for something like Bethel to be constructed in their hometowns, they all declare that it would be impossible or at least very, very hard.

Bethel has a unique combination of geography, lack of resources, and personnel. Because Bethel is in the middle of nowhere, the members really have nothing to do but to focus on their own issues and support each other. As one member notes in *Bethel,* you can't die of starvation alone in your apartment in Urakawa like you could in a big city. Bethel is also blessed by the lack of resources in the town, which has meant that they have had to be creative in their solutions. Nothing will happen unless people work together. And finally, Bethel also would not have been possible without the unique combination of Dr. Kawamura, Mr. Mukaiyachi, Kiyoshi Hayasaka, and other core Bethel members.

That being said, the face of psychiatric care in Japan is definitely changing for the better. Under pressure from the government, more and more hospitals are actively trying to reduce their average lengths of stay. More and more psychiatric group homes and sheltered workshops are being created. Inspired by Bethel, there are SST workshops and self-directed research groups sprouting up across the country. With government recognition of mental illness as a psychiatric disability and the accompanying social welfare benefits and support services, it is becoming easier to live in the community with a mental illness in Japan.

Although it sounds tautological, there may be no need to recreate Bethel in other places in Japan, because there is no need to. The point of the Bethel experiment was to create a space where people with psychiatric disabilities could live *genki* (active) lives in the community. Now that this has been proven to be possible, other locales in Japan are modifying the lessons learned from Bethel to suit their own needs. There only needs to be one Bethel—the rest of the country can be psychotourists to the Bethel Holy Land.

In the final chapters of this book, I explore what our own journey to Bethel has left us with. I'll do this by taking you through the life of one more Bethel member and then concluding by looking at the future of Bethel.

Peer Support and a Meaningful Life: Gen's Story

In June of 2007, Bethel held its 14th annual Bethel Festival at the Urakawa Town Concert Hall. In front of over several hundred visitors from across Japan (and several news crews), the festival opened with self-directed research presentations, SST skits, and other depictions of life, community, and therapy at Bethel. Kiyoshi Hayasaka was given the "You Were Really *Papipupepo* Award." *Papipupepo* is Kiyoshi's term for when he is feeling a bit scrambled in the head. The award recognized his ten years of struggling with his three main issues: money, women, and his illness. The Acorn Society and three of its original members (including Yuzuru Yokoyama and Minoru Sasaki) were also recognized.

The winners of the Bethel Festival 2007 Hallucinations and Delusions Grand Prix were the residents of Kireiso, who collectively decided that there must be an invisible person living among them. This person was responsible for all sorts of bad deeds, causing clothes to go missing, leaving things in disarray, and so on. The residents had a house meeting to talk about what to do about him. This acceptance of their shared reality and the joint decision to deal with it were the reasons that the prize committee chose them.

The festival had some other highlights. As usual, Mr. Mukaiyachi had "scouted" several new recruits, and they came on stage to talk about their experiences. One woman in her twenties had been living in an institution and gave a harrowing tale of the years of sexual abuse at the hands of her father, abortions, and subsequent self-cutting. Bethel seemed like a last resort for her. The audience was stunned by her tale, which seemed quite out of place in the light atmosphere of the festival as a whole. Even some of the staff seemed surprised. This surprised me, in turn, as I had been at her initial intake briefing when she came to Bethel, and she had told much the same story to the social workers at Bethel.

Bethel had always focused on schizophrenia as its hallmark illness. I wondered if this new member represented a different direction for Bethel, toward more contemporary issues such as sexual violence, sexual abuse, and emotional disorders. More and more of the new members seemed to be coming with such issues—and the standard Bethel mantra of "discarding your garbage" (letting go of the past) wasn't as effective with these problems.

At the Bethel downtown store, members were busy selling their various products: T-shirts, videos, seaweed, books, tapestries, and knickknacks. Tsutomu Shimono was selling several CDs of songs that he had written and composed with his on-again, off-again girlfriend Kayo Yamamoto. Their two-person band was called Punch n' Glove, which was a fair depiction of their tumultuous personal relationship.[1]

A Busy Man, An Exhausted Man

Gen'ichi Nakayama was extremely busy, as usual. I saw him running around the Urakawa City Town Hall, where the festival was held. I had met Gen in the hospital the very first time I had come to Bethel, back in 2005. He was in a rush then too, discharging himself from the closed psy-

Figure 6.5 Self-directed research presentations on the main stage at the Bethel Festival in 2007. Photo by the author.

Figure 6.6 The Yonbura Store during the 2007 Bethel Festival. Photo by the author.

chiatric ward in order to fly over to Mito City to talk about schizophrenia and to show his paintings and sketches at a public presentation, then fly back and check himself back into the psych ward. In one of Bethel's books, Gen described himself as having "schizophrenia with self-explosive tendencies, over-heating type, and chronic out-of-money-itis" (Mukaiyachi 2006, 214).

In the spring of 2006, Gen had discharged himself from the hospital and moved into one of Bethel's shared living facilities, a rickety wooden structure in front of the train station called Station House. He lived there with Tsutomu Shimono and several other young men. While at Station House, Gen studied to become a psychiatric peer supporter in order to help some of the long-term psychiatric patients, his former ward mates, make the transition from the hospital to independent living. After passing the examination, he wore his peer supporter ID card around his neck constantly, proud of what he was doing and what he had become. I rarely had a chance to talk to Gen as he was always hurrying around town.

Instead, I became friends with his mother, Chika. Gen's little brother was also hospitalized at the Urakawa Red Cross Hospital, so Chika regularly made the trek from her home in Utsunomiya in central Japan to see her two sons. When she was in town, she occasionally went to the parent's meetings at the psychiatric day care unit on Fridays. After the meetings, the various mothers (and I) would go out for coffee or drive out to a local hot springs spa. So I ended up knowing Chika better than I knew Gen.

After the 2007 Bethel Festival ended, things seemed to return to normal in Urakawa. I went to the psychiatric day care center and listened to people who were working with Mr. Mukaiyachi on their self-research projects. At Bethel House, other people were preparing PowerPoint presentations for upcoming talks out of town. I walked by Shiosaiso house and found a dozen members engaged in an impromptu game of baseball.

Gen was apparently exhausted from the work he had put into the festival as one of the coordinators. I heard through the grapevine that soon after the festival ended, he checked himself into the hospital and got his usual bed in Ward 7. He had initially thought that he would stay there about a week, but his condition didn't seem to get any better so he decided to stay there a bit longer than usual.

A Bethel Fight

On a Friday night, about two weeks after the festival, I screened a revised cut of *Bethel* at Bethel House. I was nervous because previous versions that I had shown at Bethel hadn't included the fight scene at the end where Masako Yoshino was mercilessly teased by two other members for having such strong body odor. At the end of the clip, Masako storms out of the room in tears. The remaining members talked about what had happened and what they should or should not have done.

Truth be told, Masako really did smell pretty bad at the time; for the people who were sensitive to odors or already agitated by other things in their lives, the odor could push them over the brink. Bethel encouraged people to talk about things that bothered them so that they didn't store them up and explode later on. So, people argued, why not tell her directly?

There were of course multiple backstories. Masako was having a hard time because her boyfriend at the time was being abusive. He had come from an Ainu background and, like many of his generation, suffered from a history of parental and social abuse that had led to issues in the present. In that environment, Masako was having trouble maintaining her personal hygiene.

There were other tensions as well. When Masako first came to Bethel, she belonged to a Buddhist religious organization named Soka Gakkai. A good number of Bethel members were Soka Gakkai members, as it was well known that that religion tended to proselytize heavily among people and families of people with disabilities. One of Masako's tormentors was a particularly fervent member.

A split was created between the Christian and Soka Gakkai members when Masako started to go to various church events to play the keyboard. She was asked because there were so few people in the community who could play the keyboard. In the Christmas scene at the church in *Bethel,* there is a quick glimpse of Masako at the keyboard. She is also playing the keyboard in *A Japanese Funeral.* Part of the anger directed at Masako in the fight scene was because some of the members were worried that Masako might be losing her faith. One member's comment that Masako was having problems with her face and body because she wasn't living a "wholesome life" may have come from fears that she might be losing her faith and becoming a Christian.[2]

Although the fight seemed brutal, it was a normal event for Bethel, which is why the staff did not intervene—or even think of intervening; it very much reflected their philosophy that "Bethel is full of problems." Tensions flare up and strong emotions are expressed and then equilibrium is reached again. That is part of normal social life. When I told Masako and Mieko that people in the United States were surprised at the fight scene and thought that the two of them must hate each other, they wanted me to let people know that they were friends and posed for this picture.

Saturday Morning

The morning after the film screening, I was driving down the main road in the Porsche when I saw Kudo-kun, one of the younger members. I pulled over to say hello and ask him if he needed a ride anywhere.

Figure 6.7 Masako and Mieko show the world that they are still friends after the screening of *Bethel.* Photo by the author.

He told me: "Gen is gone!"

"Gen has disappeared somewhere?" Bethel members occasionally run off and leave town. Earlier in the summer, one of the members went missing and was found naked, but otherwise fine, lying in the street in the next town over.

"No, he's dead!" Kudo told me. I was stunned. Gen had seemed so full of life at the festival. I learned that his body was going to be taken to the church. Kudo-kun got into the front of the Porsche, and I dropped him off at the church. I was about to go into the church myself when the visual anthropologist in me took over, and I went back home to get my video equipment. I rushed in, grabbed my camera, threw my tripod into the back of the pickup and headed back to the church. On the way, I saw Megumi and pulled over to tell her about it, but she already knew. She was heading to the flower store to buy flowers before going to the church. In a small town, news travels fast.

Normally in Japan, people get taken home for a few nights after dying in a hospital.[3] Death is not seen as the immediate cessation of biological activity but a process through which the spirit slowly leaves the body and this world. Ideally, deceased people should spend one or two final nights resting on their own futon mattress in their own homes before being taken to be cremated. A healthy supply of dry ice keeps the body from decomposing, as most Japanese do not normally embalm or bury their dead whole in the ground. In Gen's case, his little apartment at Station House was much too small for a proper viewing, so the first floor of the church was chosen for his final nights on this earth.

The film *A Japanese Funeral* starts when I arrive at the church, just after 11 a.m. Gen is resting peacefully in a futon on the floor. Mrs. Mukaiyachi and Rika-san and some other members are setting up a small altar for him. Megumi comes in soon after with a basket of flowers, her floppy black hat framing her tears. Mrs. Mukaiyachi is busy setting up a little altar for Gen. One of her staff helps by arranging some of his drawings, photographs, and awards. She also buys some soda, coffee, and cigarettes for Gen, his favorite things in the world. By this time, a dozen Bethel members and staff, as well as Dr. Kawamura and several nurses, are in the room, keeping watch over Bethel. Stunned, people are silent at first, but after a while we start to talk about Gen and his life. The hospital social workers bring in some food and drinks. We share some of the refreshments with Gen and then dig in ourselves. We surround the doctor and ask him what had happened.

Gen's Death

Gen's death had come as a surprise to Dr. Kawamura. He told us that after the Bethel Festival had ended, Gen had come to the hospital saying that he was exhausted. He'd been exhausted before. He had a rare genetic disease that manifested itself both psychologically and physically. He was often running a fever and always had a thermometer on him. If he felt tired, he would usually go to the hospital and get Dr. Kawamura to admit him to Ward 7. After a few days, he'd rest up and discharge himself. So no one was surprised when he checked into Ward 7 right after the festival.

On June 18, 2007, Gen had checked into the hospital and been given his usual bed in Ward 7, the closed psychiatric ward. He thought that he would stay there about a week, but his condition didn't seem to get any better, so he continued to stay there. On June 29, Gen missed the final meeting when the discharge date for one of Gen's peer support clients was set (Yuzuru Yokoyama, who appears in chapter 5). It must have been a relief to Gen that his client was being discharged after thirty-seven years of institutionalized life but also bittersweet in that he was not able to be there.

That evening, Gen had trouble sleeping, so he asked for sleeping pills from the duty nurse. On June 30, the nurses doing the early morning rounds noted that Gen was sound asleep, snoring. But when 9 a.m. came around and he still hadn't come out for breakfast, they went to check on him. His body was already cold. It was estimated that his time of death was around 7 a.m. The cause of death was listed as cardiac failure.

Gen's Parents Arrive

Mr. and Mrs. Nakayama live in Mito City, which is about a hundred kilometers northeast of Tokyo, on the mainland. They immediately flew up to Sapporo as soon as they heard, but it still took them several hours to arrive in Urakawa. As soon as they walked into the living room of the church apartment where Gen was, Mrs. Nakayama broke down in tears at the sight of her son.

The Nakayamas looked lost at first, but the staff of Bethel immediately mobilized to help. They noted what funeral arrangements needed to be made and made all of the phone calls that were required. They contacted the funeral home and the city crematorium and made arrangements. Meanwhile, the Nakayamas started to talk to the other members, thanking them for being friends to Gen for so many years. They knew that he had absolutely cherished his time at Bethel.

I left around 6 p.m. that evening. Mr. and Mrs. Nakayama looked exhausted, and I wanted to give them their privacy, especially as I had been filming all that time. Just a few members remained when I departed. They were setting up futon mattresses for Gen's parents so that they could spend one final night sleeping next to their son.

The next morning, I went straight to the church. Mrs. Nakayama greeted me and thanked me for taping the previous day. She thought that it would be an important record of her son's life and life at Bethel. She was sorry that I didn't stay longer, as Gen's younger brother, Yoshihiko, had come to see him that evening. Yoshihiko also had psychiatric problems and was a resident of Ward 7. Yoshihiko had come later in the evening with some of the staff members from the hospital. His mother said that Yoshihiko was utterly moved at the sight of his brother's body. He shook Gen hard, shouting, "Wake up big brother, wake up!" He then started uttering magical spells, trying to resurrect him. She wished that I had been able to capture that last moment between the two brothers.

Sunday Service

The next day was a Sunday, so we held service in the church. Rather than holding it upstairs in the chapel, we decided to hold it in the first floor apartment so that Gen could participate. About a dozen people were there that morning. Kiyoshi led the services, occasionally stumbling over difficult words in the Bible but carrying through with his usual strength and sincerity of belief.

After service, we had the usual tea and snacks. The funeral director and his assistant showed up in the early afternoon. They shaved and prepared Gen's body. We cleaned his body with moist wipes before transferring him to a coffin. It was difficult navigating the narrow pathway of the church as he was brought to the hearse outside to be taken to the funeral home.

That evening, we held a wake (*otsūya*) for Gen at the funeral home, eating and drinking and celebrating his life. In Japanese traditional belief, one's friends and family need to have a good time at the wake, for the spirit of the dead is still nearby. If there is too much crying and sorrow, the spirit will feel sad and not want to leave this earth. Even though Gen was Christian, we still held the wake in the traditional style. One of the social workers from the hospital set up a data projector with photographs from Gen's life. The members got up one by one to share memories of Gen.

A Japanese Funeral

Gen's funeral was held the next day in town's funeral home, one of the few businesses on Urakawa's main road other than Bethel that seemed to be prospering. Reverend Yamamoto came from Sapporo to administer the last rites over Gen's body and deliver the sermon. He was the minister responsible for the entire area, so he was familiar to all of the members, as he occasionally led the Sunday mass at the Urakawa church. The funeral home's main room was packed with people wanting to give Gen a final farewell. One of the hospital staff that knew Gen had volunteered to play his cello at his funeral, and the soft, sad tones greeted us when we entered the door. Masako played the keyboard while we sang hymnals.

After the service, Gen's friends carried his body to the waiting hearse, which took it to the city crematorium. Cremating a body takes a few hours, so we had to wait for the process to finish. The worker at the crematorium prepared his bones and ashes, breaking apart the larger ones and putting them into his urn. He took out Gen's voicebox and put it in a smaller urn. In Buddhist tradition, the voicebox (*nodo botoke*) holds the seat of the soul.

Figure 6.8 Kiyoshi speaks at Gen's funeral. Photo by the author.

Then the crematorium director asked us to help with the rest of the bones. In Buddhist funerals, the bones of the dead are passed from person to person with chopsticks before being put in the urn. This is the reason that there is a strong taboo about ever passing food directly from chopstick to chopstick in China and Japan.

In this Christian funeral, the director directed us to transfer the bones from chopsticks to a folded piece of paper before going to the urn. This was confusing to many people, but we struggled as best we could. It was difficult to see our friend reduced to this form.

Mr. and Mrs. Nakayama were given the two urns, the main one and the smaller one holding his voicebox-soul. We then all returned back to the church. The Nakayamas soon went back to Mito City, carrying their son home with them.

Visiting the Nakayamas

Several months after Gen's final departure, I took the train to the Nakayamas' home in central Japan to see Gen's parents. I stayed at their house for two nights, sleeping next to the room where Gen used to live. In the evening, we all got together in their living room. In a corner, Gen's ashes were in the urn, right underneath a portrait of him. I asked Mrs. Nakayama about Gen's childhood.[4] This is their story.

Many decades ago, when he was a young man, Gen's father had trained as a medical doctor. Stubborn and opinionated, he didn't make many friends while he was in medical school, and his adviser suggested that he go to Germany after graduation, since it was unlikely that he'd get hired in Japan. From long before the war, Germany had been seen as the center of medical expertise in Japan. As already mentioned, many classically trained Japanese doctors still write their patients charts or *karte* in German.

Taking his professor's advice, Muneharu Nakayama went to Munich. There he met a strikingly beautiful young Japanese college student who was studying music there. Chika was the daughter of a very prominent scholar of German literature. Few people knew that her father was an alcoholic and an abusive one at that. Chika had been brought up in wealth and education, as befitted her station, but without much warmth in her family. The dashing, handsome young doctor must have presented an irresistible opportunity for her to forge her own path in life.

They married a year after they returned from Munich. As Muneharu's college adviser had suspected, he had a lot of trouble holding down jobs and went through over a dozen different posts at various hospitals in the first couple of years of their married life. He invariably fought with his superiors and had to leave.

Their family life was happier. The Nakayamas' first son, Gen'ichi, was born in March of 1968. Many years later, Chika would tell me that they named him Gen'ichi because he looked like Shingen Takeda, a famous Japanese warrior. They took the *Gen* from Shingen and added *ichi* which means first, as he was their first son. Listening to our conversation, Chika's husband, Muneharu, grumbled that he remembered it a bit differently. He says that Chika's rather imperious father gave Gen'ichi his name, overriding his own desire for a different name.

The following year, Gen had a little sister, Aya. Soon after that, though, Gen'ichi's father decide that he had had enough of Japan and left for Germany again. His wife and his children followed him a few months later. They ended up spending four years in Munich, ones that they look back upon with much fondness.

Swaddled with love, Gen was just two years old when they left Japan. His mother remembers that Gen was afraid to go outside at first because he thought that the Germans, with their wild red hair and big noses, looked like Japanese *oni,* or ogres. But he loved to stare out the window and was especially excited when fire trucks rolled by. He didn't want to leave the house, so he stayed inside and drew pictures of the cars and trucks that drove by.

After a few years, Gen and his little sister found themselves with a little brother. Yoshihiko was born in 1972 in Germany. The following year, the entire family returned to Japan. Gen's dad found a job at the Saiseikai Hospital in Mito, a position that he managed to keep until he retired almost forty years later. They bought a large house in the center of town and moved in. With three children and finally some stability, the Nakayama's family life seemed perfect. They were achieving the Japanese Dream.

A good part of the Japanese Dream, though, was achieving educational success for their children. There was a lot of unspoken pressure on Gen'ichi to follow in his father's footsteps as a physician. That wasn't going to be too difficult, though, as he had shown a lot of promise in school. Quiet and hating any type of violence, Gen'ichi was a very diligent student and always got good grades.

Dreams and Realities

All of the dreams of the Nakayamas came to a crashing end in 1986. It is difficult to imagine a more horrendous year—and succeeding decade—for any family.

In February of 1986, Gen's little brother suddenly started to refuse to go to school, saying that he was terrified of it. He was 14 at the time, in middle school. Mrs. Nakayama didn't think it was the usual acting out, so she went to the hospital to ask a psychiatrist for help (her son refused to leave the house to go with her), but the matter was unresolved.

In August of 1986, the Nakayamas invited several family friends over for a luncheon at their house. They were just about to sit down to eat when they heard a loud crashing sound upstairs. They ran up to see what had happened. Gen's little sister was lying on the floor by the window with the curtains around her neck. She had tried to hang herself, but the curtain rods gave out instead. She wasn't making any sense, saying that she was afraid of something that was coming after her. The Nakayamas rushed her to a hospital. She was only seventeen, in high school. The doctors diagnosed her with schizophrenia and started her on antipsychotics.

By that time, as the oldest sibling, Gen'ichi had just finished high school. He said he wanted to go to medical school, just like his father. He had passed the entrance exam for a private medical school but his father said that they couldn't afford a private university, so Gen took a year off to attend a residential "cram school" to study for the more difficult public medical universities. In March of 1987, the Nakayamas got a phone call. Gen had come back from the university entrance exams and was found in his cram school dorm room, spinning in circles, oblivious to the world around him. Something was wrong.

The doctors that saw the children were totally at their wits' end. All three were put on antipsychotics. Aya had the worst symptoms and had to be closely monitored. Gen'ichi was slightly better—he was content to hole himself up in his room, furiously smoking cigarettes, scribbling notes, making wild drawings, and storing his urine in soda bottles.

In 1989, on the recommendation of a friend, the three siblings went to the preeminent Tsukuba University Medical Hospital for tests. There the doctors gave them an extensive battery of tests including blood tests and a test called an electromyogram, which measures muscle response. They also received painful muscle biopsies. What the doctors found surprised everyone.

The three siblings had red blood cells with strange spikes and thorns on them. In addition, one of their blood enzymes, creatine phosphokinase

(CPK), was off the charts. Normal values were between 60–400 IU/L (international units per liter), but the siblings all had CPK readings over 5,000 IU/L. And then there were their neurological symptoms, most notably psychosis (the hallucinations and delusions). The doctors gave the bad news to the Nakayamas: Their children all had a very rare genetic disease called acanthocytosis.

Acanthocytosis comes from the Greek word *acantha*, which means thorns, and it describes the signature misshapen red blood cells. The degenerative neuroacanthocytosis that was affecting all three Nakayama children was extremely rare, and there was no known cure or even known treatment for it.

With the blood CPK levels so high, doctors recommended against the use of antipsychotics. But without the antipsychotics, the three children were unmanageable. The Nakayamas found themselves in a very difficult situation.

Still, Gen seemed to be doing better. Giving up on medical school, he was admitted to Toyo University in Tokyo to study Indian philosophy. He took evening classes there and went to the Tokyo University Hospital for their psychiatric day care program. He also started going to a Christian chapel to pray. But while he was taking classes, it was hard for him to commute to Tsukuba University Hospital for his regular checkups. His condition worsened, and he had to be hospitalized again.

Gen was admitted to the psychiatric ward of a public hospital located on the outskirts of Mito City, where his parents lived. Because his CPK levels were so high, he couldn't take any antipsychotics and yet he refused to eat. The doctors at the hospital strapped him down to a gurney and forced an IV into his arm. The IV leaked, and his left arm started swelling from the fluid. His mother remembers coming into the hospital and seeing her son lying crucified like Jesus Christ to a gurney, his arm swollen beyond recognition. By the time his parents managed to discharge him (which took quite some effort), his left arm had become paralyzed.

Through the entire decade of the 1990s, all three children were repeatedly hospitalized. Feeling at her wits' end, in 2002 Mrs. Nakayama started to see a prominent family psychiatrist in Tokyo. Both Gen'ichi and his sister were living at home, and they were driving their parents up the wall. After hearing her pour out her story, the psychiatrist told Chika on her first visit, "Let's try to get Gen'ichi to leave your house by the end of the year. I think Bethel would be perfect for your family."[5]

Chika remembers thinking at the time that this was an entirely unreasonable proposition. Gen'ichi had been living in their home as a total shut-in for the previous seven years. The only time their son ever left the house was to go two hundred meters to the local convenience store and for his biweekly hospital visits. Chika had heard about Bethel through one of their books and one of their videos, but she wasn't quite sure why her new psychiatrist was so emphatic that it'd be perfect for them. In fact, her new family psychiatrist recommended Bethel so many times during their sessions that Chika started thinking about not seeing her anymore.

By coincidence, a talk was held in the area by a man who had set up a farm up north in Hokkaido to give youth from all across Japan an opportunity to work with nature. Interested in the subject, Gen'ichi went with his mom to listen to this person. But when Gen introduced himself to the speaker after the talk, the man brusquely told him that there was no use for "someone like him" at his farm. This hit Gen hard.

When Chika mentioned this incident to her psychiatrist, she said that this was an opportunity to talk to Gen about Bethel—and perhaps to go meet Dr. Kawamura. Chika shared the materials on Bethel that she had with Gen. After reading the book and watching the video intensely, he stood up and told her, "I have to go to the travel agent to buy our airplane tickets."

The Pilgrimage

Two days later, Mrs. Nakayama and her son packed their bags and went to Urakawa. They didn't know anything about Bethel except what they had read about in the book and seen in the video. They arrived on a Sunday night and walked about the town. They decided that while they were there, they might as well try to see the psychiatrist.

On Monday morning, the two walked into Dr. Kawamura's office. Their conversation ended up lasting an hour and a half.[6] Dr. Kawamura took an immediate liking to Gen and remarked that it was such a waste that a fine young man like him was whiling away his time in Mito. He should come up to Urakawa and enroll as an "exchange student at Bethel University." He'd find that he would have a lot to learn there.

Kiyoshi Hayasaka happened to be seeing the doctor that day. When Kiyoshi poked his head into the doctor's office, Gen leapt up and said, "Wow! I know you, you're famous! Can I shake your hand?!" The doctor asked Kiyoshi to show Gen and his mother around the hospital. While visiting the psychiatric day care and the inpatient ward, Gen'ichi quickly became friends with Kiyoshi and was greatly saddened when they had to return to Mito.

Mrs. Nakayama knew that at the time Dr. Kawamura rarely took new patients. Riding on the popularity of Bethel's books and the glowing television shows about Bethel, many people had moved to Urakawa in the hopes of being accepted into Bethel or at the Red Cross Hospital. But the hospital psychiatric ward was full, and so was Bethel. Some people waited for several years to get into Bethel. Dr. Kawamura said he would make an exception for Gen, but only if he really was up to the challenge. He told Gen to go back to Mito and think about it carefully.

Gen'ichi returned to Mito and thought about it for a month. He wrote to Dr. Kawamura that he had decided that this is what he wanted to do. The doctor had asked him if he wanted to do research together on Gen's problems, and Gen wrote that the thought of doing this type of research excited him. The doctor called him back and said he was welcome to come. In November of 2002, Gen'ichi flew up and checked into the Urakawa Red Cross Hospital, Ward 7.

Gen ended up being hospitalized for almost four years. During that time, he became an accomplished artist and public speaker. He was discharged in March of 2006. His little brother, Yoshihiko, was next on the hospital waiting list and was accepted the next month.

Gen'ichi lived at Station House for only fifteen more months before his death on June 30, 2007.

Four years later, Gen's little brother is still in Ward 7 of the Red Cross Hospital. His condition has improved a lot since coming to Urakawa. One of Gen's housemates at Station House is now a peer supporter and sees Yoshihiko regularly.

Gen's little sister is in a residential care facility in Mito City.

Mr. and Mrs. Nakayama are still living in their house, now very quiet, in Mito City. They still regularly go up to Urakawa to see their son. When I last talked to them, they were planning to go to Urakawa over New Year's. They were looking forward to pounding rice cakes at the New Year's festival at Dr. Kawamura's house again.

CHAPTER SEVEN

Departures

> They danced down the streets like dingledodies, and I shambled after as I've been doing all my life after people who interest me, because the only people for me are the mad ones, the ones who are mad to live, mad to talk, mad to be saved, desirous of everything at the same time, the ones that never yawn or say a commonplace thing, but burn, burn, burn like fabulous yellow roman candles exploding like spiders across the stars and in the middle you see the blue centerlight pop and everybody goes "Awww!"
>
> —JACK KEROUAC, *On the Road*

At a morning staff meeting, Eriko Itoh, one of the psychiatric social workers, commented that there had been a change in the makeup of the psychiatric patients that had been coming to Urakawa over the years. There was a decrease in schizophrenia and other psychotic disorders and an increase in personality and emotional disorders (such as borderline personality disorder and depression). She added that she thought that while schizophrenia was easy to incorporate into the Bethel system, depression and personality disorders were more difficult.

I asked her what she meant. She said people with schizophrenia could learn to accept their illness and live with themselves. But people with emotional and personality disorders had a much harder time. To illustrate the point, she mentioned a patient that she was working with. This woman had worked in a company before she lost her job and came to Urakawa. Bethel and Urakawa are famous for their seaweed packaging occupational therapy. But this woman couldn't stand working while everyone else chatted near her. And being a seaweed packager didn't fit in with her ideal image of herself. The point of the seaweed packaging at Bethel wasn't the work itself but communicating and cooperating with others, an aspect that was especially salient for people with schizophrenia who are often locked in a mental world of their own. Having people to connect with is salvation. But for people with depression (speaking from experience here), the gap between what they know they could do if they were well and where they find themselves in the present is often just more depressing.

There are several identifiable generational cohorts in the thirty-year span of the Urakawa-Bethel experiment. The first generation is the people who had grown up in Urakawa or the southeast Hokkaido area and had been hospitalized in the Red Cross Hospital for several years before encountering Mr. Mukaiyachi and Dr. Kawamura in the 1980s. This group, which includes Kiyoshi Hayasaka and Minoru Sasaki, formed the core of the first Bethel House.

The second generation consists of those people who trickled into Urakawa in the 1990s, drawn by the first series of newspaper articles and books on Bethel. Like the first generation, they also had been diagnosed with schizophrenia and, not finding the type of care they wanted on the mainland, had moved to Urakawa. Many of the young people in this generation had gone to college before becoming sick, so they brought expertise and skills with them, allowing Bethel to expand its efforts in all directions, especially in self-promotion. This group included Rika Shimizu, Kohei Yamane, and Gen'ichi Nakayama.

Starting in the 2000s, Bethel expanded to several times its original size. Television crews were regularly featuring Bethel as the cutting edge of psychiatric care and independent living in Japan. Michio Saito's *The Ability to Worry,* which discussed how Bethel gave its members back the ability to worry about things in their lives and to voice their concerns, won the prestigious 2002 Kodansha Non-Fiction Award. The same year, Bethel formally incorporated as a social welfare nonprofit, which gave it an additional revenue source for running sheltered workshops and an incentive to bring in more members. The number of books and articles on Bethel increased rapidly. By 2005, Bethel was running at full capacity at over one hundred members, with several dozen on the waiting list. Many had moved to Urakawa even though they were still on the waiting list, hoping in the meantime to absorb Bethel through osmosis just by living there. The rapid expansion of Bethel as well as the influx of new people in this third cohort (many of whom were not schizophrenic but had other emotional and personality disorders that Bethel was not used to treating) caused all sorts of growing pains for the organization.

Other Signs of Social Change

About the same time that Eriko made her comment, I walked into New Bethel and noticed that a complaint box had been put up on the wall on the first floor. A sign above it indicated that it was for anonymous complaints or suggestions. I was greatly saddened when I saw it. That anonymous complaints box represented the failure of several core principles of Bethel. Bethel itself was supposed to have been run by and for the members. People should have felt free to voice their complaints in public (or private) at any moment. The complaint box in a sense signaled that people no longer trusted the openness of the environment, that a distance had grown between the members and the organizational staff.

This was not the first sign of the growing pains that Bethel was encountering. In November of 2003, just over a year after Bethel incorporated as a nonprofit social welfare organization and moved into its new facilities at New Bethel, they were surprised by a special audit by the Hokkaido prefectural government on suspicion of accounting fraud and violating the articles of its nonprofit incorporation. According to newspaper accounts of the raid, two external members of Bethel's own board of directors had gone to the social welfare office in the town hall to file a complaint about Bethel's sloppy bookkeeping and business practices.[1]

The most serious allegation involved the purchase of office equipment costing over one million yen (approx. US$12,000). In 2002, Bethel had received a grant from a nonprofit foundation for the purchase of some computers, but the grant agency had not yet deposited the funds when the invoice for the equipment came due. In order to not be in arrears, one of the staff members paid the bill out of pocket in advance, but as the grant agency required evidence of equipment purchase *after* their funds were deposited, Bethel ending up paying the office equipment vendor *again* so that they would have a bank statement and receipt with the appropriate date. They had reached a special agreement with the vendor that the double payment would be refunded at a later date.

The special audit took four months, from November of 2003 to March of 2004. The investigation eventually cleared Bethel of the most serious charges of fraud, but it resulted in a cloud over the organization. In particular, the government required a fundamental restructuring of Bethel's business practices, especially its system of allowing its members (that is, those with psychiatric disabilities) to make fundamental business decisions rather than giving those responsibilities to the governing board of directors or to a chief executive officer. The two whistleblowers on the board resigned, as did two other board members.

I asked Mr. Mukaiyachi about this incident. Now, with several years of distance from the event, he felt that most of it was caused by the lack of experience on the part of the Bethel staff and members in running a nonprofit corporation. In the early days of Bethel, the members had a much larger role in the running the organization. There were only three volunteer staff then—Mr. and Mrs. Mukaiyachi and Mrs. Miyajima—and none of them were engaged full-time in Bethel, which was much more like a clubhouse than a company. Money was very tight then, and they had to scramble to make ends meet. They were used to robbing Peter to pay Paul, to borrow a Christian phrase.

After they incorporated, they were able to file for grants and contracts from the prefectural government and other nonprofits to run workshops and training programs, but they were not used to the accounting procedures that these grants required. In addition, Mr. Mukaiyachi felt that the special auditors were taken aback when they came to Bethel and found out that the president of Bethel, Minoru Sasaki, and many of the staff and board members, including Kiyoshi Hayasaka, were people with psychiatric disabilities. Bethel's lack of hierarchy and unclear channels of decision-making responsibility were also frustrating. Mr. Mukaiyachi felt that all of this had resulted in alarm and suspicion on the part of the government auditors.

The effect of the audit and the resulting administrative guidance was to normalize not only Bethel's accounting practices but also its most fundamental operations. Bureaucratization started to creep in. While it was still true that any member could take over any other member's job in seaweed production and that many of events were run cooperatively, the government required the hiring of specialized staff positions for accounting and management that were opaque to the members. Bethel House became Bethel, Inc.

While walking around the office, I noticed a pile of large books stacked in the corner, each several inches thick. I took one down. It was titled *An Easy-to-Understand Index to Health Insurance Laws*. It was 1,700 pages of very fine print. Piled on top of that book were other equally thick books with similarly thrilling titles such as *A Guidebook to Accounting Classifications Based on Type of Business (Vols. 1 and 2)* and *Social Welfare Insurance—Application Guide with Examples*. The accounting guidebooks were 2,400 pages long; the social welfare insurance guide was just under 1,900 pages. It takes a special type of mind to read these.

The losers in the growing specialization of jobs were the member-staff.[2] Bethel had always had members (that is, those with diagnosed psychiatric disabilities) in their staff ranks in the administrative office as well as the caretakers for the group homes and so on. In the early years, the member-staff were the core of the organization, with Mr. Mukaiyachi, Mrs. Miyajima, and others serving as catalysts. But after Bethel incorporated, it hired several able-bodied staff, and Mrs. Mukaiyachi became the de facto office manager. New government regulations required that certain posts be held by people with particular qualifications—requirements that made it harder to keep member-staff in positions of responsibility. In addition, it has become increasingly difficult for member-staff to keep up with the growing workload, and they find their positions being replaced by able-bodied staff. While Bethel has portrayed itself as a "workplace where you can goof off," this is now only true of the sheltered workshops.

An Unintentional Intentional Community

> From the moment a utopian community is founded, its members face the question of what to do about the rest of the world. Most utopian groups seem more eager to reform that world than to resign from it, even when they flee to hinterlands where its importunings are weakest. So, short of losing themselves in Space, they must find ways to regularize or "routinize" their dealings with the rest of humanity, especially that portion of it close at hand. Since a utopian community typically is small and weak, it must actively adapt to the present norms and institutions of the ambient great society. But it must do so in ways that are at the same time consonant with the community self-image. This is the double burden of adaptive tactics.
>
> —David W. Plath[3]

Intentional communities are groups of people who live and work together in shared residential or communal facilities with common goals, agendas, and concerns.[4] There is usually a strong emphasis on sociality and horizontal social relations and networks. Communes and kibbutzim are two well-known forms of intentional communities, but the broad definition also includes some forms of coops, ecovillages, and group homes. There often is a conscious and shared intent to create a better—if not utopian—community and society.[5]

Intentional communities based on utopian ideals often run into difficulties as they age (Kanter 1972; Bouvard 1975). The initial group of committed members gives way to a larger group of newcomers with different backgrounds, goals, and dreams. The expansion of the community leads to growing bureaucratization and specialization of roles. Multiple centers of power and schisms develop. The original core principles get lost or twisted.

Bethel started off as an unintentional intentional community. Its original goals were simply to provide a place where former psychiatric patients from the Red Cross hospital could live and work in the community. Unlike many other intentional communities that start from a core set of principles or central philosophies, Bethel developed these only after several years of growth, and they still remain very much in flux.

What is remarkable that although it has lost some of its idealistic qualities as it has grown larger, it is not a failed experiment by any means. Bethel, Inc., is successful financially and is not at risk of fiscal implosion. The mechanism for complaints has become bureaucratized, but the grousing has not reached a fever pitch. And still, more than anywhere else in Japan, the town of Urakawa has to be one of the least restrictive environments for people with psychiatric disabilities. The very existence of Bethel shows that people with even severe symptoms of schizophrenia and other mental illnesses can live in the community and do not have to be permanently institutionalized.

To a great degree, Bethel has stayed together up to now because of three charismatic men: Kiyoshi Hayasaka, Ikuyoshi Mukaiyachi, and Dr. Kawamura. But where Kiyoshi was much more visible and active in a small community of twenty members, he now faces a Bethel where he doesn't always know all of the new people. And Ikuyoshi Mukaiyachi, the social worker at the center of Bethel, is also being torn in different directions. His full-time teaching position at the Health Sciences University of Hokkaido means a grueling commute each week, and he is also constantly being requested for consultations at facilities across Japan. Somehow, he manages to publish a book or two on Bethel every year, but the search for new topics and new subjects has him scrambling. I doubt that he can continue to maintain this pace.

Like many intentional communities, Mr. Mukaiyachi's family has also been pulled into the business. His wife, who was formerly a nurse at the hospital, is now the de facto office manager of Bethel. Their son runs the communications and publications branch in Tokyo. Mr. Mukaiyachi and his wife also own two of Bethel's residential facilities—their former house, which is now a shared residential facility, and the small apartment units attached to their new home. The extent to which Bethel, Inc., has become Mukaiyachi, Inc., has brought some criticism from patients and family members, although it's difficult for me to parse the degree to which this is the usual grumbling that one would find in any large institution. Still, the old Bethel by virtue of its small size and strong interpersonal connections would likely have developed more personal mechanisms for defusing these criticisms.

There are also growing complaints at Bethel's work units. Sheltered workshops and other make-work facilities at institutions for people with disabilities are not themselves novel. What made Bethel unique was that *profit* was a central motivator for those that were participating and that *control* was decentralized. In capitalist terms, profit-sharing was a core goal and, in Marxist terms, the members were not alienated from the products they were making. But rules established by the new Bethel have alienated people from their products of their labor. A good part of this is the growing bureaucratization and rationalization that came in the aftermath of the audit, meaning workers were paid more transparently, by the hour. As the seaweed production was organized under the rubric of sheltered workshops, the hourly wage was the paltry ¥220 (US$2) per hour stipulated by social welfare regulations.

Unwittingly, Bethel's growth has been the cause of many of Bethel's problems. Here, the organization seems divided on what to do. On one hand, it has capped the number of sheltered workshops to two, which limits the membership to a hundred people (fifty in each workshop, per government rules).[6] But at the same time, Bethel has been aggressively purchasing real estate as it becomes available in Urakawa. A larger Bethel will only become more bureaucratic and risks becoming a total institution as it controls all aspects of the members' lives.

At the same time that Bethel is becoming more like other places in Japan, other places in Japan are becoming more like Bethel. Various group homes, sheltered workshops, and independent living support centers are springing up for people with psychiatric disabilities, many with very progressive leaders and full community participation. Some have been inspired by Bethel's principles, but others developed on their own. While Bethel will perhaps remain the poster child for community-based psychiatric care in Japan, there are now alternatives to traveling to the remotest edge of northern Japan.

A Japanese Community

I'm often asked if there are any elements of Bethel that are uniquely Japanese. My response is that Bethel is very much focused on the social aspects of recovery in the context of mental health. While there has been much discussion of independent living for people with disabilities, the reality is that all of us (disabled or not) are social beings, and no one can live without other people. The relentless group meetings, house meetings, and social skills workshops all work toward helping members recover their ability to live and work together.

Almost every aspect of Bethel focuses on the social—indeed, far from shying away from the problems of sociality, it welcomes them as a fundamental part of being humans in society. Because the notion of independence is very much a core principal in the West, many readers might see the importance of recovering sociality as evidence of Bethel's embeddedness in Japanese society. Like many at Bethel, I don't view independence and sociality as oppositional terms. In order to be a full social being, you have to come to terms with your own needs and desires and balance those against the needs and desires of others. True independence isn't possible without this balance.

Much of Bethel exists in communal memory as well as social relations. Bethel encourages the development of myths and stories. Events such as the Hallucinations and Delusions Grand Prix help solidify these within the communal memory. A weekly comic strip, *Papipupepo,* put out by Bethel depicts the escapades of the members visually. Even the mind-numbingly boring daily recitals of reports and sales data at the morning meetings help develop the transactive memory of social science—a shared memory and skill bank that allows individual members to work (and goof off) more freely, knowing that everyone knows what is going on, such that no single member is critical and thus irreplaceable. Each person gives as much time as they can; from each according to his ability, to each according to his needs.

The Hotel California

One of the reasons the Urakawa-Bethel model is successful is that it covers all of the stages of a person who makes significant progress grappling with a severe mental illness. The hospital can seamlessly discharge a patient into a full-service Bethel group home. Then, when he or she is better, that person can move into a Bethel shared living facility and work in a Bethel workshop or store. If the patient gets worse, he or she can easily move back into the hospital for a shorter or longer stay. This takes away much of the anxiety that usually accompanies hospital intakes and discharges for people with severe mental illnesses. But to some readers, the all-encompassing nature of Bethel can seem troubling.

As Mr. Mukaiyachi noted in chapter 4, the point of Bethel is not to get better. The goal is not to be "cured" and to return back to a job at a Japanese company on the mainland. I personally have had a hard time myself struggling with the idea that one doesn't leave Bethel. One can be an alcoholic but, through a 12-step program, recover one's life and career. The members at Bethel left their old lives and dreams when they came to Urakawa and are being told that they need to accept a new life with more limited possibilities. This may in fact be realistic pessimism but it is also depressing.

It is here that Bethel is different from all of the other community-based living facilities for people with mental illness that I saw on the mainland. The ultimate goal of Yadokari no Sato (the home for hermit crabs) and other programs is that people learn how to return to their own communities, not create an entirely new one separate from the world.

Bethel works in large part because the town of Urakawa is in the middle of nowhere; the only ways out are by car (which few people have), by (expensive) train, or by (expensive) bus. There are few things to do in Urakawa except for Bethel itself. Some Americans, after hearing about Bethel, have asked me if being in Urakawa was like the Eagles' "Hotel California," where "you can check out any time you like, but you can never leave."

I raised this question with several Bethel members, and their response was fairly uniform—why would they want to return to a society and social/familial conditions that made them ill in the first place? For them, Bethel allows them to live their lives happily. Perhaps a life without high aspiration, perhaps a life in slow descent, but at least they had a life worth living.

When Gen Nakayama died, many of my friends at Bethel told me that his was a life and death worth emulating. He died doing what he loved and doing something that was socially valued. He died surrounded by his friends and people who understood him. Gen's mother said it was fortunate that he died in Urakawa because if he had died at their home on the mainland, the only people who would have gone to the funeral would be family relatives who felt obligated to go. In Urakawa, he died with his friends. Rika and other Bethel members have told me that they expect to die in Urakawa too. Bethel itself plans on buying a joint funeral plot for its members, since so many are disconnected from their families and want to spend their afterlife with their friends instead.

Furthermore, it's not the case that people never leave Urakawa. People regularly leave for short visits back home or on the lecture circuits for Bethel. So they know what life is like back home or on the outside, and they choose not to participate in it. For example, Kohei Yamane, the engineer who wanted to meet the UFOs, left Bethel and worked for several years on disability issues in Tokyo at the National Rehabilitation Center for Persons with Disabilities. He came back in 2007 to run some earthquake evacuation drills, since Urakawa was chosen as a model community. All of the Bethel members, even the ones with the most serious conditions, were able to evacuate successfully to the top of the bluff overlooking the town in the allocated fifteen minutes.

On March 11, 2011, that training came in very handy when the Fukushima earthquake happened. The evacuation wasn't as orderly as the drills—some people forgot their meds—but everyone made it up to the top of the bluff unharmed. The tsunami had lost most of its force by the time it reached Urakawa, but it still managed to damage some buildings and boats in the low-lying areas of town.

In addition to Kohei, there are some other members who have left Bethel to return to their lives or begin new ones. When I talk about these people with the members who have stayed, they don't seem to regard them with any jealousy, just sadness that these people are no longer in the community. There was also a quiet confidence that these people would return. In fact, I was dismayed to learn that in 2011, Kohei indeed planned to move back to Bethel to resume life there.

Bethel is far from the types of "total institutions" such as prisons and mental hospitals that sociologist Erving Goffman described back in 1961. While Bethel does provide housing, food, and jobs for its members, they are all optional. Bethel does not tell you when to wake up, you can decide what to eat and wear, you don't have to go to your job if you want to, and you only have to work as much as you want, and you can pretty much do whatever you want with your life. One of Bethel's core principles that remains is that of non-support (*hienjo*)—"help" is never pushed onto people who don't want it. In this way, Bethel has resonance to the spirit of the first half of that last line from "Hotel California": "You can check out any time you like."

Paradise Lost, Paradise Found

Is it an American tendency to distrust utopias? Certainly, the history of the United States is scattered with the remains of failed intentional communities: the Oneidas, the Shakers, and Jamestown scar our communal memory.

When is a utopia actually a dystopia? Perhaps that is entirely a moral rather than an objective distinction. There were many times when I felt that Bethel had many similarities with religious cults. It had charismatic leaders, a strong belief system, and an emphasis on a tight-knit community life. Unlike in a cult, though, everyone was free to do whatever he or she wanted.

I remember sitting in New Bethel one day when a member came in, distraught. She was homesick and missed her teenage daughter, who was staying with her parents on the mainland. She went to the Bethel accountant, withdrew all her funds from her account, and left in a taxicab. No one tried to stop her, although someone there did ask her, just once, if this was what she really wanted to do. Fundamentally, Bethel believes that people are in control of their own lives and that they should be allowed to make their own decisions so that they can own both their mistakes and successes.

Even if there are some negatives to life in Bethel, it is important to balance this against the reality that life outside of Bethel is much worse for most people with severe mental illnesses. Whether it is in the United States or Japan (the two countries in which I have spent the most time), people with schizophrenia face discrimination, forced institutionalization, forced medication, and social ostracization.

The woman who went to the mainland came back to Bethel a couple of weeks later. Her teenage daughter was much happier living with her grandparents and didn't want her mother in her life. Her family did not want her around either, so she sadly decided to go back to Urakawa.

The feeling of despair that no one understands is perhaps the worst pain for people with severe mental illnesses. With very few options available outside of long-term institutionalization, some have suggested that the creation of "enclave communities" such as Bethel may be the best route for social inclusion (Mandiberg 1993, 2010).

Bethel provides a sense of community, belonging, and sanctuary for its members. For many, it provides the only alternative to long-term institutional living. Furthermore, because Bethel has a good working relationship with the hospital, the town, the schools, local landlords, and local employers, Bethel members are able to get help for any number of possible scenarios that would otherwise disrupt an attempt at independent living. While the pay is meager at Bethel and many make do with social welfare checks, many have a good amount saved up for a rainy day and therefore no longer have to fear for their futures. They know that when the end comes—and given the life-shortening effects that mental illness and psychotropic medications have on the body, it will come relatively soon—that they will die among friends.

CHAPTER EIGHT

Beyond Bethel: A Postscript

I finished the major fieldwork for this book in 2008 but kept in contact with my friends at Bethel. Over the past years, life seemed to continue as normal in Urakawa: some of my friends got better, some got sicker, some people got discharged from the hospital, others went back in. Some people left Bethel to see if they could live on their own; others went back to their families. Some of these were temporary departures, others were permanent. New members came to the Holy Land of Urakawa to replenish their numbers, while Mr. Mukaiyachi continued to scout the country for new talent to bring to Bethel.

In November of 2010, Rika sent me a sad message by e-mail. Tsutomu Shimono, my friend the guitar player, was found dead on Urakawa's seashore. He had a habit of walking along the seawall at night when he was drunk, and most people think that he either slipped or was swallowed up by a wave. He had just turned 41 and had appeared on a popular television show *Connecting Hearts* a few weeks before his death. He was given his final farewell at the Urakawa funeral home surrounded by his friends. I was deeply saddened by the news and struck again by how precious life was at Bethel.

In 2012, I returned to Bethel to talk with its members about this book. I wanted to obtain permission again from everyone who was mentioned by name as well as get permission for the photographs that are used. I stayed at Sunshine House with Rika and her housemates. We had pizza and talked late into the night. It was like old times again.

Figure 8.1 Mana Mukaiyachi, Masako Yoshino, Mikio Honda, Tsutomu Shimono, and Rika Shimizu on the set of the television show *Connecting Hearts*, September 27, 2010. Tsutomu died just a few weeks later. Photo by Ikuyoshi Mukaiyachi.

While I was in Urakawa, I went to see Dr. Kawamura at the hospital. I was surprised to see major construction being done on the Red Cross hospital and had difficulty finding the entrance to the building that I once knew so well. Dr. Kawamura sat down with me, and I asked him about where he saw Bethel and Urakawa going. The doctor noted that he had just turned 62 and that he had been thinking a lot about his retirement in a few years.

The hospital had finally gotten the funds to rebuild after the disastrous 2003 earthquake had destroyed one of its wings. The 2011 earthquake in Fukushima also prompted concerns that the old building was no longer safe. The new hospital would be a modern high-rise structure rather than the squat ferroconcrete design of its predecessor.

Dr. Kawamura noted that when he was asked for input in the design of the new building, he suggested that they consider closing the psychiatric inpatient ward altogether. He wasn't sure who was going to replace him when he retired, and he was worried that the new chief of psychiatry might want a return to the warehousing days of years past.

I mentioned that when I read some of the older books about Bethel or watch the early videos that they made, the doctor was much more of a presence in the Bethel community than he is now. Was this deliberate? Dr. Kawamura nodded his head and responded:[1]

> I noticed that if a doctor is present [at an event], everyone places some kind of expectation on him. It's the same thing that needs to happen when children leave the home and become independent of their parents. In some ways, they [my patients] still want to be like children . . . or, how to put it . . . they want to make all of the difficulties that they are going through someone else's responsibility. There is still a childish quality there. So if I were to respond to those expectations, it would only help to sustain that sort of immature relationship. So I consciously pulled myself back a bit from the community.
>
> I have to say that the ability of the members [to cope with issues] has increased over the years, so I think the expectation and need to rely on medical care [psychiatry] has really gone down compared to the old days. In the past, there was too much that was entrusted to the hospital and to the medical care, to the point where people would say things like, "I don't feel anything emotionally" or "I can't even feel despair."
>
> The members here have really matured and become smarter. So I think that the role that the hospital and medical care has to play has in turn grown smaller. I wonder how much smaller still it can go.
>
> After I retire, I don't know what kind of doctor will come to Urakawa to replace me and what type of role they might want. I do know that it would be impossible for them to duplicate the same type of thing that I have been doing for thirty years. To help them, I want to continue to reduce the role that medical care is playing within the community.
>
> If I don't, I think potential new doctors won't want to come here. There are both positive and negative aspects to the fact that I've been such a large presence here for the past thirty years. Whoever replaces me will need to take several years in order to effect any change. In order to support whoever is replacing me, I need to gradually fade away in the background.

I also asked Dr. Kawamura about all the changes I had noticed at Bethel over the years. The various workgroups were starting to look and sound more and more like some of the sheltered workshops that I had seen on the mainland. There was much less laughter and conversation than in the old days. Dr. Kawamura responded:

> To be honest, to use the label "Bethel" to talk about. . . .

[He stopped for a moment and then continued.]

> I've been here for thirty years now. There was "Bethel" then and there is "Bethel" now. In the past, I had spare time, and we all wanted to try new things. Most importantly, we laughed at all of the mistakes we were making. Everything was fresh and new to us, and we were always rolling on the floor with laughter. When people would bring stories about their mistakes to share with others in spaces of conversation[2], we would all feel that these were crucial new experiences.
>
> There was a freshness to all of it back then. These days, they are still using the same forms[3], they are still using the same language of Bethel, but I feel that there is a lot of slipperiness to those words. They are just superficial, without any depth.
>
> These days, the members, the staff, and the families of those involved have all become really good at using the right words, [but they have forgotten that] the most important thing is laughter, being filled with humor, and a certain degree of being able to let things go.
>
> In the old days, having a sense of humor was essential for just being to move forward day by day. How else were we going to deal with the realities we faced? The only way we knew was to turn these things into things we could laugh about. And it was in that space that courage was able to grow.
>
> Right now there are so many new programs and benefits that there are alternatives to laughter. The necessity for humor has changed. But I think that one day there will be a need for everyone to once again contemplate what "Bethel-like" [*Beteru rashisa*] means as well as what "Bethel" itself means.
>
> We're at a critical step right now. It's now been thirty years since we began this initiative. I think it's inevitable that in any enterprise, a time comes when you become exhausted and lose the substance that defines who you were. I think that if the older members—those who knew who we were at the beginning—can teach the younger members, then we can recover important components of our being as well as our sense of humor.

On the day that I left Urakawa, Mr. Mukaiyachi offered to drive me to Sapporo, as the Hidaka Main Line had closed down because of a snowstorm. Along the way, I asked Mr. Mukaiyachi if he ever regretted Bethel's incorporation as a nonprofit, which seemed to have marked its normalization to government rules. He thought over this a bit. In many ways, Mr. Mukaiyachi responded, it was better when there were no funded programs, and they could do things their own way. But what was most important wasn't Bethel itself but Bethel's principles, and because of Bethel's success, their principles were making it out to broader society. In several years or decades, Bethel might no longer exist as a physical entity, but its ideas will keep going on.

Bethel has certainly changed. I'm not talking about its transformation through bureaucratization in the past decade, but rather that it has become something bigger than just the small community in Urakawa that sits next to a Red Cross hospital. It is has become more than just the members and staff. It is more than the books that they write, the lectures that they give, and the seaweed that they package. It is more than the members, their parents, their relatives, and the supporters in towns across Japan who voraciously study Bethel's principles. It is more than the psychiatrists and social workers who join other pilgrims and psycho-tourists to travel to Bethel or who watch it from afar.

Bethel, Inc., itself is at a critical stage in its thirty years of existence and will need to recreate itself or perhaps perish. But to paraphrase Mr. Mukaiyachi, the soul of Bethel has grown to become much richer than they could have ever thought possible and will continue to exist well past the death of its tangible body.

In anthropological terms, Bethel is a field of practices and a field of discourse and imagination. By becoming part of the growing dialogue and debate about Bethel, this book and the films I made are now part of Bethel, and by reading this book and watching the film, you as the reader/viewer have also been drawn into the Bethel community.

Welcome to Bethel.

♪ Welcome to Bethel, everybody! (PAPAYA)
♪ We're the face of Bethel, how are you?
♪ Whatever you learn here, please don't be surprised.
♪ Isn't mental illness terrible? (PAPAYA)
♪ It's our gift from God.
♪ Even if we're different from normal people,
♪ We're all first-class sickos.
Thank you very much!

Notes

A Note on Language

1. For instance, the controversy over Alan Gribben's revisions to *The Adventures of Huckleberry Finn* in which the word *nigger* is replaced with *slave.* Michiko Kakutani, "Light Out, Huck, They Still Want to Sivilize You," *New York Times,* January 6, 2011, C1.

Chapter 1

1. This was in stark contrast to the independent living centers for people with physical disabilities, which were extremely politically active at the time.
2. Westerners tend to think futons as only the mattresses you sleep on, but in Japanese *futon* refers to mattresses, heavy comforters, and quilts.
3. The *-chan* honorific is similar to *-san* (Asami-san, Asami-chan), but is used to show affection or when referring to someone younger and female.
4. The number of Bethel members varies depending on what is being discussed. The number of registered Bethel members who are working at Bethel sheltered workshops, in their group homes, or receiving benefits is a little less than a hundred. The greater Bethel community of people who go to Bethel events, which includes people in the hospital and those living in town in private residences, is over a hundred and fifty.
5. Walter Edwards (1989), writing about the ideal role of husbands and wives in Japanese marriages.
6. This is not to say that it is impossible to create ethnographic films that are historically deep, rich in social context, or analytically complex, just that it is very difficult to do all three of these within the confines of a single 40-minute piece and still remain accessible to lay viewers. Similarly, polyvocality, juxtaposition, and montage are certainly available to ethnographic writers, although they are much more difficult to achieve in text than a visual medium.

Memory and Catharsis

1. Junko Kitanaka (2012) noticed similar types of interactions between patients suffering from depression and their psychiatrists.

2. In Japan, there is no legal concept of joint custody after divorce. One parent or the other has full legal custody, although some parents may continue to share parental duties. In Kiyoshi's case, his father disappeared from his life entirely after the divorce.

3. Menko is a game played with stiff cards, the object of which is to slap down the cards so that the opponent's cards flip over or are pushed out of a ring. Children in the West used to do this with cardboard milk tops.

4. Kiyoshi used the word *hisuteri-hossa* (hysterical attack), but a contemporary American psychiatrist would most probably use the terms such as a disassociative or conversion episode. The American Psychiatric Association in 1980 changed the name of the diagnosis of "hysteria" to "conversion disorder," but the international ICD-10 (F-44) retains the term, as not all countries (including Japan) associate hysteria specifically with women.

5. Middle school (ninth grade) is the last year of compulsory education in Japan. Kiyoshi did not have the grades, the inclination, or the money to continue on to high school.

6. About US$2 an hour. Like many other countries, Japan gives sheltered workshops for the disabled an exemption from minimum wage laws.

7. The average exchange rate between the Japanese yen and the U.S. dollar in 2005–2006 was about ¥115 yen to the dollar.

Chapter 2

1. For example, Lewis et al. (1992) found that the incidence of schizophrenia was 1.65 times higher in urban populations than rural populations, even with adjustments for various demographic factors and social stressors. Another study by McGrath et al. (2008) found similar data with urban residents having higher rates than their rural counterparts, also noting that migrants were more likely to have schizophrenia than native-born residents.

2. Jonathan Metzl's fascinating works on depression (2003) and schizophrenia (2009) are particularly good examples of the social constructionist perspective.

3. The writings of Thomas Szasz (1963, 1970, 1978) are a good example of a radical humanist approach to psychiatry.

4. Eguchi (1991) has a wonderful article on fox possession and mental illness. Japanese folklorist Kunio Yanagita's (1910) *Tōno Monogatari* is a wonderful source of these legends, many of which have made their way into popular culture through manga and anime artists such as Shigeru Mizuki and Hayao Miyazaki.

5. According to the translator, William Naff, Hanzo is modeled after Shimazaki's own father. Shimazaki (1987), xxv.

6. There is a striking similarity in the treatment of people with mental illness in Europe in the early nineteenth century. Edward Shorter (1997) cites a description of home treatment in 1817: "There is nothing so shocking as madness in the cabin of the Irish peasant. . . . When a strong man or woman gets the complaint, the only way they have to manage is by making a hole in the floor of the cabin, not high enough for the person to stand up in, with a crib over it to prevent his getting up. This hole is about five feet deep, and they give this wretched being his food there, and there he generally dies."

7. It was preceded two years earlier in 1871 by a medical affairs bureau (*imukyoku*) in the Japanese Imperial Army.

8. Insanity was defined as "depression, lack of emotion, confused speech, laughing without reason, eyes that stare without movement, etc. Lunacy is defined as agitation, anger and abuse, or excitement and alarm" (Iwanami 2009, 60).

9. Mental Patient Custody Act [*Seishin Byōsha Kango Hō*] of 1900 (Meiji 33).

10. The term for confinement and protection (監護 *kango*) is a homonym for nursing (看護 *kango*), leading some to quip that psychiatric nursing (*seishinkango*) is still just psychiatric confinement and protection with different Kanji characters.

11. Home confinement or *shitaku kanchi*. The bird cages were *torikago*.

12. Hashimoto (2008) and Matsumura (2004) have addressed the efforts of Kure Shuzo and others to bring early modern Japanese psychiatry up to Western standards.

13. Sugamo Hospital in Tokyo was perhaps the largest of the public facilities, with four hundred beds in 1919 (Yamada 2004, 27). This was roughly comparable to the number at Bedlam Hospital in London in the mid-nineteenth century. Neither Sugamo nor Bedlam were close to the same scale as Pilgrim State Hospital on Long Island, New York, which, at its peak in 1954, housed 13,875 psychiatric patients (OMH-NY 2011).

14. David Reynold (1976, 1980) are good introductions to these methods. Chikako Ozawa de Silva has also written on Naikan extensively, having gone through the training herself.

15. The Mental Hygiene Law [*Seishin Eisei Hō*] of 1950, Public Law 123. Full text available at http://hourei.hounavi.jp/seitei/hou/S25/S25HO123.php, accessed September 26, 2011.

16. A 1954 revision removed addictions to stimulants and opiates.

17. The mental health consultation centers are known as *seishin eisei sōdanjo*.

18. In 2006, the law was revised with the introduction of the Services and Supports for Persons with Disabilities Act (*Shōgaisha Jiritsu Shien Hō*). The copay for medical services was raised to 10%, and it became difficult to apply for and receive coverage. As most Bethel members were on the social welfare, which also guaranteed medical services, they were not significantly affected by the new law.

19. The guardians are known as the *hogogimusha* and are defined in Article 20.

20. Protective hospitalization is known as *sochi nyūin*.

21. It was shared 50/50 between the prefectural and national government.

22. From MHLW (1956) Welfare Whitebook [*Kōsei Hakusho*], Chapter II Section III Subsection II.

23. From MHLW (1964) and MHLW (1965).

24. In Japanese, the agency is called the *Iryō Kinyū Kōko*. I am indebted to Kazuo Okuma for introducing me to this idea at a talk given in Saitama on September 10, 2011. Early data on the *Iryō Kinyū Kōko's* funding can be found at MHLW (1961).

25. From MHLW (1966).

26. From MHLW (1966). An earlier 1960 report put the number requiring beds at 430,000 based on 1.3 million people with mental illness and 33.9% requiring institutionalization (MHLW 1960).

27. The title of his book was *An Explosive Psychiatrist: A Challenge to the Breakdown of the Health Care System*.

28. The United States beat both countries by more than thirty years. Connecticut was the first with a law in 1896 forbidding the marriage of "epileptic, imbecile, or feeble-minded" (*JAMA* 1896). Indiana called for the compulsory sterilization of unfits in 1906, the first of many states to do so.

29. This was in the 1940 Eugenics Law for National Citizens (*Kokumin Yūsei Hō*), Public Law 107.

30. Citing Matsubara (1998), Kitanaka notes that sterilization of the mentally ill was not actively pursued because of the lack of institutional facilities for it during the war (2012, 53n14).

31. It should be noted that the Japanese nation was still under Allied occupation when this law was passed. Kimura (1991, 158) notes that the Allied General Headquarters supported this measure, which they saw as an important tool for controlling the postwar population. Controversially, this law existed on the books until 1996, when it was replaced with the Motherhood Protection Act.

32. Eugenic abortion itself was apparently very rare. A 1953 study showed that only 0.4% of abortions in the sample were for "eugenic reasons," with the vast majority (80%) for economic reasons (Burch 1955, 146). Of course, women may not have given the true

reason for the abortions, especially given the stigma surrounding any of the conditions which would have lead them to choose a eugenic abortion.

33. The full text of the Clark report can be found at www.max.hi-ho.ne.jp/nvcc/CK5a.HTM, accessed September 26, 2011.

34. There was an antipsychiatry movement associated with leftist student movements that raged for almost thirty years from the 1950s to the 1980s at public medical universities and their associated university hospitals (see Kitanaka 2012), but the movement did not broaden to significantly affect the majority of private psychiatric hospitals where the vast majority of inpatient care is performed.

35. Metzl (2009) is required reading for understanding the transformation of psychiatric institutions in the 1950s and 1960s.

36. Okuma Kazuo talk in Saitama on September 10, 2011. See also www15.big.or.jp/˜frenz/tada.html, accessed September 17, 2012.

37. Apparently not satisfied with psychiatric patients, the Hotokukai hospital group branched out into elder care and in 2002 succeeded in killing eight senior citizens in a single summer through *E. coli* food poisoning. "Eighth E. Coli Death Linked to Medical Complex," *Japan Times*, August 19, 2002.

38. This statement was presented in the findings before the National Diet on June 25, 1984, available at http://kokkai.ndl.go.jp/SENTAKU/sangiin/101/1410/10106251410009a.html, accessed September 17, 2012.

39. This last item usually raises some eyebrows in the West, since epilepsy isn't usually considered a psychiatric disorder but a neurological condition.

40. This gap can be explained by the fact that most public hospitals are integrated hospitals with psychiatric wards, whereas private psychiatric hospitals tend to be specialized in just that field.

41. For data from the government-run WAM net, see www.wam.go.jp/wamappl/bb15GS60.nsf/vAdmPBigcategory50/A3DBD0DA84EF4179492576E0001BAB4B?OpenDocument, accessed September 25, 2011. On the predominance of psychiatrist-directors as head of private mental hospitals, see also Ito and Sederer (2009).

42. Cf. Japanese data from Heisei 19 (2007) Ministry of Health, Labor, and Welfare Medical Facilities Study, available at www.mhlw.go.jp/toukei/saikin/hw/iryosd/07/kekka03.html, accessed September 17, 2012.

There is also considerable regional variation in hospital stay lengths. See www.tonashiba.com/ranking/pref_health/medicalcare_p/15030035, accessed September 17, 2012.

43. U.S. data from the CDC National Health Statistics Report No. 29, October 26, 2010, available at www.cdc.gov/nchs/data/nhsr/nhsr029.pdf, accessed September 17, 2012.

44. From OECD.Stat Extracts—Health Care Utilization—Mental and Behavioral Disorders. Available at http://stats.oecd.org/index.aspx?DataSetCode=HEALTH_STAT, accessed September 25, 2011.

45. Sim et al. (2004). This is compared with 496 days in Korea, 554 in Hong Kong, and 816 in Singapore.

46. On efforts to pressure hospitals to limit hospitalizations to less than 90 days by revising rules for payment, see Ito and Sederer 1999, 213.

47. Data available at http://www8.cao.go.jp/shougai/data/data_h22/zuhyo56.html, accessed September 25, 2011.

48. Glaze and James (2006) points out that, according to the U.S. Bureau of Justice Statistics, a quarter of American jail and prison inmates have a mental health problem. Furthermore, Scott (1993) notes that 30%–50% of British homeless had significant mental illness.

49. REAP data cited in Sim et al. (2009). In an earlier study, Sim found that patients in Japan were more heavily medicated, with a full third (36.5%) of the sample receiving a clinical level of high-dose antipsychotics. This was in comparison with 3.7% in Hong Kong, 3.9% in China, and 20% in Korea. Shinfuku and Tan (2008) found that Japan had the highest dosing of antipsychotics of all the comparison countries (Asia).

If you were a patient in Japan, you were much more likely to be prescribed more than three types of antipsychotics (41.3%) at the same time, usually a cocktail of atypical and anticholinergic drugs—first- and second-generation antipsychotics (Shinfuku and Tan 2008). This was unlike Hong Kong where no one (0%) received more than three prescriptions, China only 1% of patients, Taiwan 1.6%, and Singapore 14.3%.

50. See Rijcken 2003. An earlier study by the U.S. Department of Health and Human Services Schizophrenia Patient Outcomes Research Team (PORT) showed that acute patients should receive between 300–1000 mg CPZ equivalent doses and maintenance patients 300–600 mg CPZ. See www.ahrq.gov/clinic/schzrec.htm, accessed September 25, 2011.

51. Kitanaka (2003) has a fascinating discussion of the early introduction of psychoanalysis to Japan in the 1910s.

52. The Japanese legal tradition relies heavily on the confession in prosecution of crimes, but I am not aware of any scholarship that addresses the broader social impact of this type of confession. I would argue that there is a critical difference between the confession of a crime in Japan and the confession of a criminal or sinner that Foucault talks about in his works, which he links to Christian religious tradition and thought. In the latter, it is the articulation of an identity rather than of an action—a key theme in his work on sexuality vis-à-vis the shift from sodomy to sodomite.

53. See www8.cao.go.jp/shougai/data/data_h22/zuhyo24.html, accessed September 25, 2011.

54. See www8.cao.go.jp/shougai/data/data_h22/zuhyo43.html, accessed September 25, 2011.

55. See www8.cao.go.jp/shougai/data/data_h22/zuhyo54.html, accessed September 25, 2011.

Coming of Age in Japan

1. Full disclosure: Although my grandfather was a Methodist minister in the United Church of Christ in Japan, my father and mother did not baptize their children or raise us as Christians. In acts of rebellion, my sister subsequently joined the Eastern Orthodox Church while my brother became a Quaker. I received a catechism in the Catholic Church in middle school and was almost baptized before my parents found out and vetoed it. I find myself still drawn to Christian beliefs and rituals and occasionally go to services, but as I was not baptized, I do not identify as Christian. This complex family history was, of course, disclosed to the Bethel members.

2. WA can be pronounced in Japanese as *wa* which means circle, community, or peace. I'm very honored to be part of the initial formation of WA at Urakawa. However, I was a member of WA because I have a mental illness (depression), not because I was a researcher. This was clearly spelled out when I joined WA as well as SA. I was given permission to talk about the broad outlines of WA and SA but not about the particulars of who attended or what was said.

3. The rules are titled "Urakawa Schizophrenics Anonymous—The Eight Steps toward Recovery for People with Experience with Psychiatric Disabilities (Urakawa Version)," dated August 2001. The Urakawa SA differs in many ways from the American Schizophrenics Anonymous Six Steps in the language of the original six steps as well as the inclusion of steps seven and eight. Also, both Urakawa SA and WA are explicitly open to "anyone who wishes to get better"—not just people with schizophrenia. For the American version, see www.recovery-world.com/Schizophrenia-6-Steps-for-Recovery.html, accessed September 17, 2012.

4. The Urakawa SA manual is notable in avoiding the word *God* (*kami*) in any of the translated texts, even though the American version notably uses the word *God* in Step 6.

Instead, God is translated in Japanese as "a power greater than myself," a phrase that often caused members to scratch their heads when they read it. It's worth stating that not all SA and WA members were Christian, and members did not see either of the groups as having a Christian connotation.

5. There were two problems with my "Porsche" mini-truck: it seated only two people, and the crows that stalked the area around the grocery store knew that groceries in the truck bed were easy pickings at traffic lights.

6. There were no fast food restaurants in Urakawa; the nearest chain burger shop (a MOS Burger franchise) was a forty-five-minute drive away in Shizunai.

7. Rika uses the term *higai mōsō,* which can be translated as "feelings of persecution," "feeling like a victim," or "paranoid delusions." I've chosen the nonclinical "feelings of persecution" as I think it's closest to her intent and the least susceptible to misinterpretation by readers.

8. Rika uses the phrase *tōgōshicchōshō ni nattekara,* which literally means "after I became schizophrenia." I have chosen to translate it as, "I became schizophrenic" as the nearest idiomatic English. I'm always puzzled that one "catches" a disease but one "becomes" a disability: "I caught pneumonia" or "I got AIDS," but "I became blind" or "I am depressed."

9. Social worker Eriko Ito organized a parent's support group that met weekly at the hospital for both parents who had psychiatric issues as well as parents of children with psychiatric issues.

Chapter 3

1. These twenty-six martyrs of Japan were canonized by Pope Pius XI in 1862.

2. So many people died at Shimabara in 1638 and the resident population was so cleanly wiped out that 350 years later researchers noticed that the current residents in the Shimabara area had a significantly different proclivity to retinal cancer compared to residents in other districts of Nagasaki Prefecture (Takano et al. 1991), testament to a different genetic pool having been created.

3. For a fascinating history of these "hidden Christians" (*kakure Kirisutan*), see Turnbull et al. (2000).

4. There have been seven Christian prime ministers of Japan in the modern period: Hara Takashi, Takahashi Korekiyo, Shigeru Yoshida, Tetsu Katayama, Ichiro Hatoyama, Masayoshi Ohira, and Taro Aso.

5. As a side note, my father's family is from Nagasaki, and my grandfather was a minister in the United Church of Christ in Japan. When the nuclear bomb was dropped on Nagasaki, it killed a great number of Christians in the city. Fortunately for my family, my grandfather and his family were part of the occupation in Manchuria and so were not killed.

6. For more information about the Ainu, Fitzhugh and Dubreuil (1999) is a wonderful start. See also Ohnuki-Tierney (1974) and Walker (2001).

7. This is a gross simplification of the Jōmon culture. For a more in-depth account, see Junko (2004).

8. Despite Ohnuki-Tierney's use of the generic *he,* it should be noted that in Hokkaido all of the shamans were women.

9. Kirmayer and Minas (2000), 438–439. I am indebted to Junko Kitanaka for this reference.

Chapter 4

1. The donor to the church appears in the final scene of *Bethel* when the members give him an annual gift of thanks, as they go around town caroling to their neighbors.

2. In Mukaiyachi 2009 (*Yuru Yuru Slow*) p 61, Mr. Mukaiyachi also notes that after the war, many Koreans who had been brought over to Hokkaido to be used as forced laborers by the Japanese fled their work posts and some settled in the Hidaka area of Hokkaido, where Bethel is situated.

3. Available at www.town.urakawa.hokkaido.jp/cgi-bin/odb-get.exe?WIT_template=AC020000&WIT_oid=icityv2::Contents::3166, accessed September 28, 2011.

Unfortunately, import quotas on seaweed have been removed by free trade agreements, decimating the industry. It's likely that it will decline further in the aftermath of the 2011 Fukushima nuclear accident, because of fears of irradiated material entering the food supply.

4. Literally, trust in the power of the "place" (*ba*).

5. This is one of the themes of Kaysen (1993).

UFOs and Other Mass Delusions

1. See for example, Sir James Frazer's *The Golden Bough* or Joseph Campbell's *The Hero with a Thousand Faces.*

2. Japan Railways called these re-education sessions *nikkin kyōiku* (workday training). They involved psychological and physical bullying and harassment. Part of the goal of the bullying was undoubtedly to convince the employees to quit of their own volition, as lifetime employment practices and union contracts made it very difficult to fire full-time employees. But the practice also had the beneficial side effect of making sure that the entire workforce remained compliant to management whims. Some victims of these bullying tactics have committed suicide. On the legal debates over the responsibility of companies toward workplace suicide victims, see Kitanaka (2008, 2012).

3. Readers interested in the topic should read Kitanaka (2003, 2008, 2012).

4. Based on his time at Bethel, Michio Saito wrote a book, *The Ability to Worry: The People of Bethel* (2002) that won the prestigious Kodansha Non-Fiction Book Award and brought a great deal of attention to Bethel.

5. Personal conversation with Mr. Mukaiyachi.

6. Constantin Tranulis et al. bring up the unique case of a South Asian woman and her husband who use the "the 'stories' of her psychotic experiences to construct a shared and even 'safe' and familiar means of spousal connection" (2009: 608). This case is dissimilar from Yamane's in that the husband did not believe the "stories" that his wife (who had schizophrenia) was telling him. Also, unlike the majority of the interlocutors in Yamane-san's story, the husband was not himself schizophrenic.

Chapter 5

1. Private conversation with an eminent psychiatrist who graduated around the same time as Dr. Kawamura, who wishes to remain anonymous, January 28, 2012.

2. This paragraph based on personal conversations with the doctor, as well as Kawamura (2005), 261.

3. Here it differs from the American Red Cross, which does not provide primary care in the United States.

4. Ukigaya (2009), 53; further information from www.urakawa.jrc.or.jp, accessed September 17, 2012; and conversations with Dr. Kawamura.

5. Another euphemism used by psychiatric wards at other hospitals is *shinryō naika*, which my medical dictionary translates as "Department of Psychosomatic Internal Medicine"!

6. Unlike the United States, you do not need a referral to see a specialist in a general hospital.

7. I observed several clinical interactions with Dr. Kawamura, always with the permission of the Bethel members he was seeing (with whom I was familiar in contexts outside of the hospital). During these clinical interactions, I did not take notes nor record the interactions, with the single exception of the scene in *Bethel* in which the member talks with the doctor. Because their conversation was innocuous (they were talking about his love of chocolate milk), I recorded it with permission and included it as a typical clinical interview in the film, again with permission from the individual.

8. In her groundbreaking study of depression in contemporary Japan, medical anthropologist Junko Kitanaka also noted the importance of the therapeutic affirmation when psychiatrists acknowledge the suffering of the patient: "The patients talked about the acknowledgment from a psychiatrist to be a defining, transformative moment. As one woman said to me: 'I knew, at the moment, that he understood, that I could entrust myself to him'" (Kitanaka 2012, 94).

9. *Urakawa Red Cross Hospital Overview* 2007.

10. At other institutions for the physically disabled, my informants remembered, you had to apply a week in advance in writing if you wanted visitors—or if you wanted to leave for the day. This was for the benefit of the nursing staff who had to plan around these things, they were told. They asked—quite rightly—what about our freedom to have friends come visit or to be able to go outside and breathe some fresh air when we felt like it? Who considers *our* needs?

11. Another example was when a taxi driver told me during the short ride to the hospital that a former psychiatric patient from the Urakawa Hospital had stabbed someone else in a fight. That incident had happened quite a while earlier, before Bethel's time, but it continued to haunt the memories of the town's citizens.

12. By 2007, the Red Cross Hospital had three social workers, one of whom was assigned to the psychiatric day care unit.

13. I often thought that the doctor pretended to go to sleep in meetings so that he wouldn't be seen as the central authority in the room, and all decisions would cease to be deferred to him. Or he could have just been narcoleptic. I wasn't able to prove it either way during my fieldwork.

14. Even if it were possible with the severe budget constraints and understaffing in American social welfare departments, such cooperation might be actually illegal given health information and education information confidentiality laws such as HIPAA and FERPA.

Thirty-Seven Years of Institutionalization

1. The hospital had a fourth social worker, but as his responsibility was elder care in the area, he did not attend the psychiatric day care meetings.

2. The hospital and the school are still right next to each other, but Ward 7 was moved in 2003 due to the earthquake; it no longer faces the school.

3. Mukaiyachi (2008), 186. Kiyoshi also related similar stories to me.

4. Sakai-san's peer support work is visible in the clip of group home life in the bonus section of *Bethel*.

5. Kawamura and Mukaiyachi (2008), 65. I'm not sure if Yuzuru was making a reference to the old tradition of the courtesans in the Yoshiwara brothel district of Edo, who were not permitted to leave the grounds of the red light district except once a year to watch the spring cherry blossoms in Ueno Park.

Chapter 6

1. In addition to the main fieldwork period in 2007–2008, I visited Bethel several times on much shorter occasions in 2005 and 2011. I also hosted some Bethel members

when they came to stay at my house in New Haven, Connecticut, and met with others when they came to Tokyo.

2. Road Traffic Law (1960.6.25 Public Law Number 105), Article 19, Section 1, Section 1-I; and Road Traffic Law Enforcement Ordinance (1960.10.11 Ordinance Number 270).

3. The other patients almost always recognized me as a non-patient. I'm not sure if this is a validation of the famous 1973 Rosenhan experiment, in which the "pseudopatients" in a psychiatric ward fooled the doctors but not the patients. Rather, I think the active grapevine tipped them off long before I introduced myself to them formally.

4. There were a few reasons that Bethel members gave as to why they might see the junior doctor in the hospital or go to the private mental health clinic. Notably, they said that the other doctor and the private clinic were usually more willing to prescribe medication on demand than Dr. Kawamura. Also, many people who had moved to Urakawa as psychopilgrims found that Bethel was at capacity and wasn't taking new members and Dr. Kawamura was also not accepting new patients, so their choices for care were limited to the other doctor in the hospital or the private clinic. Since the hospital's psychiatric ward was associated with Bethel, many townspeople went to the private mental health clinic instead.

5. Disability activist Shoji Nakanishi and feminist activist Chizuko Ueno cowrote a famous (2003) book called *Tōjisha Shuken* or *The Sovereignty of Tōjisha* in which they linked the civil rights of people with disabilities, women, and other *Tōjisha.*

6. I tried to look at parallels in Western history for similar terminology. Consciousness raising in 1970s feminist circles seems the most similar, but in the context of Bethel, each person's self-directed research is very much focused on individual experience and not linked to broader political awareness of discrimination to people with psychiatric disabilities as a whole.

7. This last one is viewable in the bonus section of the *Bethel* DVD.

8. Noriyuki Itoh describes himself as having "Schizophrenia: Running-at-full-speed type," as he is always scurrying from one thing to another, constantly out of breath. His schizophrenia first appeared when he was a college student, but he managed to graduate and become a civil servant in the Social Welfare Department of Urakawa City, of all places. His symptoms worsened, and he had to resign his position, but he was picked up by Bethel and became one of their *tōjisha* staff. He is unrelated to Eriko Itoh, the psychiatric social worker, and Yu Itoh, the psychiatric nurse who retired at the same time as Yuzuru Yokoyama. Itoh is a very popular last name in Japan.

9. I love that Mai uses a verb form: "I am doing schizophrenia" (*tōgōshō wo yatteite*) rather than saying that she *has* schizophrenia (*tōgōshicchōshō wo motteimasu*).

10. *Waruo* literally means "bad guy."

11. Ellipses indicate portions that I have redacted for length reasons.

Peer Support and a Meaningful Life

1. One of their songs appears in the *Bethel* film.

2. When I brought up the theory of religious schism with Mr. Mukaiyachi, he didn't think that it was the cause of the fight. He thought that the issue of body odor itself was enough of a trigger.

3. People who live in small apartments might instead go directly to a funeral home or lie in rest in the hospital. 99% of Japanese are cremated these days, because of the lack of space for larger burial plots.

4. This biography is a condensation of my interview at the Nakayama home on August 20, 2007 and a follow-up telephone interview on December 14, 2011. It also draws on Nakayama (2005).

5. This section where the Nakayamas go to Bethel is drawn largely from Nakayama (2005), 244; it is used with permission.

6. Such a long consultation would normally be unheard of anywhere but Urakawa.

Chapter 7

1. This account is based on newspaper accounts of the time as well as conversations with Bethel staff and Mr. Mukaiyachi. The newspaper accounts are *Hokkaido Shimbun,* November 13, 2003 (prefectural morning edition), 33; November 18, 2003 (prefectural evening edition), 13; November 22, 2003 (regional evening edition), 33; December 27, 2003 (regional morning edition), 21; and March 26, 2004 (prefectural evening edition), 18. Also *Asahi Shimbun,* November 10, 2003 (Hokkaido morning edition); *Kaikei Shori Meguri, Dō ga Tokubetsu Kansa, Urakawachō no Shakai Fukushi Hōjin* ("Examination of Financial Management: [Hokkaido] Prefectural Government Engages in a Special Audit of a Urakawa Town Social Welfare Organization").

2. Member-staff *(tōjisha sutaffu)* and able-bodied staff (*kenjōsha sutaffu*).

3. Plath (1996), 1152.

4. For various definitions of intentional communities, see Williams (2002).

5. The most famous intentional community in Japan is the Yamagishi Association, which is a network of ecotopias and ecovillages founded in 1953 on the principles of sustainable living in which all property is held in communal trust, with no personal belongings. There are also a number of smaller cooperatives and religious communities in Japan, but like the United States the peak of communal living in Japan was in the 1960s, and the ardor has somewhat worn off (Plath 1966), especially in the aftermath of the Aum religious cult.

6. In addition, Dr. Kawamura has severely limited the number of new admits to the inpatient ward of Ward 7 of the hospital and new consults to his outpatient department.

Chapter 8

1. Interview with Dr. Kawamura on February 22, 2012. Dr. Kawamura's words have been edited for clarity and flow.

2. *Katari no ba* literally means "space of narration," but in Japanese the concept of "narration" (*katari*) implies the existence of an audience to witness.

3. He uses the Japanese word *kata,* familiar to anyone who has done the various choreographed patterns of forms and movements in karate or judo practice.

References

Links to more resources about Bethel House and psychiatric care in Japan, video clips, errata and additions, a teacher's guide, and additional photographs about life in Urakawa can be found on the book's website: http://www.disabilityofthesoul.org.

Allison, Anne. 1994. *Nightwork: Sexuality, Pleasure, and Corporate Masculinity in a Tokyo Hostess Club.* Chicago: University of Chicago Press.

Anesaki, Masaharu. 1936. "Psychological Observations on the Persecution of the Catholics in Japan in the Seventeenth Century." *Harvard Journal of Asiatic Studies* 1(1): 13–27.

Bethel House (ed.). べてるの家1992. べてるの家の本: 和解の時代 [A book about Bethel House: An era of compromise]. Urakawa, Japan: Bethel House.

——. 2002. べてるの家の「非」援助論 : そのままでいいと思えるための25章 [Bethel House's philosophy of non-support: 25 chapters of accepting things as they are]. Tokyo: Igaku Shoin.

——. 2005. べてるの家の「当事者研究」[Bethel House's self-directed research]. Tokyo: Igaku Shoin.

——. 2009. レッツ!当事者研究 1 [Let's do self-directed research, vol. 1]. Ichikawa, Chiba: COMHBO.

——. 2010. べてるの家の恋愛大研究: Bethel House's Studies of Love. Tokyo: Otsuki Shoten.

——. 2011. レッツ！当事者研究2 [Let's do self-directed research, vol. 2]. Ichikawa, Chiba: COMHBO.

Bethel House (dir.). べてるの家 1997. キヨシどん斯く語りき [Kiyoshi's incidents and stories]. VHS Videotape. Distributed by Bethel House.

Bouvard, Marguerite Guzman. 1975. *The Intentional Community Movement: Building a New Moral World.* Port Washington, NY: Kennikat Press.

Burch, Thomas K. 1955. "Induced Abortion in Japan." *Eugenics Quarterly* 2(3): 140–151.

Charon, Rita. 2006. *Narrative Medicine: Honoring the Stories of Illness.* New York: Oxford University Press.

Cornell, John B. 1964. "Ainu Assimilation and Cultural Extinction: Acculturation Policy in Hokkaido." *Ethnology* 3(3): 287–304.
Culter, Suzanne. 1999. *Managing Decline: Japan's Coal Industry Restructuring and Community Response.* Honolulu: University of Hawaii Press.
Daiunji Temple. 2011a. Home page. http://www.daiunji.org/. Accessed September 15, 2011.
——. 2011b. ご利益 [Benefits]. http://www.daiunji.org/new_page_18.htm. Accessed September 15, 2011.
DeMille, Cecil B. (dir.). 1956. *The Ten Commandments.* 220 minutes. Distributed by Paramount Pictures.
Dower, John W. 1999. *Embracing Defeat: Japan in the Wake of World War II.* 1st ed. New York: W.W. Norton/New Press.
Eguchi, Shigeyuki. 1991. "Between Folk Concepts of Illness and Psychiatric Diagnosis: Kitsune-Tsuki (Fox Possession) in a Mountain Village of Western Japan." *Culture, Medicine and Psychiatry* 15(4).
Fanon, Frantz. 1968. *Black Skin, White Masks.* New York: Grove Press.
Fitzhugh, William W., and Chisato O. Dubreuil, eds. 1999. *Ainu: Spirit of a Northern People.* Washington, DC: Arctic Studies Center, National Museum of Natural History, Smithsonian Institution in association with the University of Washington Press.
Foucault, Michel. 1975. *Surveiller et Punir: Naissance de la Prison.* Paris: Gallimard.
——. 1985. *Madness and Civilization: A History of Insanity in the Age of Reason.* London: Tavistock Publications.
——. 1990. *The History of Sexuality.* London: Penguin Books.
——. 2003. *The Birth of the Clinic: An Archaeology of Medical Perception.* London: Routledge.
Glaze, Lauren E., and Doris J. James. 2006. "Mental Health Problems of Prison and Jail Inmates." Bureau of Justice Statistics (BJS), NCJ 213600.
Goffman, Erving. 1961a. *Asylums: Essays on the Social Situation of Mental Patients and Other Inmates.* Garden City, NY: Doubleday.
——. 1961b. "On the Characteristics of Total Institutions." In *The Prison.* Edited by Donald R. Cressey. New York: Holt, Rinehart and Winston.
Habu, Junko. 2004. *Ancient Jōmon of Japan.* New York: Cambridge University Press.
Hagemann, Edward. 1942. "The Persecution of the Christians in Japan in the Middle of the Seventeenth Century." *Pacific Historical Review* 11(2): 151–160.
Hashimoto, Akira. 2008. "People, Community, and Memories of Madness in the Amami Islands, Japan." Social Welfare Studies (Department of Social Welfare, Faculty of Literature, Aichi Prefectural University) 10:37–41.
Haumonté, M. Th. 1967. "Treatment of Alcoholic Patients in a Psychiatric Hospital." *British Journal of Addiction to Alcohol and Other Drugs* 62(1–2): 49–53.
Howell, David L. 2004. "Making 'Useful Citizens' of Ainu Subjects in Early Twentieth-Century Japan." *Journal of Asian Studies* 63(1): 5–29.
Hurd, Henry Mills, William Francis Drewry, Richard Dewey, Charles Winfield Pilgrim, George Alder Blumer, and Thomas Joseph Workman Burgess. 1916. *The Institutional Care of the Insane in the United States and Canada.* Baltimore: Johns Hopkins Press.
Ito, Hiroto, and Lloyd I. Sederer. 1999. *Mental Health Services Reform in Japan. Harvard Review of Psychiatry* 7(4): 208–215.
Itoh Emi 伊藤絵美, and Mukaiyachi Ikuyoshi 向谷地生良. 2007. 認知行動療法、べてる式 [Cognitive behavioral therapy, Bethel style]. Tokyo: Igakushoin.
Iwanami Akira. 岩波 明. 2009. 精神障害者をどう裁くか [How to judge people with psychiatric disabilities]. Tokyo: Kobunsha.
Jilek, Wolfgang G. 1995. "Emil Kraepelin and Comparative Sociocultural Psychiatry." *European Archives of Psychiatry and Clinical Neuroscience* 245(4).

Journal of the American Medical Association (JAMA). 1896. "Public Health." *JAMA: The Journal of the American Medical Association* 2624): 1138. June 6.
Kanter, Rosabeth Moss. 1972. *Commitment and Community: Communes and Utopias in Sociological Perspective.* Cambridge, MA: Harvard University Press.
Kawamura Toshiaki 川村敏明. 1992. 「べてる」に学ぶもの [What Bethel can teach us]. In べてるの家の本: 和解の時代 [A book about Bethel House: An era of compromise]. Edited by Bethel House, 160–167. Urakawa, Japan: Bethel House.
——. 2005. わきまえとして「治せない医者」[Having the sense to know that "I am a doctor who cannot cure"] In べてるの家の「当事者研究」[Bethel House's self-directed research]. Edited by Bethel House, 256–277. Tokyo: Igaku Shoin.
Kawamura Toshiaki 川村敏明 and Ikuyoshi Mukaiyachi. 向谷地生良. 2008. 退院支援, べてる式 [Helping people leave the hospital, Bethel style]. Tokyo: Igaku Shoin.
Kaysen, Susanna. 1993. *Girl, Interrupted.* 1st ed. New York: Turtle Bay Books.
Kindaichi Kyōsuke 金田一 京助. 1925. アイヌの研究 [Research on the Ainu]. Tokyo: Naigai Shobō.
Kimura, Rihito. 1991. "Jurisprudence in Genetics." *Ethical Issues of Molecular Genetics in Psychiatry* 11: 157–167.
Kirmayer, Laurence J. 2007. "Psychotherapy and the Cultural Concept of the Person." *Transcultural Psychiatry* 44(2): 232–257.
Kirmayer, Laurence J., and Harry Minas. 2000. "The Future of Cultural Psychiatry: An International Perspective." *Canadian Journal of Psychiatry/Revue Canadienne De Psychiatrie* 45(5): 438–446.
Kitanaka Junko. 2003. "Jungians and the Rise of Psychotherapy in Japan: A Brief Historical Note." *Transcultural Psychiatry* 40(2): 239–247.
——. 2008 "Diagnosing Suicides of Resolve: Psychiatric Practice in Contemporary Japan." *Culture, Medicine. and Psychiatry* 32(2): 152–176.
——. 2012. *Depression in Japan: Psychiatric Cures for a Society in Distress.* Princeton, NJ: Princeton University Press.
Kiyoshi Hayasaka 早坂潔. 1992.「べてる」と共に歩んで [Walking together with Bethel]. In べてるの家の本: 和解の時代 [A book about Bethel House: An era of compromise]. Edited by Bethel House, pp. 51–57. Urakawa, Japan: Bethel House.
Kleinman, Arthur M. 1977. "Depression, Somatization, and the 'New Cross-Cultural Psychiatry.'" *Social Science and Medicine* 11(1): 3–10.
——. 1988a. *The Illness Narratives: Suffering, Healing, and the Human Condition.* New York: Basic Books.
——. 1988b. *Rethinking Psychiatry: From Cultural Category to Personal Experience.* New York: Free Press.
Kure Shuzo 呉 秀三. 1973 [1918]. 精神病者私宅監置ノ実況及ビ其統計的観察 [The current situation of home confinement of the mentally ill as well as statistical observations]. Edited by Goro Kashida. Chofu, Japan: Sozo Shuppan.
Leamer, Laurence. 1994. *The Kennedy Women: The Saga of an American Family.* 1st ed. New York: Villard Books.
Lehman, Anthony F., Donald M. Steinwachs, and the Co-Investigators of the PORT Project. 1998. "At Issue: Translating Research into Practice: The Schizophrenia Patient Outcomes Research Team (PORT) Treatment Recommendations." *Schizophrenia Bulletin* 24(1): 1–10.
Lewis, G., A. David, S. Andréasson, and P. Allebeck. 1992. "Schizophrenia and City Life." *The Lancet* 340 (8812): 137–140.
Liberman, Robert Paul. 1992. 精神障害者の生活技能訓練ガイドブック [A social skills training guidebook for people with psychiatric disabilities]. Edited by William J. DeRisi, Kim Tornvall Mueser, and Emi Ikebuchi. Tokyo: Igakushoin.
Liberman, Robert Paul, William J. DeRisi, and Kim Tornvall Mueser. 1989. *Social Skills Training for Psychiatric Patients.* New York: Pergamon Press.

Mamiya, Ikuko 間宮郁子. 2005. 地域社会に棲みはじめた精神障害者—通所授産施設を中心とした地域生活支援の動態 [People with psychiatric disabilities starting to live in the community: The movement towards community living support centered around non-residential sheltered workshops]. Ph.D. thesis, Graduate School of the Social Sciences and Humanities, Chiba University.

Mandiberg, James M., ed. 1993. *Innovations in Japanese Mental Health Services.* San Francisco: Jossey-Bass.

——. 1993. "Between a Rock and a Hard Place: The Mental Health System in Japan." In *Innovations in Japanese Mental Health Services,* 3–12. San Francisco: Jossey-Bass.

——. 1996. "The Japanese Mental Health System and Law: Social and Structural Impediments to Reform." *International Journal of Law and Psychiatry* 19(3–4): 413–435.

——. 2010. "Another Way: Enclave Communities for People with Mental Illness." *American Journal of Orthopsychiatry* 80(2): 170–176.

Matsubara, Yoko. 1998. "The Enactment of Japan's Sterilization Laws in the 1940s: A Prelude to Postwar Eugenic Policy." *Historia Scientiarum: International Journal of the History of Science Society of Japan* 8(2): 187–201.

Matsumura, Janice. 2004. "Mental Health as Public Peace: Kaneko Junji and the Promotion of Psychiatry in Modern Japan." *Modern Asian Studies* 38(4): 899–930.

McGrath, John, Sukanta Saha, David Chant, and Joy Welham. 2008. "Schizophrenia: A Concise Overview of Incidence, Prevalence, and Mortality." *Epidemiology Review* 30(1): 67–76.

Metzl, Jonathan. 2003. *Prozac on the Couch.* Durham: Duke University Press.

——. 2009. *The Protest Psychosis: How Schizophrenia Became a Black Disease.* Boston: Beacon Press.

Ministry of Health, Labor, and Welfare (MHLW). 厚生労働省. 1956. 厚生白書 [Welfare Whitebook]. Tokyo: Ministry of Labor. Available at http://wwwhakusyo.mhlw.go.jp/ wpdocs/ hpaz195601/body.html, accessed September 21, 2011.

——. 1960. 厚生白書 [Welfare Whitebook]. Tokyo: Ministry of Labor. Available at http://wwwhakusyo.mhlw.go.jp/wpdocs/hpaz196001/b0155.html, accessed September 17, 2011.

——. 1961. 厚生白書 [Welfare Whitebook]. Tokyo: Ministry of Labor. Available at http://wwwhakusyo.mhlw.go.jp/wpdocs/hpaz196101/b0148.html, accessed September 17, 2011.

——. 1964. 厚生白書 [Welfare Whitebook]. Tokyo: Ministry of Labor. Available at http://wwwhakusyo.mhlw.go.jp/wpdocs/hpaz196401/b0110.html, accessed September 21, 2011.

——. 1965. 厚生白書 [Welfare Whitebook]. Tokyo: Ministry of Labor. Available at http://wwwhakusyo.mhlw.go.jp/wpdocs/hpaz196501/b0044.html, accessed September 21, 2011.

——. 1966. 厚生白書 [Welfare Whitebook]. Tokyo: Ministry of Labor. Available at http://wwwhakusyo.mhlw.go.jp/wpdocs/hpaz196601/body.html, accessed September 17, 2011.

——. 2010. 精神保健医療福祉の改革ビジョン進捗状況 [The progress of the reformation of mental health medical welfare]. Tokyo: Ministry of Labor. Available at www.mhlw.go.jp/shingi/2010/05/dl/s0531-14c_2.pdf, accessed May 30, 2012.

Miyajima, Michiko 宮島美智子. 1992. 私の出会った人たち [The people I met]. In べてるの家の本: 和解の時代 [A book about Bethel House: An era of compromise]. Edited by Bethel House, 34–44. Urakawa, Japan: Bethel House.

Mizuki Shigeru 水木 しげる. 1998. 水木しげるの妖怪伝大画集 [A visual encyclopedia of Mizuki Shigeru's monsters and apparitions]. Tokyo: Shinkigensha.

Morton, Kramer. 1969. "Statistics of Mental Disorders in the United States: Current Status, Some Urgent Needs, and Suggested Solutions." *Journal of the Royal Statistical Society*, Series A (General) 132(3): 353–407.

Mukaiyachi, Ikuyoshi 向谷地生良. 1992.「べてる」を支えるもの [What supports Bethel]. In べてるの家の本: 和解の時代 [A book about Bethel House: An era of compromise]. Edited by Bethel House, 12–33. Urakawa, Japan: Bethel House.

——. 2006a.「べてるの家」から吹く風 [Winds blowing from Bethel House]. Tokyo: Inochi no Kotobasha.

——. 2006b. 安心して絶望できる人生 [Giving up hope in life without fear]. べてるの家, ed. Tokyo: NHK Publishing.

——. 2008. べてるな人びと [The people of Bethel, vol. 1]. Sapporo, Japan: Ichibaku Shuppan.

——. 2009a. ゆるゆるスローなべてるの家 ： ぬけます、おります、なまけます [Bethel House slowly swinging back and forth: Avoiding, descending, neglecting]. Edited by Shinichi Tsuji. Tokyo: Otsuki Shoten.

——. 2009b. 技法以前: べてるの家のつくりかた [Before techniques: How Bethel House was built]. Tokyo: Igaku Shoin.

——. 2010. べてるな人びと [The people of Bethel, vol. 2]. Sapporo, Japan: Ichibaku Shuppan.

Nagaoka Yasushi 長岡 和. 2008.「爆弾精神科医」医療崩壊への挑戦状 [An explosive psychiatrist: A challenge to the breakdown of the health care system]. Tokyo: Joho Center Publishing.

Nakamura, Karen. 2006. *Deaf in Japan: Signing and the Politics of Identity*. Ithaca, NY: Cornell University Press.

Nakanishi Shoji and Chizuko Ueno 中西 正司 、上野千鶴子. 2003. 当事者主権 [The rights of Tōjisha]. Tokyo: Iwanami Shoten.

Nakatani, Yoji. 2000. "Psychiatry and the Law in Japan: History and Current Topics." *International Journal of Law and Psychiatry* 23(5–6): 589–604.

Nakayama, Chika 中山 周. 2005.「当事者」としてのわたしは、何に悩み、苦しんできたのか [What I, as a "Tojisha," have worried about and suffered]. In べてるの家の「当事者研究」[Bethel House's self-directed research]. Edited by Bethel House べてるの家, 243–253. Tokyo: Igaku Shoin.

Noda, Fumitaka, Campbell Clark, Hisako Terada, Naoki Hayashi, Keiko Maeda, Mikiko Sato, Keiko Ito, Junko Kitanaka, Takeshi Asal, Takashi Nishimura, Kenji Kushigami, Kazushi Okada, Yosuke Taniguchi, and Tomoyuki Mantani. 2004. "Community Discharge of Patients with Schizophrenia: A Japanese Experience." *Psychiatric Rehabilitation Journal* 28(2): 143–149.

Office of Mental Health, New York (OMH-NY). 2011. "Pilgrim Psychiatric Center." Electronic document, www.omh.state.ny.us/omhweb/facilities/pgpc/facility.htm, accessed January 12, 2012.

Ohnuki-Tierney, Emiko. 1974. *The Ainu of the Northwest Coast of Southern Sakhalin*. New York: Holt, Rinehart, and Winston.

——. 1981. *Illness and Healing among the Sakhalin Ainu: A Symbolic Interpretation*. New York: Cambridge University Press.

Okuma Kazuo 大熊一夫. 1973. ルポ・精神病棟 [Report: A psychiatric ward]. Tokyo: Asahi Shimbunsha.

Omata Waichiro 小俣 和一郎. 2005. 精神医学の歴史 [A history of psychiatry]. Tokyo: Daisanbunmeisha.

Osawa Sakae 大澤 榮. 2010. べてるの家の先駆者たち: 苦労を大切にする生き方 [The pioneers of Bethel House: How to live while valuing your suffering]. Tokyo: Inochi no Kotobasha.

Ozawa-de Silva, Chikako. 2002. "Beyond the Body/Mind? Japanese Contemporary Thinkers on Alternative Sociologies of the Body." *Body and Society* 8(2): 21–38.
——. 2006. *Psychotherapy and Religion in Japan: The Japanese Introspection Practice of Naikan*. New York: Routledge.
——. 2007. "Demystifying Japanese Therapy: An Analysis of Naikan and the Ajase Complex through Buddhist Thought." *Ethos* 35(4): 411–446.
Parsons, Talcott. 1951. "Illness and the Role of the Physician: A Sociological Perspective." *American Journal of Orthopsychiatry* 21(3): 452–460.
Pettee, James H. 1895. "A Chapter of Mission History in Modern Japan being a Sketch for the Period since 1869 and a Report for the Years since 1893 of the American Board's Mission and the Kumiai Churches in their Affiliated Work." S.l.: s.n.
Plath, D. W. 1969. "Modernization and Its Discontents: Japan's Little Utopias." *Journal of Asian and African Studies* 4(1): 1–17.
——. 1966. "The Fate of Utopia: Adaptive Tactics in Four Japanese Groups." *American Anthropologist* 68(5): 1152–1162.
Reynolds, David K. 1976. *Morita Psychotherapy*. Berkeley: University of California Press.
——. 1980. *The Quiet Therapies: Japanese Pathways to Personal Growth*. Honolulu: University Press of Hawaii.
——. 1983. *Naikan Psychotherapy: Meditation for Self-Developmen*t. Chicago: University of Chicago Press.
Robertson, J. 2002. "Blood Talks: Eugenic Modernity and the Creation of New Japanese." *History and Anthropology* 13(3): 191–216.
Rosenhan, D. L. 1973. "On Being Sane in Insane Places." *Science* 179(4070): 250–258.
Russell, John Gordon. 1988. "The Descendants of Susano: Marginalization and Psychiatric Institutionalization in Japan." Ph.D. dissertation, Harvard University.
Saito Michio 斉藤 道雄. 2002 悩む力: べてるの家の人びと [The ability to worry: The people of Bethel]. Tokyo: Misuzu Shobo.
——. 2010. 治りませんように: べてるの家のいま [I hope I don't get cured: Contemporary life at Bethel]. Tokyo: Misuzu Shobo.
Sasaki, Minoru 佐々木実. 1992.「べてる」に生きて [Living in Bethel]. In べてるの家の本: 和解の時代 [A book about Bethel House: An era of compromise]. Edited by Bethel House, 45–50. Urakawa, Japan: Bethel House.
Scott, J. 1993. "Homelessness and Mental Illness." British Journal of Psychiatry 162(3): 314–324.
Shimazaki, Tōson. 1987. Before the Dawn. Ed. and trans. William E. Naff. Honolulu: University of Hawaii Press.
Shimizu Rika. 清水里香 2005. 被害妄想の研究：幻聴さんだって自立する [Research into delusions of persecution: Even Gencho-san voices can be independent]. In べてるの家 「当事者研究」[Bethel House's self-directed research]. Edited by Bethel House, 93–109. Tokyo: Igaku Shoin.
Shinfuku, Naotaka, and Chay-Hoon Tan. 2008. "Pharmacotherapy for Schizophrenic Inpatients in East Asia: Changes and Challenges." *International Review of Psychiatry* 20(5): 460–468.
Shinichirō, Takakura, and John A. Harrison. 1960. "The Ainu of Northern Japan: A Study in Conquest and Acculturation." *Transactions of the American Philosophical Society* 50(4): 1–88.
Shorter, Edward. 1997. *A History of Psychiatry: From the Era of the Asylum to the Age of Prozac*. New York: John Wiley & Sons.
Siddle, Richard. 1996. *Race, Resistance and the Ainu of Japan*. London: Routledge.

Sim, Kang, A. Su, J.Y. Leong, K. Yip, M.Y. Chong, S. Fujii, S. Yang, G.S. Ungvari, T. Si, E.K. Chung, H.Y. Tsang, N. Shinfuku, E.H. Kua, and C.H. Tan. 2004. "High Dose Antipsychotic use in Schizophrenia: Findings of the REAP (Research on East Asia Psychotropic Prescriptions) Study." *Pharmacopsychiatry* 37(4): 175–179.

Sim, Kang, Hsin Chuan Su, Senta Fujii, Shu-yu Yang, Mian-Yoon Chong, Gabor Ungvari, Tianmei Si, Yan Ling He, Eun Kee Chung, Yiong Huak Chan, Naotaka Shinfuku, Ee Heok Kua, Chay Hoon Tan, and Norman Sartorius. 2009. "High-Dose Antipsychotic Use in Schizophrenia: A Comparison between the 2001 and 2004 Research on East Asia Psychotropic Prescription (REAP) Studies." *British Journal of Clinical Pharmacology* 67(1): 110–117.

Smith, William L. 2002. "Intentional Communities, 1990–2000: A Portrait." *Michigan Sociological Review* 16: 107–131.

Sugimoto Akira 杉本 章. 2008. 障害者はどう生きてきたか: 戦前・戦後障害者運動史 [How people with disabilities used to live: A history of disability activism before the war and after the war]. Tokyo: Gendai Shoten.

Szasz, Thomas Stephen. 1963. *Law, Liberty, and Psychiatry: An Inquiry into the Social Uses of Mental Health Practices.* New York: Macmillan.

——. 1970. *The Manufacture of Madness: A Comparative Study of the Inquisition and the Mental Health Movement.* 1st ed. New York: Harper and Row.

——. 1978. *The Myth of Psychotherapy: Mental Healing as Religion, Rhetoric, and Repression.* 1st ed. Garden City, NY: Anchor Press/Doubleday.

Takano, J., K. Akiyama, N. Imamura, M. Sakuma, and T. Amemiya. 1991. "Incidence of Retinoblastoma in Nagasaki Prefecture, Japan." *Ophthalmic Paediatrics and Genetics* 12(3): 139–144.

Takei, N., A. Inagaki, and JPSS-2 Research Group. 2002. "Polypharmacy for Psychiatric Treatments in Japan." *The Lancet* 360(9333): 647.

Tomita Mikio 富田 三樹生. 1992. 精神病院の底流 [The undercurrents beneath psychiatrist hospitals]. Tokyo: Sekyusha.

——. 2000. 東大病院精神科の30年：宇都宮病院事件・精神衛生法改正・処遇困難者専門病棟問題 [The 30-year history of Tokyo University Hospital's psychiatric ward: The Utsunomiya incident, the revisions to the Mental Health Care Act, and the problems with the ward for treatment-resistant patients]. Tokyo: Seikyusha.

Totsuka, Etsuro. 1990. "The History of Japanese Psychiatry and the Rights of Mental Patients." *The Psychiatrist* (14): 193–200.

Tranulis, Constantin, E. Corin, and Laurence J. Kirmayer. 2008. "Insight and Psychosis: Comparing the Perspectives of Patient, Entourage, and Clinician." *International Journal of Social Psychiatry* 54(3): 225–241.

Tranulis, Constantin, L. Park, L. Delano, and Byron Good. 2009. "Early Intervention in Psychosis: A Case Study on Normal and Pathological." *Culture, Medicine and Psychiatry* 33(4): 608–622.

Tsuchiya, Takashi. 1997. "Eugenic Sterilizations in Japan and Recent Demands for Apology: A Report." *Newsletter of the Network on Ethics and Intellectual Disability* 3(1): 1–4.

Turnbull, Stephen. 2000. *Japan's Hidden Christians, 1549–1999.* Stephen R. Turnbull, ed. Surrey: Curzon.

Ukigaya Sachiyo 浮ケ谷 幸代. 2009. ケアと共同性の人類学: 北海道浦河赤十字病院精神科から地域へ [An anthropology of care and communal living: From Hokkaido's Urakawa Red Cross Hospital to the community]. Tokyo: Seikatsu Shoin.

Urakawa Red Cross Hospital 浦河赤十字病院.1990. 地域医療を支えて五十年: 創立50年史 [50 years of supporting regional healthcare: In commemoration of our 50 years since founding]. Urakawa, Japan: Urakawa Red Cross Hospital.

——. 2007. 病院概要 [Hospital overview]. Urakawa, Japan: Urakawa Red Cross Hospital.

Vickery, George Kendall. 2005. "A Cold of the Heart: Japan Strives to Normalize Depression." Ph.D. dissertation, University of Pittsburgh.

Walker, Brett L. 2001. *The Conquest of Ainu Lands: Ecology and Culture in Japanese Expansion, 1590–1800.* Berkeley: University of California Press.

Wegner, Daniel M. 1986. "Transactive Memory: A Contemporary Analysis of the Group Mind." In *Theories of Group Behavior.* Edited by B. Mullen and G.R. Goethals, 185–208. New York: Springer-Verlag.

Wegner, Daniel M., T. Giuliano, and P. Hertel. 1985. "Cognitive Interdependence in Close Relationships." In *Compatible and Incompatible Relationships.* Edited by W.J. Ickes, 253–276. New York: Springer-Verlag.

White, James W. 1988. "State Growth and Popular Protest in Tokugawa Japan." *Journal of Japanese Studies* 14(1): 1–25.

Wolf, Margery. 1990. "The Woman Who Didn't Become a Shaman." *American Ethnologist* 17(3): 419–430.

Yanagita Kunio 柳田 国男. 2010 [1910]. 遠野物語 [Stories of Tōno]. Tokyo: Daiwa Shobo.

Yanaka, Teruo. 1993. "The Village of the Hermit Crab." In Innovations in Japanese Mental Health Services. Edited by James M. Mandiberg, 57–66. San Francisco: Jossey-Bass.

Yoshimoto Ishin. 吉本 伊信. 1983. 内観への招待: 愛情の再発見と自己洞察のすすめ [An invitation to Naikan: Rediscovering love and advancing self-knowledge]. Osaka, Japan: Toki Shobo.

Index

CPSIA information can be obtained
at www.ICGtesting.com
Printed in the USA
LVHW031721211221
706846LV00008B/1098